HIDDEN®
OAHU

Ray Riegert

SIXTH EDITION

Ulysses Press

EXPLORE THE HIDDEN REALM

There's a reason that Oahu, the most populated of the Hawaiian Islands, became "The Gathering Place." Its first inhabitants arrived to find her shorelines bountiful, her earth fertile and her forests resource-rich. Today, Oahu shows some wrinkles, the result of centuries of wear and tear and runaway construction. But beyond the highrises of Honolulu and Waikiki, you'll still find her lush, pristine valleys, spectacular undersea wonderlands and wide, unspoiled beaches. Oahu has a hidden realm, and when you get to know her, you'll discover she harbors the heartbeat of Hawaiian islands.

Hidden Oahu points you to destinations that offer unique Oahu experiences. Some are off the beaten path, literally hidden from view. Others are locally tried and true—a bakery that turns out the island's best pastries or a sacred place steeped in Hawaiian legend. Oahu's four coastlines are quite distinct, and with specialized maps, detailed descriptions and accurate information, you'll be equipped to explore each of them.

Oahu's burgeoning population regulates Hawaii's pulse, so keep your eyes open for opportunities to engage in the local lifestyle—attend an art opening, enter a swim race, "talk story" with the roadside vendors. Aloha, after all, comes from the generous hearts of the friendly island people.

CULTURAL SIGHTS

Iolani Palace was the official resident of Hawaii's last two monarchs.

Hawaiians believe strongly in a sense of place, and every place has a story. Physically being at a cultural site can put its story into context. You are able to exercise your senses—observe the setting, breathe the air, listen to what's around you. At many *heiau*, sacred temples and mystic ruins of ancient Hawaii, you can sense the spiritual energy that lingers. It lends truth to the belief that these places are alive, still telling the stories of the island people and perpetuating their culture.

Some cultural sights are found in remote areas while others, like **Iolani Palace** *(p. 101)* stand sentinel in the middle of urban Honolulu. An outstanding tour of the royal residence takes visitors through its storied corridors, even past the bedroom where Queen Liliuokalani was imprisoned following the overthrow of the monarchy. On the Windward Coast, an ancient **Huilua Fishpond at Kahana Bay** *(p. 160)* reveals how the Hawaiians who inhabited the area ensured that their population would remain fed. A cluster of coconut and eucalyptus trees in central Oahu guards the sacred stones of **Kukaniloko** *(p. 188)*, a site where royal women gave birth to high chiefs. Even today, many people believe the stones hold mystical powers. In Makaha Valley, the well-preserved **Kaneaki Heiau** *(p. 195)* was built to honor Lono, the Hawaiian god of agriculture.

The sacred grounds of the faithfully restored Kaneaki Heiau is a step back in time to ancient Hawaii.

BEACHES

The ocean is an integral part of island life, especially on Oahu where most of the shoreline is readily accessible. The sea's omnipresence is easy on the eyes and therapeutic for the soul. With a water temperature that hovers around 75 degrees, ocean sports are enjoyable year-round. Whether you want to swim, surf, paddle, fish, kayak, dive or just bob up and down in the waves, you can find a beach on Oahu that's suited to your preference. Even if all you do is sit and gaze at the distant horizon, rarely does a trip to the beach disappoint.

First-time visitors will be happy to learn that not all of Oahu's beaches are as crowded as Waikiki. For a romantic excursion, visit **Halona Cove Beach** *(p. 150)*, tucked beneath the main highway in Southeast Oahu, a secluded spot to exchange saltwater kisses like Burt Lancaster and Deborah Kerr did when they filmed *From Here to Eternity*. The shoreline at **Mokuleia Beach Park** *(p. 186)* stretches for miles in either direction and is ideal for long, leisurely walks uninterrupted by encroaching development. At **Lanikai Beach** *(p. 168)*, you'll find what is truly one of the world's most idyllic strands—an unmatched coastline of powder-fine sand bordered by crystalline turquoise water.

With its soft white sand and gorgeous views, Lanikai Beach is the perfect place to catch some rays.

A steep descent from Kalanianaole Highway brings you to rocky Halona Cove Beach, a fine choice to lay your mat.

GARDENS AND NATURE PRESERVES

Plentiful on all the islands, aromatic plumerias are often used to make leis.

Hawaiians believe that if you take care of the land, the land will take care of you. Thanks to state and federal conservation areas and the organizations that manage them, many of Hawaii's delicate ocean and forest areas are being actively protected. The botanical gardens and arboretums around Oahu offer brilliant introductions to the tropical plants you see growing in the wild, showcasing unique varieties of orchids, heliconia, hibiscus, anthuriums, birds of paradise, plumerias, ginger and so much more. These contained habitats also play a critical role in preserving native plant species, and it's worth a visit to get a glimpse of what once grew wild on the islands. Walking through these nature preserves can give you a deeper appreciation for the stark diversity of flora that colors the island landscape.

Take a guided nature hike through **Hoomaluhia Botanical Garden** *(p. 157)*, a 400-acre botanical garden in Kaneohe that has an extensive native plant collection. At **Lyon Arboretum** *(p. 127)*, keep an eye out for white-rumped Shama thrushes, cockatoos, cardinals, mynas and other singing birds as you stroll past towering breadfruit trees and exotic palms. **Kaena Point Natural Area Reserve** *(p. 177)* is a breathtaking, rugged outpost where you can explore Oahu's ecosystem on your own.

Explore the winding hiking paths at Lyon Arboretum, located in lush Manoa Valley.

HAWAIIAN CRAFTS

Ancient Hawaiians were expert craftsmen, as evidenced by their handiwork—koa canoes that crossed oceans, durable baskets plaited from *lauhala* leaves, cowry-shell octopus lures and deadly shark-tooth clubs. The elaborate feather cloaks worn by the *alii* were woven from hundreds of thousands of feathers hand-plucked by specialized bird catchers, hinting at a standard of meticulous perfection. Today, skilled artisans continue in the Hawaiian tradition, sewing intricate quilts, ornate

Woven lauhala *goods are a Hawaiian craft specialty.*

shell jewelry, exotic wooden bowls and other decorative items. Galleries islandwide sell fine art by island residents, but the best places to find local handicrafts are at farmers markets and community craft fairs, typically held on weekends.

Natural dyes are used for the decorative patterns on tapa, traditional Polynesian cloth made from tree bark.

Na Mea/Native Books Hawaii *(p. 138)* has the most comprehensive selection of books, music, and DVDs relating to Hawaii and the Pacific, as well as homemade crafts that make thoughtful gift items. At **Polynesian Treasures** *(p. 183)* on the North Shore, you'll find island-inspired jewelry and knickknacks, wood carvings, locally made soaps and candles, and other cultural handicrafts. If you're mesmerized by the serene strumming of island music, **The Ukulele House** *(p. 93)* in Waikiki has a wide range of instruments, not to mention the world's largest ukulele.

LOCAL-STYLE GRINDS

Listen carefully to the lyrics of reggae-inspired island pop, and you'll find a lot of them celebrate local food. "I like my fish and poi, I'm a big boy…" "Beef stew on the stove, *lomi* salmon with the ice…" "I love you like a mango…" You get the picture. Food is a big part of life in Hawaii, where eating is both a popular pastime and a way to share cultures. There's nothing that says local more than the classic plate lunch—a generous helping of meat, "two scoops rice" and a mound of mac salad. There's a lot more to local-*kine* grinds than plate lunches, though. A long list of ethnic treats that were introduced during plantation days

A traditional plate lunch always includes white rice, macaroni salad and a healthy portion of meat.

are now mainstays of local cuisine—so much so that you'll find Spam, *musubi* and *mochi* at convenience stores and Portuguese sausage and *saimin* at McDonalds.

You won't regret finding your way to **Kaka'ako Kitchen** *(p. 133)*, where local dishes get a gourmet touch, like seared *ahi* steak on a purple taro bun with local greens. For authentic island eats just steps from Waimanalo's beaches, try **Keneke's Plate Lunch** *(p. 148)*. On the North Shore, **Giovanni's Aloha Shrimp Truck** *(p. 179)* serves up roadside plate lunches that some claim are the best on Oahu. Located on Honolulu's waterfront, **Nico's Pier 38** *(p. 110)* puts a slightly upscale twist on familiar local dishes, like fried rice with ham, Portuguese sausage, bacon and *kamaboko* (Japanese fishcake).

Locals feast on ahi sandwiches like these from Nico's Pier 38.

Laulau, kalua pork and grilled mahimahi are a favorite lunch order.

Top: The lemon-and-butter shrimp at Giovanni's Aloha Shrimp Truck is a to-die-for ocean-fresh treat.

Bottom left: Plate lunches from Kaka'ako Kitchen get a healthy upgrade with a mesclun salad.

Bottom right: There's no pretension at Keneke's, where a hand-written menu greets diners.

HAWAII REGIONAL CUISINE

The blend of Hawaii's cultural diversity and the bountiful fresh fish, game animals, vegetables and tropical fruit of the islands gave rise to a distinct style of cooking known as Hawaii Regional or Pacific Rim cuisine. It's expressed in both

true Hawaiian classics, such as *imu*-roasted pig, *laulau* and poi, and innovative Asian-influenced menus that use fresh, local ingredients in palate-pleasing meals. The islands are the place to try delicate fish like *opah* paired with mango chutney or desserts like cheesecake served with tangy-sweet passionfruit sauce. For a unique cultural experience, indulge in these lush, upscale flavors as they're prepared by chefs who have made names for themselves around the world.

Orchids pairs its elegant, island-inspired menu with an unbeatable view of the Pacific.

At **The Pineapple Room by Alan Wong** *(p. 133)*, local-style favorites reach astonishing new heights. Try the *kalua* pig BLT or crispy calamari *somen* salad, modern twists on old classics. Seafood lovers will appreciate **Sam Choy's Breakfast Lunch & Crab** *(p. 113)* sensible island treatment—coconut-breaded shrimp, fresh flash-fried *poke* and fresh sashimi with a wasabi *shoyu*. In Kahala, **Hoku's** *(p. 136)* chef Wayne Hirabayashi masterfully brings out the intricate flavors of fresh island ingredients in dishes like *kiawe* cold-smoked Kurobata pork chops with Kahuku corn and haricots verts.

Complemented by a panoramic ocean view, it's perfect for a special occasion. The oceanfront **Orchids** *(p. 89)* in Waikiki serves a mix of Hawaiian and international cuisine like broiled *ono* with a roasted garlic, ginger and soy vinaigrette.

This sweet chili–glazed monchong from The Pineapple Room by Alan Wong demonstrates the subtle Asian influence on Hawaiian cuisine.

COTTAGES AND INNS

There's no place in the world like Waikiki, and its beachfront resorts offer unbridled luxury and convenience. While some visitors appreciate the area's extensive nightlife, dining and shopping options, others are looking for a more intimate experience—a slice of paradise they don't have to share with hundreds of other guests. That's what a handful of charming cottages on Oahu have to offer. Many are built in a simple plantation-house style, designed to utilize the tradewind flow and usually featuring an outdoor lanai where guests can gather and "talk story." Some are beachfront, so you can be lulled by the wash of the waves from the comfort of your own hammock. Inns, too, overflow with country charm—fresh flowers, local art, homemade meals—rather than trendy elegance, giving guests a sense of old Hawaii and sharing the same aloha that existed then.

A short drive from the beach is **Manoa Valley Inn** *(p. 130)*, a charming, century-old country inn surrounded by lush vegetation that promises quiet serenity. On the other side of the Koolau Range, there are numerous bed and breakfasts in the seaside town of Kailua. Check with **Pat's Kailua Beach Properties** *(p. 162)* for an affordable cottage 100 yards from the dazzling aquamarine water. You might recognize the North Shore's **Ke Iki Beach Bungalows** *(p. 178)* from its many Hollywood appearances. This cluster of oceanfront duplexes is an excellent alternative to the pricey resort down the street.

The ocean is just steps away from your room at Ke Iki Beach Bungalows.

SURFING

It's no surprise that surfing is an integral part of Oahu's identity. The North Shore is widely considered the Mecca of modern surfing, and Waikiki Beach its legendary birthplace. From Duke Kahanamoku to Eddie Aikau, surfing's most renowned heroes rose to fame riding Oahu's magnificent waves. Today, visitors can still enjoy the rolling breakers once reserved for Hawaiian royalty, but you don't have to be a pro to ride Oahu's waters. Waikiki Beach has spots for all levels—ask a local beach boy or girl to point you to the right break for you. Beginners can also head up to the North Shore surf schools for a day of fun in the summer. As much as the ancient tradition has evolved, the invigorating "stoke" that surfing produces remains the same, and enthusiasts from around the world come to experience it.

Summer swells bring lively waves to the south shore, and spots along **Kakaako Waterfront Park** *(p. 116)* are among Honolulu's finest. Here, bodysurfers enjoy a private peak called "Point Panic" while shortboarders rip up Kewalo's abundant left and right walls. Away from the crowds, the Leeward Coast's **Keaau Beach Park** *(p. 201)* has a long break known as "Free Hawaii." Along the famous North Shore, experienced surfers can tackle the powerful waves at **Haleiwa Alii Beach** *(p. 185)*, where the world's best come to compete every winter.

If you couldn't squeeze your surfboard into your carry-on, beachside rental places dot Oahu's beaches.

Beginners enjoy the North Shore's calm summer waves, while pros venture out into colossal winter swells.

SNORKELING

Snorkeling in Hawaiian waters is akin to floating in a teeming aquarium of rare species. The offshore reefs abound with colorful blue and green spectacled parrotfish and rainbow-colored lagoon triggerfish—just to name a few. You can't go anywhere else in the world to see some of these underwater creatures: 25 percent of the fish swimming here can only be found on the reefs in this volcanic paradise. You may be lucky enough to hang out with ancient sea turtles or skim the waves with a few spinner dolphins.

If you're lucky, you'll spot a honu (green sea turtle) or even swim with one.

Fringing reefs off Oahu's shoreline provide excellent opportunities to explore this undersea universe. Calm summer conditions on the North Shore make **Pupukea Beach Park** *(p. 184)* one of the best snorkeling destinations in Hawaii. The marine life conservation district boasts large schools of reef fish, giant coral formations, and excellent visibility. In Southeast Oahu, you'll find the labyrinth of vibrantly colored coral at **Hanauma Bay Nature Preserve** *(p. 149)*, Oahu's iconic snorkeling destination. Off the beaten path at **Kaena Point State Park** *(p. 149)*, the sparkling aquamarine waters of Yokohama Bay make glimpsing the world beneath the waves irresistible.

There's plenty of colorful marine life to spot when snorkeling Oahu's waters.

Top: Moray eels are common in Oahu waters.
Bottom: Pupukea Beach Park features pristine coves ideal for underwater adventure.

SUNSET COCKTAILS

What's a fabulous Hawaiian sunset without a mai tai in one hand and your sweetheart's hand in the other? Okay, if you don't have the sweetheart, a soothing serenade from a slack-key guitar may be every bit as satisfying. Oahu's dreamy sunsets are not to be missed—pretty shades of pastels overtake the sky, and the coconut palms become shadowy silhouettes as the deep-orange sun drops beneath the distant horizon. A marvelous curtain call for another glorious day.

The ocean views from Waikiki's Mai Tai Bar are as refreshing as the cocktails.

Viewing spots abound in the Waikiki corridor, and the **Mai Tai Bar** *(p. 96)* is no exception to the rule, with its patio tables providing front-row seats for watching the sun set over the ocean. Far and away the best place to hear some of Hawaii's most talented musicians is **Chai's Island Bistro** *(p. 115)* at Aloha Tower Marketplace, where you can enjoy exquisite contemporary island cuisine in an intimate concert setting. And at **Duke's Canoe Club**'s *(p. 96)* beachside lanai, you can raise an umbrella-topped glass to Duke Kahanamoku, one of surfing's legends, while listening to the likes of island favorite Henry Kapono.

Duke's Canoe Club boasts exotic tropical drinks just steps from the beach.

HIDDEN®
OAHU

Including Waikiki, Honolulu and Pearl Harbor

Ray Riegert

SIXTH EDITION

"*Hidden Oahu* offers a glimpse at the Hawaiian island's
one-of-a-kind lodging and dining opportunities,
as well as innovative outdoor activities."
—*Denver Post*

"This guide focuses on the unique rather than the obvious."
—*San Antonio Express-News*

Ulysses Press
BERKELEY, CALIFORNIA

Published by: ULYSSES PRESS
                 P.O. Box 3440
                 Berkeley, CA 94703
                 www.ulyssespress.com

ISSN 1524-5934
ISBN-13 978-1-56975-585-3

Printed in Canada by Transcontinental Printing

20 19 18 17 16 15 14 13 12 11 10 9

UPDATE AUTHOR: Catharine Lo
EDITORIAL DIRECTOR: Leslie Henriques
MANAGING EDITOR: Claire Chun
EDITORIAL ASSOCIATES: Lauren Harrison, Abigail Reser,
    Emma Silvers, Elyce Petker
PRODUCTION: Judith Metzener, Abigail Reser
CARTOGRAPHY: Pease Press
HIDDEN BOOKS DESIGN: what!design @ whatweb.com
INDEXER: Sayre Van Young
COVER PHOTOGRAPHY: front © Pacific Stock/Dave Fleetham;
    back © Douglas Peebles
COLOR INSERT: *page i* © Pacific Stock/Vince Cavataio; *page ii* ©
Douglas Peebles; *page iii* top © Pacific Stock/William Waterfall,
bottom © istockphoto.com/Kimberly Greeleaf; *page iv* © istock
photo.com/Tomás del Amo; *page v* © Pacific Stock/Greg Vaughn;
page vi top © Rodd M. Halstead, bottom © Douglas Peebles; *page vii*
top © istockphoto.com/kazsano, bottom © istockphoto.com/
BigZenDragon; *page viii* top © Mike Burnett, middle © Nico's Pier
38/Shane Kaneshiro, bottom© Christian Razukas; *page ix* top ©
Douglas Peebles, bottom left © Franco Salmoiraghi/PhotoResource
Hawaii.com, bottom right © Monica S. Lee; *page x* top © Orchids,
courtesy of Halekulani, bottom © Donna Shiroma Nakasue; *page xi*
© Ke Iki Beach Bungalows/John McDaniel; *page xii* © istock
photo.com/David Lewis; *page xiii* top © istockphoto.com/Jacom
Stephens, bottom Dave Bjorn/PhotoResourceHawaii.com; *page xiv*
© istockphoto.com/Joanna Witczak, bottom © istockphoto.com/
qldian; *page xv* top © Roy Niswanger, bottom © Photo Resource
Hawaii/DanitaDelimont.com; *page xvi* top © Justin Kane, bottom ©
Pacific Stock/Kyle Rothenborg

Distributed by Publishers Group West

The author and publisher have made every effort to ensure the accuracy of information contained in *Hidden Oahu*, but can accept no liability for any loss, injury or inconvenience sustained by any traveler as a result of information or advice contained in this guide.

For Claire,
my favorite kamaaina

CONTENTS

10 CENTRAL OAHU & LEEWARD COAST 187

MAPS

OUTDOOR ADVENTURE SYMBOLS

The following symbols accompany national, state and regional park listings, as well as beach descriptions throughout the text.

▲	Camping	🏄	Surfing
🚶	Hiking	🎿	Waterskiing
🏊	Swimming	⛵	Windsurfing
🤿	Snorkeling or Scuba Diving	🐟	Fishing

HIDDEN LISTINGS

Throughout the book, listings that reveal the hidden realm—spots that are away from tourists or reflect authentic Oahu—are marked by this icon:

There are also special maps at the start of each section that guide you to some of these hidden listings. Each place is identified with this symbol:

THE GATHERING PLACE

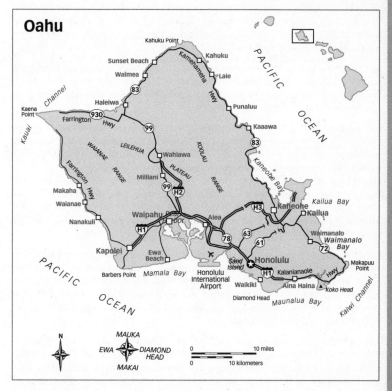

Oahu

Oahu is the centerpiece of the Hawaiian archipelago that stretches more than 1500 miles across the North Pacific Ocean. In a sense, it's a small continent. Volcanic mountains rise in the interior, while the coastline is fringed with coral reefs and white-sand beaches. In the parlance of the Pacific, it is a "high island," very different from the low-lying atolls that are found elsewhere in Polynesia.

The northeastern face of the island, buffeted by trade winds, is the wet side. The contrast between this side and the island's southwestern sector is sometimes startling. In the northeast, the landscape teems with exotic tropical plants, while across the island you're liable to see cactus growing in a barren landscape!

2   Dominated by the capital city of Honolulu, Oahu is the meeting place of East and West. Today, with its highrise cityscape and crowded commercial center, Honolulu is more the place where Hong Kong meets Los Angeles. It's the hub of Hawaii—a city that dominates the political, cultural and economic life of the islands.

And it's the focus of Oahu as well. Honolulu has given Oahu more than its nickname, The Capital Isle. The city has drawn three-fourths of Hawaii's population to this third-largest island, making Oahu both a military stronghold and a popular tourist spot.

With military installations at Pearl Harbor and outposts seemingly everywhere, the armed forces control about one-quarter of the island. Most bases are off-limits to civilians; and tourists congregate in Honolulu's famed resort area—Waikiki. Both defense and tourism are big business on Oahu, and it's an ironic fact of island life that the staid, uniformly dressed military peacefully coexist here with crowds of sun-loving, scantily clad visitors.

The tourists are attracted by one of the world's most famous beaches, a seemingly endless white-sand ribbon that has drawn sun worshippers and water lovers since the days of Hawaiian royalty. In ancient times Waikiki was a swamp; now it's a spectacular strand of world-class resorts.

Indeed, Waikiki is at the center of Pacific tourism, just as Honolulu is the capital of the Pacific. Nowhere else in the world will you find a population more varied or an ambience more vital. For instance, the Japanese continue to flock to Waikiki (especially during Golden Week, which usually falls at the end of April), and as a result, a large number of shops maintain Japanese-speaking staff; many services, from shopping trolleys to surf lessons, cater to Japanese visitors. There are times when Waikiki's Parisian-size boulevards seem ready to explode from the sheer force of the crowds. People in bikinis and wild-colored aloha shirts stroll the streets, while others flash past on mopeds.

But, the secret of this island is that just beyond Honolulu's bustling thoroughfares stretches a beautiful island, featuring countless beaches and two incredible mountain ranges. Since most of the tourists (and a vast majority of the island's 905,600 population) congregate in the southern regions around Honolulu, the north is rural. You can experience the color and velocity of the city, then head for the slow and enchanting country.

As you begin to explore for yourself, you'll find Oahu also has something else to offer: history. *Oahu* means "gathering place" in Hawaiian, and for centuries it has been an important commercial area and cultural center. First populated by Marquesans around A.D. 500, the island was later settled by seafaring immigrants from Tahiti. Waikiki, with its white-sand beaches and luxurious coconut groves, became a favored spot among early monarchs.

Warring chiefs long battled for control of the island. Kamehameha I seized power in 1795 after landing troops along the coast just east of Waikiki, proceeding inland and sweeping an opposing army over the cliffs of Nuuanu Pali north of Honolulu. Several years earlier the British had "discovered" Honolulu Harbor, a natural anchorage destined to be one of the Pacific's key seaports. Over the years the harbor proved ideal first for whalers and sandalwood traders and eventually for freighters and ocean liners.

By the 1840s, the city, originally a village called Kou, had grown into a shipping port and the commercial and political capital of the Hawaiian kingdom. Here in 1893 a band of white businessmen illegally overthrew the native monarchy. Almost a half-century later, in an ill-advised but brilliantly executed military maneuver, the Japanese drew the United States into World War II with a devastating air strike against the huge naval base at Pearl Harbor.

There are some fascinating historical monuments to tour throughout Honolulu, but I recommend you also venture outside the city to Oahu's less congested regions. Major highways lead from the capital along the east and west coasts of this 608-square-mile island, and several roads bisect the central plateau en route to the North Shore. Except for a five-mile strip in Oahu's northwest corner, you can drive completely around the island.

Closest to Honolulu is the east coast, where a spectacular seascape is paralleled by the Koolaus, a jagged and awesomely steep mountain range. This is Oahu's rainswept Windward Coast. Here, traveling up the coast past the bedroom communities of Kailua and Kaneohe, you'll discover beautiful and relatively untouched white-sand beaches. On the North Shore are some of the world's most famous surfing spots—Waimea Bay, Sunset, the Banzai Pipeline—where winter waves as high as 20 to 30 feet roll in with crushing force.

Kapolei, the planned "second city" built to relieve some of the pressure that a growing population placed on Honolulu, continues to grow. Further along Route 1, the residential enclaves of Ewa Beach and Makakilo and the Ko'olina Resort mark the end of the south shore and the beginning of the west side.

The Waianae Range, rising to 4040 feet, shadows Oahu's western coast. The sands are as white here, the beaches as uncrowded, but I've always felt slightly uncomfortable on the Leeward Coast. Low-income Leeward residents suffer most in economically trying times, and theft can be a problem here. In response to concerns about safety, the city has closed several of the beach parks at night. Avoid dangerous situations by being sensitive and respectful to families living on the beach.

Between the Koolau and Waianae ranges, remnants of the two volcanoes that created Oahu, spreads the Leilehua Plateau. This fertile region is occupied by current pineapple plantations as well as several large military bases.

Geologically, Oahu is the second-oldest island in the chain; two million years ago it was two individual islands, which eventually were joined by the Leilehua Plateau. Among its geographic features is the *pali*, an awesome wall of sheer cliffs along the windward coastline, and three famous tuff-cone volcanoes—Diamond Head, Punchbowl and Koko Head. The coastline of Oahu is 112 miles, offering approximately 130 different beaches to swim, surf, boogieboard, snorkel, dive or just plain relax.

WHERE TO GO

Although many visitors bypass Oahu to vacation on the Neighbor Islands, it has much to offer. From the hustle and bustle of the largest city in the Pacific Islands to the quiet beaches of the Windward Coast and the mountains of the interior, the island's diversity allows a variety of experiences unavailable elsewhere in Hawaii.

Waikiki is where the action is. People come from all over the world to stroll along its beaches, shop in its malls and be part of the scene. The competition among the vast number of hotels means there are good bargains in accommodations, which means most people stay here. Restaurants range from inexpensive fast food to elegant five-star hotel dining rooms highlighting Hawaiian regional cuisine to diverse ethnic fare. Shopping opportunities are endless.

The buildings of **Downtown Honolulu** trace the city's history from its early days as a mission outpost and royal capital to its current incarnation as a modern port and commercial center. This eclectic collection of architectural treasures includes old homes, commercial buildings, churches, the shops of Chinatown and the only royal palace ever to be built in the United States.

Greater Honolulu is the Honolulu of the locals. It is where they live and play in neighborhoods like Kalihi, a working class enclave to the west of downtown, inhabited by Hawaiians and Samoans, among others. Or in Kahala, the tony coastal district with its beachside homes and perfectly manicured lawns. Or Manoa, a neighborhood that stretches from the University of Hawaii campus to a valley verdant with tropical rainforest.

Beyond the hustle and bustle of Honolulu lies the rural tropical terrain of **Southeast Oahu**. This region of volcanic craters towering overhead, cliffs plunging into the sea and beaches strung out along the shoreline is waiting to be explored. Waimanalo, a rural town of fruit farmers and cowboys, sports another side of Oahu's many faceted personality.

Heading north along the **Windward Coast**, the spectacular scenery continues. The bedroom community of Kailua has become a low-key destination for windsurfers, kayakers and swimmers, with lots of bed and breakfasts and restaurants catering to the watersport crowd. Kamehameha Highway hugs the coast, passing a series of sandy beaches on one side and small farms on the other. The Mormons developed the town of Laie with its branch of Brigham Young University and the Polynesian Cultural Center, which brings to life, in a fashion, the traditional customs of the Pacific islanders.

Perhaps nowhere is more legendary among surfers than Oahu's **North Shore**. Surfers from around the world come to try their skills at Waimea Bay and Sunset Beach. The area is also noted for its farms and ranches. Haleiwa, a mostly gentrified plantation town, serves as the commercial center of the North Shore and has a number of shops and restaurants that cater to surfers, farmers and counterculturalists, all who call this beautiful coastal region home.

Central Oahu and the **Leeward Coast**, which together comprise the western half of Oahu, are the only parts of the island that have been relatively untouched by tourism. The last of Oahu's major plantations occupy the high central plateau that is nestled between two mountain ranges. The isolated Leeward Coast, with its rugged landscape, has some of the most beautiful beaches on Oahu. The area also serves as home to rugged, independent people, and a large concentration of na-

Obama's Oahu

It wasn't long after Barack Obama became Hawaii's first native-born U.S. President that Obamamania hit the streets of Honolulu. Even if you don't intend to, you'll likely run into places the President likes to frequent, many of them sentimental reminders of his youthful days on Oahu. Local establishments proudly proclaim that the President once came to call, and custom walking tours and specialized maps allow visitors to follow in his footsteps.

Close to his childhood home in Makiki is the sprawling campus of Obama's distinguished alma mater, Punahou School. There's no doubt about the President's island roots when you see where he skillfully bodysurfed the shorebreak at Sandy Beach or regularly treated his family to shave ice. He paid his respects at the National Memorial Cemetery of the Pacific where his grandfather is buried and at an isolated rocky outcropping on the south shore where his mother's ashes were strewn. Obama has taken his daughters to snorkel at Hanauma Bay, and they lunched on hamburgers from Kua Aina Sandwich Shop. A round of golf at Olomana Golf Links gave him a chance to catch up with old friends, and dinner at Alan Wong's brought back the distinct, familiar flavors of Hawaii Regional cuisine.

For additional local Obama trivia, consult Franko's Obama Oahu Guide (www. obamahawaiimap.com), a colorful and informative waterproof map, or Ron Jacobs's detailed scrapbook Obamaland, which relates more personal stories and candid photographs of Obama than his greatest fans could wish for.

tive Hawaiians, who are determined to preserve the customs and traditions of the past that have disappeared elsewhere.

WHEN TO GO

SEASONS

There are two types of seasons on Oahu, one keyed to tourists and the other to the climate. The peak tourist seasons run from mid-December until Easter, then again from mid-June through Labor Day. Particularly around the Christmas holidays and in August, the visitors centers are crowded. Prices increase, hotel rooms and rental cars become harder to reserve, and everything moves a bit more rapidly.

If you plan to explore Oahu during these seasons, make reservations several months in advance; actually, it's a good idea to make advance reservations whenever you visit. Without doubt, the off-season is the best time to hit the island. Not only are hotels more readily available, but campsites and hiking trails are also less crowded.

Climatologically, the ancient Hawaiians distinguished between two seasons—*kau*, or summer, and *hooilo*, or winter. Summer extends from May to October, when the sun is overhead and the temperatures are slightly higher. Winter brings more variable winds and cooler weather.

The important rule to remember about Oahu's beautiful weather is that it changes very little from season to season but varies dramatically from place to place. The average yearly temperature is about 78°, and during the coldest weather in January and the warmest in August, the thermometer rarely moves more than 5° or 6° in either direction and there's usually a cooling breeze. Similarly, seawater temperatures range comfortably between 74° and 80° year-round. Seeking a cooler climate? Head up to the mountains; for every thousand feet in elevation, the temperature drops about 3°.

Crucial to this luxurious semitropical environment are the trade winds that blow with welcome regularity from the northeast, providing a natural form of air conditioning. When the trades stop blowing, they are sometimes replaced by *kona* winds carrying rain and humid weather from the southwest. These are most frequent in the winter, when the Hawaiian islands receive their heaviest rainfall.

While summer showers are less frequent and shorter in duration, winter storms are sometimes quite nasty. I've seen it pour for five consecutive days, until hiking trails disappeared and city streets were awash. If you visit in winter, particularly from December to March, you're risking the chance of rain.

A wonderful factor to remember about this wet weather is that if it's raining where you are, you can often simply go someplace else. And I don't mean another part of the world, or even a different island. Since the rains generally batter the northeastern sections of each island, you can usually head over to the south or west coast for warm, sunny weather.

CALENDAR OF EVENTS

Something else to consider in planning a visit to Oahu is the amazing lineup of annual cultural events. For a thumbnail idea of what's happening when, check the calendar below. You might just find that special occasion to climax an already dynamic vacation. For a comprehensive listing with current updates, check the Hawaii Visitors & Convention Bureau website at www.gohawaii.com. Once you're on Oahu, you can pick up a free copy of *Honolulu Weekly*, which spotlights just about everything that's happening, and the Friday editions of the *Honolulu Advertiser* and the *Honolulu Star Bulletin*, the city's major newspapers.

JANUARY
Mid-January The opening of **Hawaii's legislature** on the third Wednesday in January is marked by traditional pageantry. The week-long **Sony Open**, a full-field PGA tour event held at the Waialae Country Club, features some of the world's best golfers.

Mid-January or February The month-long **Narcissus Festival** begins the Chinese New Year with street parties and parades in Honolulu's Chinatown.

Late January In Waikiki, people come from throughout the islands to compete in ancient games, a quarter-mile outrigger canoe race and tug-of-war competitions at the **Ala Wai Challenge** at Ala Wai Park. The **Pipeline Bodysurfing Classic** takes place on the North Shore.

FEBRUARY

Early February   The **Pro Bowl** draws fans to Aloha Stadium for one of football's annual traditions. The **Punahou Carnival**, one of the best county fair–style events, features games, rides and events and a chance to mingle with local folks.

Late February   The world's greatest bodyboarders compete in the **IBA Pipeline Pro** at the birthplace of the sport, the North Shore's Pipeline.

February through March   The Japanese community in Honolulu celebrates the **Cherry Blossom Festival** with tea ceremonies, kabuki theater presentations, martial arts demonstrations and crafts exhibits.

MARCH

Early March   On the first Saturday of the month, a small group of kite afficionados gather in Kapiolani Park for the **Oahu Kite Festival**.

Mid-March   Japanese street performers, food booths, sumo wrestling and dancing celebrate Asian, Pacific and Hawaiian culture during the **Honolulu Festival**, which culminates a major parade.

March 17   The **St. Patrick's Day Parade** makes its way from Fort DeRussy to Kapiolani Park in honor of the state's large Hawaiian-Irish population.

APRIL

Early April   Buddhist temples on the island mark **Buddha Day**, the Buddha's birthday, with special services. Included among the events are pageants, dances and a flower festival. Sample a taste of the Highlands at the **Hawaii Scottish Festival** in Kapiolani Park, where you're bound to see a bagpipe or two along with contests of strength, food booths and crafts.

MAY

May 1   **Lei Day** is celebrated on the island by people wearing flower leis and colorful Hawaiian garb. The Brothers Cazimero, one of Ha-

A Circle of Aloha

The lei. A symbol of Hawaii, along with grass skirts and shimmering palm trees. If you are fortunate enough to be met at the airport by someone you know, chances are you will be wreathed in fragrant blossoms and kissed on both cheeks. But if you come to the island as a stranger, give yourself this aromatic gift. At some point venture downtown to Maunakea Street where you will find a row of small shops selling a variety of flower leis, including the fragrant plumeria or ginger leis. Lei-giving is a tradition that dates back to ancient times, when they were used as head wreaths as well as flower necklaces in religious ceremonies and were presented to the *alii*. And as in ancient times, the craft of lei-making is thriving today. You can still find leis that incorporate ferns, *pukiawe* (red berries), *lehua* blossoms and *maile* leaves into intricate works of art, some having hundreds of blossoms and all made with aloha.

waii's popular singing groups, gives an annual **May Day Concert** at the Waikiki Shell.

Mid-May *Mabuhay!* Kapiolani Park hosts the **Filipino Fiesta and Parade** where you'll find live entertainment, food and crafts. Top dancers from Hawaii, Samoa and the mainland compete in the **World Fire Knife Dance Competition and Samoan Festival** at the Polynesian Cultural Center in Laie.

JUNE

During June Starting on Memorial Day and lasting for four weekends, the **50th State Fair** highlights Hawaii's agriculture, farm animals, flowers and products in Aloha Stadium. There are also rides, games and commercial booths.

Early June A floral parade with floats and marching bands, a ceremony decorating Kamehameha's statue with leis, and an all-day festival of Hawaiian entertainment in Kapiolani Park commemorate Hawaii's first king with the **King Kamehameha Celebration**.

Mid-June to mid-July Athletes from throughout the state come to compete in 40 various Olympic sports at locations around the island as part of the **Aloha State Games**. The **Matsuri Festival** focuses on Japanese culture, with Bon dance performers in full regalia, a parade and other activities and events in Waikiki.

Late June More than 20 hula *halau* from around the islands and as far away as Japan compete in the **King Kamehameha Hula Competition**, an annual event that showcases chanting as well as both traditional and contemporary hula styles. The three-day **Taste of Honolulu** food and wine festival raises money for charities.

JULY

Early July Military and high school bands interspersed with floral floats make their way through the streets of Kailua during the city's **4th of July Weekend Parade**. The **4th of July All Star Rodeo** at the New Town & Country Stables in Waimanalo showcases professional rodeo events, with the crowd as colorful as the competing *paniolo* (Hawaiian cowboys). Oahu's biggest watersports carnival, **BayFest**, takes place at Kaneohe Bay on the Marine Corps base, with live entertainment, food booths and a carnival, in addition to, you guessed it, watersports events.

Mid-July The contestants in the **TransPacific Yacht Race** start arriving in Honolulu from Los Angeles to be greeted by festivities and parties at the city's marinas. In Honolulu, dancers six to twelve years old gather to compete in the **Queen Liliuokalani Keiki Hula Festival**.

Mid- to late July The **Hawaii All-Collectors Show** at the Blaisdell Exhibition Hall provides hours of fun for browsers as well as buyers of Hawaiiana. Both locals and visitors can browse and purchase visual arts, and discover new talent at the North Shore's Annual **Haleiwa Arts Festival**, highlighted by "talking story" with the artists and children's hands-on activities.

Late July   Dancers from all the islands come to Moanalua Gardens to participate in the **Prince Lot Hula Festival** in honor of Prince Lot.

AUGUST

During August   The dramatic **Haleiwa Cup**, a one-mile ocean swim from Haleiwa Beach Park to Puena Point and back, draws more than 350 swimmers. The **Wahine Bodyboard Championships** take place on designated beaches on the island.

Early August   The **Hawaii Dragon Boat Festival**, held at Ala Moana Beach Park, is a colorful spin on an oriental nautical theme, with races, crafts, multicultural entertainment and food. **Duke's Ocean-Fest** offers more than a week of watersport competitions between individuals and teams from around the world at locations along Waikiki Beach, ending in a celebration of Duke Kahanamoku's birthday.

Mid-August   The three-day **Made in Hawaii Festival** highlights local products at the Blaisdell Exhibition Hall.

SEPTEMBER

Early September   Iolani Palace celebrates **Queen Liliuokalani's Birthday** with island entertainment. The **Queen Liliuokalani Canoe Regatta** is also staged early this month.

Mid-September and October   The highlight of Hawaii's cultural season is the **Aloha Week** festival, a series of week-long celebrations featuring parades, street parties and pageants.

OCTOBER

Early October   About 100 teams of the top male outrigger canoe paddlers in the world compete in the 40.8-mile Molokai-to-Oahu outrigger canoe race, the **Annual Molokai Hoe**, which ends at Fort DeRussy Beach in Waikiki.

Late October   The **Hawaii International Film Festival** provides a showcase of 100 foreign, independent, short and premiere films, seminars and workshops.

NOVEMBER

November through December   The world's greatest surfers compete on the North Shore in a series of contests, including the **Triple Crown of Surfing**.

DECEMBER

During December   **Honolulu City Lights** at City Hall marks the start of the Christmas season with a tree-lighting ceremony, a parade and a wreath exhibit. **A Candlelight Christmas** at Mission Houses is an old-fashioned celebration of the season. The two-day Festival of Art & Fine Crafts at Thomas Square Park features over 110 vendors.

Early December   Buddha's enlightenment is commemorated with **Bodhi Day** ceremonies and religious services. Runners by the thousands turn out for the **Honolulu Marathon**.

BEFORE YOU GO

VISITORS CENTERS

HAWAII VISITORS & CONVENTION BUREAU ✉*2270 Kalakaua Avenue, Room 801, Honolulu, HI 96815* ✆*808-923-1811, 800-464-2924* ⌂*www.go hawaii.com, info@hvcb.org* This state-run agency is a valuable resource from which to obtain free information on Oahu. The Bureau can help plan your trip as well as offer advice once you reach the island.

OAHU VISITORS BUREAU ✉*733 Bishop Street, Suite 1520, Honolulu* ✆*808-524-0722, 877-525-6248* ⌂*www.visit-oahu.com* This visitors bureau offers tourist information specific to this island.

HAWAII STATE PUBLIC LIBRARY SYSTEM ⌂*www.librarieshawaii. org* With a network of libraries, this government agency is an excellent resource and provides facilities for residents and non-residents alike. The libraries are good places to find light beach-reading material as well as books on Hawaii. On Oahu, libraries can be found in Honolulu, Kailua, Waimanalo and many other communities. Visitors can check out books by simply applying for a library card with a valid identification card (non-residents must pay $10 for a three-month membership). Most books do not have to be returned to the same branch where they were originally checked out.

PACKING

When I get ready to pack for a trip, I sit down and make a list of everything I'll need. It's a very slow, exact procedure: I look in closets, drawers and shelves, and run through in my mind the activities in which I'll participate, determining which items are required for each. After all the planning is complete and when I have the entire inventory collected in one long list, I sit for a minute or two, basking in my wisdom and forethought.

Then I tear the hell out of the list, cut out the ridiculous items I'll never use, halve the number of spares among the necessary items, and reduce the entire contents of my suitcase to the bare essentials.

Before I developed this packing technique, I once traveled overland from London to New Delhi carrying two suitcases and a knapsack. I lugged those damned bundles onto trains, buses, jitneys, taxis and rickshaws. When I reached Turkey, I started shipping things home, but by then I was buying so many market goods that it was all I could do to keep even.

I ended up carrying so much crap that one day, when I was sardined in a crowd pushing its way onto an Indian train, someone managed to pick my pocket. When I felt the wallet slipping out, not only was I unable to chase the culprit—I was so weighted down with baggage that I couldn't even turn around to see who was robbing me!

I'll never travel that way again, and neither should you. Particularly when visiting Oahu, where the weather is mild, you should pack very light. The airlines vary on how much luggage you can take, so check with your carrier. Try to take one suitcase and maybe an accessory bag that can double as a beach bag. Dress styles are very informal in the islands, and laundromats are ubiquitous, so you don't need a broad range of clothing items, and you'll require very few extras among the essential items.

Remember, you're packing for a semitropical climate. Take along a sweater or light jacket for the mountains, and a poncho to protect against rain. But otherwise, all that travelers on Oahu require are shorts, bathing suits, lightweight slacks, T-shirts, short-sleeved shirts and blouses, and summer dresses or muumuus. Rarely do visitors require sports jackets or formal dresses. Wash-and-wear fabrics are the most convenient.

For footwear, I suggest soft, comfortable shoes. Low-cut hiking boots or tennis shoes are preferable for hiking; for beachgoing, there's nothing as good as sandals.

Aloha Ambassadors

You'll see them strolling down the streets of Waikiki, from the Kalakaua Bridge all the way to Kapahulu Avenue. They are highly visible in lime green shirts and are frequently on duty in front of the police station at Kuhio Beach Park. They're "Aloha Ambassadors," and they're here to help you.

Crime ranks near the top of the list of problems facing Honolulu residents. Whenever you meet the locals they're likely to talk about the rise in robberies and car break-ins. If you rent a car in Hawaii the company will warn you not to leave valuables inside, and you'll be reminded at the parks and the beaches by signs stating the same thing. Although your chances of being ripped off are probably pretty slim, as a tourist you are a prime target, so it's something to be wary of.

Tired of having crime tarnish their island's reputation, the citizens of Oahu took action. In late 1996, they formed the Aloha Patrol, a citizen's watchgroup and the eyes and ears of the police in Waikiki. Their intention was also to embody the spirit of aloha for guests. Early the next year, they expanded their work to the North Shore. Today, these "sidewalk ambassadors" have become a professional security force for the Waikiki Business Improvement District.

In Waikiki, the Aloha Ambassadors walk the streets from 10 a.m. to 11 p.m. daily, answering questions, giving directions, telling people about themselves and the Aloha Patrol and, if they see any problems, alerting the police by two-way radio. On the North Shore, they patrol the beach parking lots each afternoon to prevent car break-ins. And it seems to work. Since the program began, there have been no robberies in the afternoons at the patrolled beaches and visitors to Honolulu can be assured that the streets of Waikiki are safer because of the folks in the bright green shirts. For assistance, call 808-216-5947.

There are several other items to squeeze in the corners of your suitcase—sunscreen, sunglasses, a towel and, of course, your copy of *Hidden Oahu*. You might also consider packing a mask, fins and snorkel. Note that if you're not using a digital camera, you'll want to buy your film on the island and have it developed before you leave to avoid x-ray damage. Never carry undeveloped film in your checked luggage. Also remember that the maximum amount of liquid permitted in carry-on luggage is 3 oz. per container; all liquids must also be sealed in a quart-size Ziploc bag.

If you plan on camping, you'll need most of the equipment required for mainland overnighting. On Oahu, you can get along quite comfortably with a lightweight tent and sleeping bag. You'll also need a knapsack, canteen, camp stove and fuel, mess kit, first-aid kit (with insect repellent, water purification tablets and lip balm), toilet kit, a pocket knife, hat, waterproof matches, flashlight and ground cloth.

LODGING

Accommodations on Oahu range from funky cottages to bed-and-breakfast inns to highrise condos. You'll find inexpensive family-run hotels, middle-class tourist facilities and world-class resorts. Generally, the farther a hotel is from the beach, the less it costs.

Whichever you choose, there are a few guidelines to help save money. Try to visit during the off-season, avoiding the high-rate periods during the summer and from Christmas to Easter. If you must travel around Christmas and during the summer high season, it's wise to book reservations as far in advance as possible. Rooms with mountain views are less expensive than oceanview accommodations. Another way to economize is by reserving a room with a kitchen. In any case, try to reserve far in advance.

To help you decide on a place to stay, I've described the accommodations not only by area but also according to price (prices listed are for double occupancy during the high season; prices may decrease in low season). *Budget* hotels ($) are generally less than $90 per night for two people; the rooms are clean, basic and comfortable, but lack amenities. The *moderately* priced hotels ($$) run $90 to $160, and provide larger rooms, plusher furniture and more attractive surroundings. At *deluxe*-priced accommodations ($$$) you can expect to spend between $160 and $240 for a homey bed and breakfast or a double in a hotel or resort. You'll check into a spacious, well-appointed room with modern facilities; downstairs the lobby will be a fashionable affair, and you'll usually see a restaurant, lounge and a cluster of shops. If you want to spend your time (and money) in the island's very finest hotels, try an *ultra-deluxe* facility ($$$$), which will include all the amenities and price well above $240.

Bed-and-Breakfast Inns

The bed-and-breakfast business on Oahu becomes more diverse and sophisticated every year. Today there are several referral services that can find you lodging.

"Lost" in Hawaii

Oahu has been the site of numerous films and television shows, most recently *Lost*, a popular drama series airing on ABC. On the show, a plane crashes on a mysterious tropical island and, when no one comes to their rescue, the survivors are faced with numerous challenges. Locals and frequent visitors will recognize many of the locations as Oahu landmarks, although they've been given new names—and sometimes a new look—in true Hollywood fashion.

The scenic North Shore has gotten the most screen time. A section of Mokuleia Beach that lies across from Dillingham Airfield was used as the plane's crash site, and sand was spread on Kamehameha Highway to cover the asphalt and create the illusion of a larger beach. The spot has since been abandoned in favor of Papailoa Beach (also called Police Beach), near Haleiwa Beach Park, which isn't subject to such high winter surf. Waimea Falls and Valley also have been featured extensively.

Other scenes have been shot on Kualoa Ranch and in Waikane Valley, both on the windward side, as well an unused piece of land at a Hawaiian Electric power station near Kaneohe. These sites are closed to the public, as are the old Army bunkers inside Diamond Head crater that were used in several scenes.

Crews also filmed at Valley of the Temples Memorial Park, where they were drawn to its bamboo grove and Byodo-In, a replica of a 950-year-old Japanese Buddhist temple. The starkly scenic Ka Iwi coast, near Hanauma Bay, has gotten air time, too.

Loyal viewers who visit Oahu will recognize other locales, as scenes have been shot at Waikiki, Manoa Valley and Manoa Falls Trail, the convention center, Waikiki Yacht Club dock, Chinatown and Aloha Stadium.

Bed & Breakfast Hawaii ⊠*P.O. Box 449, Kapaa, HI 96746* ☎*808-822-7771, 800-733-1632* ✉*808-822-2723* ⏍*www.bandb-hawaii.com, reservations@bandb-hawaii.com* The original association, Bed & Breakfast Hawaii, claims about 20 locations on Oahu. Founded in 1979, this Kauai-based service is well known throughout Hawaii.

Affordable Accommodations ⊠*2825 Kauhale Street, Kihei, HI 96753* ☎*808-879-7865, 888-333-9747* ✉*808-874-0831* ⏍*www.affordablemaui.com, info@affordablemaui.com* You can also try Affordable Accommodations, which is based on Maui and has a number of listings on Oahu.

All-Islands Bed & Breakfast ☎*808-263-2342, 800-542-0344* ✉*808-263-0308* ⏍*www.all-islands.com, inquiries@all-islands.com* Or call this Oahu-based reservation service that represents more than 250 bed and breakfasts on the island.

Hawaii's Best Bed & Breakfasts ⊠*571 Pauku Street, Kailua, HI 96734* ☎*808-263-3100, 800-262-9912* ✉*808-262-5650* ⏍*www.bestbnb.com, reservations@bestbnb.com* While the properties represented by these agencies range widely in price, Hawaii's Best Bed & Breakfasts specializes in small, upscale accommodations. With a handful of Oahu-based establishments to choose from, it places guests in a variety of privately owned facilities; most are deluxe priced.

Condos

Many people visiting Hawaii, especially those traveling with families, find that condominiums are often cheaper than hotels. While some hotel rooms come with kitchenettes, few provide all the amenities of condominiums. A condo, in essence, is an apartment away from home. Designed as studio, one-, two- or three-bedroom apartments, they come equipped with full kitchen facilities and complete kitchenware collections. Many also feature washer/dryers, dishwashers, air conditioning, color televisions, telephones, lanais and community swimming pools.

Utilizing the kitchen will save considerably on your food bill; by sharing the accommodations among several people, you'll also cut your lodging bill. While the best way to see Oahu is obviously by hiking and camping, when you're ready to come in from the wilds, consider reserving a place that provides more than a bed and a night table.

Vacation Rentals

The following list offers a host of choices from hotel rooms to beachside homes.

Condo Rentals of Waikiki ☏ 800-923-0555 ✎ www.waikikicondos.com

CyberRentals ✎ www.cyberrentals.com

Gold Coast Real Estate, Inc. ☏ 808-926-7525 ✎ www.goldcoasthawaii.com

Hawaii Vacation Hosts ☏ 800-754-0905 ✎ www.vacationhosts.com

Hawaiian Beach Rentals ☏ 800-853-0787 ✎ www.hawaiianbeachrentals.com

Hawaiian Condo Resorts ☏ 800-487-4505 ✎ www.hawaiicondo.com

Hawaiian Islands Bed & Breakfast ☏ 800-258-7895 ✎ www.lanikaibeachrentals.com

Luxury Vacation Homes ☏ 800-262-9013 ✎ www.luxuryvacationhomes.com

Marc Resorts ☏ 800-535-0085 ✎ www.marcresorts.com

Marina Hawaii Vacations ☏ 808-946-0716 ✎ www.marinahawaiivacations.com

SandSea Inc. Vacation Homes ☏ 800-442-6901 ✎ www.sandsea.com

Tropical Villa Vacations ☏ 888-875-2818 ✎ www.tropicalvillavacations.com

DINING

A few guidelines will help you chart a course through Oahu's countless dining places. Within a particular chapter, the restaurants are categorized geographically, with each restaurant entry describing the establishment as budget ($), moderate ($$), deluxe ($$$) or ultra-deluxe ($$$$) in price.

To establish a pattern for Oahu's parade of dining places, I've described not only the cuisine but also the ambience of each establishment. Restaurants listed offer lunch and dinner unless otherwise noted.

Dinner entrées at *budget* restaurants usually cost $8 or less. The ambience is informal café style and the crowd is often a local one. *Moderately* priced restaurants range between $8 and $16 at dinner and offer pleasant surroundings, a more varied menu and a slower pace. *Deluxe* establishments tab their entrées above $16, featuring sophisticated cuisines, plush decor and more personalized service. *Ultra-deluxe* restaurants generally price above $24.

Breakfast and lunch menus vary less in price from restaurant to restaurant. Even deluxe-priced kitchens usually offer light breakfasts and lunch sandwiches, which place them within a few dollars of their budget-minded competitors. These early meals can be a good time to test expensive restaurants.

TRAVELING WITH CHILDREN

Oahu is an ideal vacation spot for family holidays. The pace is slow, the atmosphere casual. A few guidelines will help ensure that your trip here brings out the joys rather than the strains of parenting, allowing everyone to get into the aloha spirit.

Use a travel agent to help with arrangements; they can reserve bulkhead seats on airlines and determine which flights are least crowded. They can also seek out the best deals on inexpensive condominiums, saving you money on both room and board.

Planning the trip with your kids stimulates their imagination. Books about travel, airplane rides, beaches, whales, volcanoes and Hawaiiana help prepare even a two-year-old for an adventure. This preparation makes the "getting there" part of the trip more exciting for children of all ages.

And "getting there" means a long-distance flight. Plan to bring everything you need on board the plane—diapers, food, toys, books and extra clothing for kids and parents alike. I found it helpful to carry a few new toys and books as treats to distract my son and daughter when they got bored. I also packed extra snacks.

Allow extra time to get places. Book reservations in advance and make sure that the hotel or condominium has the extra crib, cot or bed you require. It's smart to ask for a room at the end of the hall to cut down on noise. Some resorts and hotels have daily programs for kids during the summer and holiday seasons. Hula lessons, lei making, storytelling, sandcastle building and various sports activities keep *keiki* (kids) over six happy while also giving Mom and Dad a break. As an added bonus, these resorts offer family plans, providing discounts for extra rooms or permitting children to share a room with their parents at no extra charge. Check with your travel agent.

When reserving a rental car, inquire to see if they provide car seats and if there is an added charge. Hawaii has a strictly enforced car seat law. Besides the car seat you may have to bring along, also pack shorts and T-shirts, a sweater, sun hat, sundresses and waterproof sandals. A stroller with sunshade for little ones helps on sightseeing sojourns; a shovel and pail are essential for sandcastle building. Most importantly, remember to bring a good sunblock. The quickest way to ruin a family vacation is with a bad sunburn. Also plan to bring indoor activities such as books and games for evenings and rainy days.

Most towns have stores that carry diapers, food and other essentials. However, prices are much higher on Oahu than on the mainland. To

---

Time Out for Parents

When parents who are vacationing at the major resorts want to relax in a spa, golf, shop or simply have a little down time, they can send the kids to Keiki Camp. These half- or full-day programs will keep the little ones entertained. Ask your travel agent about special family packages with discounts and freebies on meals, activities and hotel rates.

HILTON HAWAIIAN VILLAGE ✉*2005 Kalia Road* ✆*808-949-4321, 800-774-1500* This resort has the most extensive *keiki* program. The year-round Rainbow Express Keiki Club runs from 8:30 a.m. to 3 p.m. for ages 5 to 12; $60 to $90. Activities include Hawaiian crafts, hula, seashell hunts, sandcastle building, fishing and trips to Waikiki attractions. Kids also can play with games and toys, join the King's Jubilee Keiki Parade on Friday nights or take a wildlife and ecology tour. Reservations required.

SHERATON WAIKIKI HOTEL ✉*2255 Kalakaua Avenue* ✆*808-921-8086* The year-round Poppins Keiki Hawaii program here runs from 9 a.m. to 6 p.m. It's open to children ages 3 months to 12 years. Activities change throughout the year, but often include visiting the Waikiki Aquarium and the Honolulu Zoo, boogieboarding, hula, lei making, surfing, bamboo pole fishing, catamaran sailing and volcano making. Fees range from $26 to $30 per hour, or $90 to $180 for half- or full-day activities. Children do not need to be hotel guests to participate. Reservations required.

KAHALA HOTEL & RESORT ✉*5000 Kahala Avenue* ✆*808-739-8608* Kids ages 5 to 12 can attend sessions from 9 a.m. to 4 p.m. at this upscale resort. The year-round program features reef walking, snorkeling, storytelling, bamboo pole fishing, lei making, hula, crabbing and Hawaiian art. Fees range from $35 to $65. Reservations suggested.

TURTLE BAY RESORT ✉*57-091 Kamehameha Highway, Kahuku* ✆*808-293-8811* The daily Keiki Turtle Club operates from late May to early September for kids ages 5 to 12. The sessions run from 9 a.m. to 3 p.m. Monday through Wednesday and 5 p.m. to 9 p.m. on Friday and Saturday and feature lei making, coconut frond weaving, hula, sponge painting, beading and night sandcrab hunts. Fees range from $55 for a half-day program to $85 for full-day programs that include lunch, supplies, a T-shirt and a backpack. Reservations suggested.

JW MARRIOTT IHILANI RESORT & SPA ✉*92-1001 Olani Street, Kapolei* ✆*808-679-0079* This secluded resort offers children's programs from June through September. The Ihilani's Keiki Beachcomber Club runs from 9 a.m. to 3 p.m for kids ages 5 to 12. Activities include treasure hunts, hula dancing, lei making, karaoke, sports and crafts. Register before 5 p.m. the day before. Fees for half-day programs are $36 without lunch and $41 with lunch; full-day programs include lunch and are $60, with discounts for additional children.

economize, some people take along an extra suitcase filled with diapers and wipes, baby food, peanut butter and jelly, etc. If you're staying in Waikiki, **ABC stores** carry a limited selection of disposables and baby food. Shopping outside Waikiki in local supermarkets will save you a considerable sum: The nearby **Safeway** (888 Kapahulu Avenue; 808-733-2600) is Hawaii's largest and is open 24 hours.

A first-aid kit is always a good idea. Also check with your pediatrician for special medicines and dosages for colds and diarrhea. If your child does become sick or injured in the Honolulu area, contact **Kapiolani Medical Center** (808-983-6000). On the Windward Coast, call **Castle Medical Center** (808-263-5500); on the North Shore, **Kahuku Hospital** (808-293-9221); and on the leeward side, **Wahiawa General Hospital** (808-621-8411). There's also a **Poison Center** (800-222-1222) hotline.

Hotels often provide access to babysitters. **Aloha Babysitting Service** (808-732-2029, fax 808-735-1958) is a bonded babysitting agency.

There are plenty of places to take kids who tire of the beach. The Honolulu Zoo, the Waikiki Aquarium, Hawaii Children's Discovery Center, The Polynesian Cultural Center and Sea Life Park are a few that come to mind, but there are many, many more. Be sure to look in the local paper for events that are occurring while you are there such as luaus, *hukilau* and island entertainment.

WOMEN TRAVELING ALONE

Traveling solo grants an independence and freedom different from that of traveling with a partner, but single travelers are more vulnerable to crime and should take additional precautions.

It's unwise to hitchhike and probably best to avoid inexpensive accommodations on the outskirts of Honolulu; the money saved does not outweigh the risk. Bed and breakfasts, youth hostels and YWCAs are generally your safest bet for lodging, and they also foster an environment ideal for bonding with fellow travelers. There are three YWCAs on Oahu: the **Kokokahi YWCA** (45-035 Kaneohe Bay Drive, Kaneohe; 808-247-2124) on the Windward Coast; the **Laniakea YWCA** (1040 Richards Street; 808-538-7061) in downtown Honolulu; and the **Fernhurst YWCA** (1566 Wilder Avenue; 808-941-2234) in Greater Honolulu, which is the only YWCA that offers lodging. Check specific lodging sections for other options.

Keep all valuables well-hidden and hold on to cameras and purses. Avoid late-night treks or strolls anywhere, even beaches, and especially through undesirable parts of town, but if you find yourself in this situation, continue walking with a confident air until you reach a safe haven. A fierce scowl never hurts.

These hints should by no means deter you from seeking out adventure. Wherever you go, stay alert, use your common sense and trust your instincts. If you are hassled or threatened in some way, never be afraid to scream for assistance. It's a good idea to carry change for a phone call or keep your cell phone on and charged. In case of emergency, contact the **Sex Abuse Treatment Center** (808-524-7273).

For more helpful hints, get a copy of *Safety and Security for Women Who Travel* (Travelers' Tales).

GAY & LESBIAN TRAVELERS

GAY HAWAII *P.O. Box 88245, Honolulu, HI 96830-8245* ☎*808-545-5252* ⌨*www.gayhawaii.com* This company's website is a good source of connections to Oahu's gay community and includes bulletin boards to help you find the best gay and lesbian hotels, bars and beaches throughout the island.

For further information, be sure to look under "gay-friendly travel" in the index at the end of the book.

SENIOR TRAVELERS

Oahu is a hospitable place for senior citizens to visit. Museums, historic sights and even restaurants and hotels offer senior discounts that can cut a substantial chunk off vacation costs. For a small fee, the national park system's Golden Age Passport, which must be applied for in person, allows free admission for anyone 62 and older to the national park facilities on the island. Once purchased, the passport is good for life.

AMERICAN ASSOCIATION OF RETIRED PERSONS ✉*601 E Street NW, Washington, DC 20049* ☎*888-687-2277* ⌨*www.aarp.org* AARP offers membership to anyone over 50. Its benefits include travel discounts with car-rental agencies, hotel chains and many other firms.

ELDERHOSTEL ✉*11 Avenue de Lafayette, Boston, MA 02111* ☎*800-454-5768* 📠*617-426-0701* ⌨*www.elderhostel.org* This national organization offers reasonably priced, all-inclusive educational programs in a variety of locations throughout the year.

We should all be extra careful about health matters when we are traveling. Consider carrying a medical record with you—including your medical history and current medical status as well as your doctor's name, phone number and address. Make sure your insurance covers you while you are away from home. It is wise to have your doctor write out extra prescriptions in case you lose your medication. Always carry your medications on board your planes, not in your luggage.

DISABLED TRAVELERS

The state of Hawaii has been conscious of access issues for many years.

DISABILITY AND COMMUNICATION ACCESS BOARD ✉*919 Ala Moana Boulevard, Room 101, Honolulu, HI 96814* ☎*808-586-8121* 📠*808-586-8129* ⌨*www.hawaii.gov/health/dcab/home, dcab@doh.hawaii.gov* The Disability and Communication Access Board publishes a survey of the city, county, state and federal parks in Hawaii that are accessible to travelers with disabilities. They also provide "Hawaii Traveler Tips Guides," which cover Oahu, Maui, Kauai and the Big Island, and give information on airports, various hotels, shopping centers, and restaurants that are accessible. Guides are available to download from their website.

✉ *347 5th Avenue, Suite 605, New York, NY 10016* ✆ *212-447-7284* 📠 *212-444-1928* 🖰 *www.sath.org* This society offers general information for travelers with disabilities.

Be sure to check in advance when making room reservations. Some hotels feature facilities for those in wheelchairs.

FOREIGN TRAVELERS

PASSPORTS AND VISAS Foreign visitors need a passport and tourist visa to enter the United States. Furthermore, tighter U.S. Department of Homeland Security regulations now mandate that all those traveling to the U.S. by air, land and sea, including U.S. citizens, must show a valid passport to enter or reenter the U.S. Contact your nearest U.S. Embassy or Consulate well in advance to obtain a visa and to check on any other entry requirements.

CUSTOMS REQUIREMENTS Foreign travelers are allowed to carry in the following: 200 cigarettes (1 carton), 50 cigars, or 2 kilograms (4.4 pounds) of smoking tobacco; one liter of alcohol restricted to checked luggage for personal use only (you must be 21 years of age to bring in alcohol); and US$100 worth of duty-free gifts that can include an additional quantity of 100 cigars (except Cuban). All containers with liquids must be enclosed in a 1-quart plastic Ziploc bag and the maximum amount of liquid permitted in each container is 3 oz. You may bring in any amount of currency, but must fill out a form if you bring in over US$10,000. Carry any 90-day supply of prescription drugs in clearly marked containers. (You may have to produce a written prescription or doctor's statement for the custom's officer.) Meat or meat products, seeds, plants, fruits, and narcotics are not allowed to be brought into the United States. For further information, contact **United States Customs and Border Protection** (1300 Pennsylvania Avenue NW, Washington, DC 20229; 202-354-1000; www.cbp.gov).

DRIVING If you plan to rent a car, an international driver's license should be obtained prior to arrival. Some rental car companies require both a foreign license and an international driver's license. Many car rental agencies require that the lessee be at least 25 years of age; all require a major credit card. Seat belts are mandatory for the driver and all passengers. Children under the age of 8 should ride in the back seat in approved child safety restraints.

CURRENCY United States money is based on the dollar. Bills come in six denominations: $1, $5, $10, $20, $50 and $100. Every dollar is divided

Agricultural Restrictions

Oahu's environment is fragile. Part of its natural beauty comes from its geographic isolation from alien ecosystems. Bringing in plants, produce or animals can introduce pests and non-endemic species that could eventually undermine the ecosystem.

into 100 cents. Coins are the penny (1 cent), nickel (5 cents), dime (10 cents), quarter (25 cents), half-dollar (50 cents) and dollar (100 cents).

You may not use foreign currency to purchase goods and services in the United States. Consider buying traveler's checks in dollar amounts. You may also use credit cards affiliated with an American company such as Interbank, Barclay Card, VISA and American Express.

ELECTRICITY AND ELECTRONICS Electric outlets use currents of 110 volts, 60 cycles. For appliances made for other electrical systems, you need a transformer or adapter. Travelers who use laptop computers for telecommunication should be aware that modem configurations for U.S. telephone systems may be different from their European counterparts. Similarly, the U.S. format for videotapes is different from that in Europe; U.S. Park Service visitors centers and other stores that sell souvenir DVDs and videos often have them available in European format.

WEIGHTS AND MEASUREMENTS The United States uses the English system of weights and measures. American units and their metric equivalents are as follows: 1 inch = 2.5 centimeters; 1 foot (12 inches) = 0.3 meter; 1 yard (3 feet) = 0.9 meter; 1 mile (5280 feet) = 1.6 kilometers; 1 ounce = 28 grams; 1 pound (16 ounces) = 0.45 kilogram; 1 quart (liquid) = 0.9 liter.

MAIL If you're staying in a particular establishment during your visit, you can usually have personal mail sent there. You can also have mail sent to a particular post office in care of general delivery.

TRANSPORTATION

GETTING TO OAHU

During the 19th century, sleek clipper ships sailed from the West Coast to Hawaii in about 11 days. Today, you'll be traveling by a less romantic but far swifter conveyance—the jet plane. Rather than days at sea, it will be about five hours in the air from California, nine hours from Chicago, or around 11 hours if you're coming from New York.

HONOLULU INTERNATIONAL AIRPORT ⊠ *Rodgers Boulevard, Honolulu* ✆ *808-861-1260* ✑ *www.honoluluairport.com* There's only one airport on Oahu and it's a behemoth. The airlines that fly in here are Air Canada, Air New Zealand, Air Pacific Airways, All Nippon Airways, American Airlines, American Trans Air, China Airlines, Continental Airlines, Continental Air Micronesia, Delta Airlines, Japan Airlines, JTB Aloha Service, Korean Airlines, NorthWest Airlines, Qantas Airways, Philippine Airlines, Rich International and United Airlines.

Honolulu International Airport is a Pacific crossroads, an essential link between North America and Asia. Honolulu International includes all the comforts of a major airport. You can check your bags; fuel up at a restaurant, coffee shop or cocktail lounge; shop at several stores; or shower.

Ground Transport

To cover the eight or so miles into Waikiki, it's possible to hire a cab for $30.

ROBERT'S HAWAII ℂ *808-954-8600, 866-898-2519* ✎ *www.robertshawaii.com* For $9 (roundtrip $15), this tour and transportation company will take you to your Waikiki hotel or condominium.

THEBUS ℂ *808-848-5555* ✎ *www.thebus.org* City buses #19 and #20 travel through Downtown Honolulu and Waikiki. This is the cheapest trans-portation, but you're only allowed to carry on baggage that fits under your seat or on your lap. So, unless you're traveling very light, you'll have to use another conveyance.

Car Rentals

Of all the islands, Oahu offers the most car-rental agencies. At the Honolulu airport, **Alamo Rent A Car** (808-833-4585, 800-327-9633), **Avis Rent A Car** (808-834-5536, 800-331-3712), **Budget Rent A Car** (808-537-3600, 800-527-0700), **Dollar Rent A Car** (808-831-2300, 800-800-4000), **Enterprise Rent A Car** (808-836-2213), **Hertz** (808-529-6800, 800-654-3011), **National Car Rental** (808-831-3800, 800-227-7368) and **Thrifty Rent A Car** (808-833-0046, 800-367-2277) all have booths. Their convenient location helps to save time while minimizing the problem of picking up your car.

There are other Honolulu-based companies offering lower rates but providing limited pick-up service at the airport. I've never found the in-convenience worth the savings. There you are—newly arrived from the mainland, uncertain about your environment, anxious to check in at the hotel—and you're immediately confronted with the Catch-22 of getting to your car. Do you rent a vehicle in which to pick up your rental car? Take a bus? Hitchhike? What do you do with your bags meanwhile?

Though not at the airport, **VIP Rental** (234 Beachwalk; 808-922-4605) is a cheaper outfit that provides airport pick-up service.

If you prefer to go in high style, book a limousine from **Cloud Nine** (808-524-7999, 800-524-7999).

Jeep Rentals

There aren't many places on Oahu where you will need a jeep, but if off-roading is your thing, check out: **Adventure Rentals** (808-921-8111), **Dollar Rent A Car** (808-944-1544) and **VIP Car Rental** (808-922-4605).

Moped Rentals

For two-wheel motorized transport, there are two outfits that rent mopeds.

ADVENTURE ON 2 WHEELS ✉ *1946 Ala Moana Boulevard, Honolulu* ℂ *808-944-3131* This Waikiki store rents mopeds for 4, 8 and 24 hours. Fee includes hotel pick-up.

BLUE SKY RENTALS ✉ *1920 Ala Moana Boulevard, Honolulu* ✆ *808-947-0101*

This facility located on the ground floor of the Inn On The Park Hotel rents mopeds.

Public Transit

Oahu has an excellent bus system that runs regularly to points all over the island and provides convenient service throughout Honolulu. Many of the beaches, hotels, restaurants and points of interest mentioned in these chapters are just a bus ride away. It's even possible to pop your money in the fare box and ride around the entire island.

THEBUS ✆ *808-848-5555* ✑ *www.thebus.org* There is perhaps no greater Hawaiian bargain than TheBus. Although you can rent a car to explore Oahu, you can also do it by the island's remarkable public transportation system.

TheBus is a great way to sightsee at a leisurely pace—and people-watch at the same time. Hop aboard the #19 (or another downtown-bound bus) from Waikiki and you'll pass Ala Moana Center, the fishing boats of Kewalo Boat Basin and the historic Mission Houses before entering Chinatown. There tiny wizened *obachans* (grandmas) speaking a patois of Japanese-English climb patiently aboard, while mothers with a child in one arm and a shopping bag in the other negotiate the steep steps.

Or take the #52 Circle Island route and get the grand tour of the island. You'll pass through sleepy villages and alongside strands of sandy beaches while getting an upclose view of local life. Roughly twice hourly buses give ample opportunity to stop and check out the sights along the way.

TheBus covers 90 percent of the 60-square-mile island. The fleet of 525 buses that are on the road travel a combined total of 60,000 miles every day, carrying 260,000 passengers daily—between 30,000 and 35,000 of them are visitors.

Buses generally operate between 5 a.m. and 10 p.m., although some lines run 24 hours. (The last Waikiki-bound bus, however, leaves the airport at 11:31 p.m. and arrives in Waikiki by 12:22 a.m.) Unless you have to be somewhere during rush hour, the best times to travel are between 9 a.m. and 3 p.m. or after 6 p.m. All of all buses operate with wheelchair lifts, making them accessible to physically disabled riders.

Because so many local residents rely on public transportation, service is reliable and buses run frequently, even outside of Honolulu. With each ticket, riders can request a transfer that must be used to transfer to a different route within one and a half hours. The transfer can't be used for another ride on the same bus route. For $20 you can purchase the Discovery Passport, which gives you unlimited bus rides for four days. It's available at ABC Stores in Waikiki or from TheBus Pass office (811 Middle Street, Honolulu).

TheBus provides a bus information service, with operators giving directions between the hours of 5:30 a.m. and 10 p.m. Those with Internet access can print out directions and time tables by contacting www.thebus.org.

Aerial Tours

The quickest way to see what Oahu has to offer is by taking to the air. In minutes you can take in the island's hidden waterfalls, secluded beaches and volcanic landmarks. Tranquil gliders and hovering whirly-birds all fly low and slow to make sure you see what you missed on the trip over from the mainland. You can also take extended flights that include the outer islands.

MAKANI KAI HELICOPTERS ✉*130 Iolana Place, Honolulu* ☎*808-834-5813, 877-255-8532* 📠*808-837-7867* 🖥*www.makanikai.com* This company offers helicopter tours of Waikiki and Honolulu, Hanauma Bay, the Koolau Mountains, Chinaman's Hat, Sacred Falls, Kahana Rainforest and the North Shore. They also take trips to the "Jurassic Park" valley, an area where parts of the movie were filmed. Reservations required.

THE ORIGINAL GLIDER RIDES ✉*Dillingham Airfield, Mokuleia* ☎*808-637-0207* 🖥*www.honolulusoaring.com, info@gliderridehawaii.com* To enjoy a one- or two-passenger glider trip, head out here and talk to Mr. Bill. On your 20-minute trip you're likely to see fields of sugar cane, marine mammals, surfers working the North Shore and neighboring Kauai. You'll also enjoy peace and quiet while working your way down from 3000 feet.

Walking Tours

OAHU NATURE TOURS ✉*P.O. Box 8059, Honolulu, HI 96815* ☎*808-924-2473* 📠*808-924-5395* 🖥*www.oahunaturetours.com, naturetours@oahunaturetours.com* Offering different daily eco-tours, Oahu Nature provides an overview of native Hawaiian birds and plants. One focuses on Oahu's volcanic history at Diamond Head Crater. Another tour takes you into the Hawaiian rainforest at 2000-feet elevation in the Koolau Mountains. Equipment, transportation and water are provided. Reservations required. Fee.

HAWAII HERITAGE CENTER ✉*1168 Smith Street, Honolulu* ☎*808-521-2749* Chinatown's rich history and culture can be experienced with the center's walking tour, which makes this exotic place come alive. Reservations required. A self-guided tour of Chinatown can be downloaded from www.chinatownhi.com.

THE LAND & OUTDOOR ADVENTURES

GEOLOGY

More than 25 million years ago a fissure opened along the Pacific floor. Beneath tons of sea water molten lava poured from the rift. This liquid basalt, oozing from a hot spot in the earth's center, created a crater along the ocean bottom. As the tectonic plate that comprises the ocean floor drifted over the earth's hot spot, numerous other craters appeared. Slowly, in the seemingly endless procession of geologic time, a chain of volcanic islands, now stretching almost 2000 miles, has emerged from the sea.

On the continents it was also a period of terrible upheaval. The Himalayas, Alps and Andes were rising, but these great chains would reach their peaks long before the Pacific mountains even touched sea level. Not until about 25 million years ago did the first of these underwater volcanoes, today's Kure and Midway atolls, break the surface and become islands. It was not until about five million years ago that the first of the main islands of the archipelago, Niihau and Kauai, broke the surface to become high islands.

For a couple of million more years, the mountains continued to grow. The forces of erosion cut into them, creating knife-edged cliffs and deep valleys. Then plants began germinating: mosses and ferns, springing from windblown spores, were probably first, followed by seed plants carried by migrating birds and on ocean currents. The steep-walled valleys provided natural greenhouses in which unique species evolved, while transoceanic winds swept insects and other life from the continents.

Some islands never survived this birth process: The ocean simply washed them away. The first islands that did endure, at the northwestern end of the Hawaiian chain, proved to be the smallest. Today these islands, with the exception of Midway, are barren, uninhabited atolls. The volcanoes that rose last, far to the southeast, became the mountainous archipelago generally known as the Hawaiian Islands.

With several distinct biological regions, there's much more to the island than meets the eye. Oahu's varied terrain makes it possible to experience all kinds of outdoor adventures in tropical forests, atop volcanic craters and on sandy beaches. But paradise also means an easy lifestyle, so slow down and you'll discover how relaxing the island experience can be.

FLORA AND FAUNA

FLORA

Many of the plants you'll see on Oahu are not indigenous. In fact, much of the lush vegetation of this tropical island found its way here from locations all over the world. Sea winds, birds and seafaring settlers brought many of the seeds, plants, flowers and trees from the islands of the South Pacific, as well as from other, more distant regions. Over time, some plants adapted to Hawaii's unique ecosystem and climate, creating strange new lineages and evolving into a completely new ecosystem. This process has long interested scientists, who call the Hawaiian Islands one of the best natural labs for studies of plant and bird evolution. Unfortunately, other new arrivals have become pests and invasive weeds.

Sugar cane arrived in Kauai with the first Polynesian settlers, who appreciated its sweet juices. By the late 1800s, it was well established as a lucrative crop. The pineapple was first planted during the same century. A member of the bromeliad family, this spiky plant is actually a collection of beautiful pink, blue and purple flowers, each of which develops into a fruitlet. The pineapple is a collection of these fruitlets, grown together into a single fruit that takes 14 to 17 months to mature. Sugar cane and pineapple were once important crops in Hawaii, but competition from other countries and environmental problems caused by pesticides have taken their toll. More recently, coffee, corn and banana have also become key components of Hawaii's agriculture.

Visitors to Oahu will find the island a perpetual flower show. Sweetly scented plumeria, deep red, shiny anthurium, exotic ginger, showy birds of paradise, small lavender crown flowers, highly fragrant gardenias and the brightly hued hibiscus run riot on the island and add color and fragrance to the surrounding area. Scarlet and purple bougainvillea vines, and the aromatic lantana, with its dense clusters of flowers, are also found in abundance.

The beautiful, delicate orchid thrives in Hawaii's tropical heat and humidity. Cultivated primarily on the Big Island, the most popular orchids are the *dendrobium*, which can come in white, purple, lavender, or yellow; the *vanda* (bamboo orchid), which is lavender with white lavender and often used for making leis; and the popcorn, which has small, yellow flowers. The wild *vanda*, with its white and lavender petals, can be spotted along the side of the road year-round.

Although many people equate the tropics with the swaying palm tree, Oahu is home to a variety of exotic trees. The state tree, the candlenut, or *kukui*, tree, originally brought to Hawaii from the South Pacific islands, is big, bushy and prized for its nuts, which can be used for oil or polished and strung together to make leis. Early Hawaiians used the oil for light and natural remedies. Covered with tiny pink blossoms, the canopied monkeypod tree has fernlike leaves that close up at night. With its cascades of bright yellow or pink flowers, the cassia tree earns its moniker—

the shower tree. The famed banyan tree, known for pillarlike aerial roots that grow vertically downward from the branches, spreads to form a natural canopy. When the roots touch the ground, they thicken, providing support for the tree's branches to continue expanding.

Found in a variety of shapes and sizes, the ubiquitous palm does indeed sway to the breezes on white-sand beaches, but it also comes in a short, stubby form, the Samoan coconut, featuring more frond than trunk. The fruit, or nuts, of these trees are prized for their oil, which can be utilized for making everything from margarine to soap. The wood (rattan for example) is often used for making furniture.

FRUITS AND VEGETABLES There's a lot more to Hawaii's tropical wonderland than gorgeous flowers and overgrown rainforests. The island is also teeming with edible plants. Roots, fruits, vegetables, herbs and spices grow like weeds from the shoreline to the mountains. Following is a list of some of the more commonly found edibles.

Avocado: Covered with either a tough green or purple skin, this pear-shaped fruit sometimes weighs as much as three pounds. It grows on ten- to forty-foot-high trees, and ripens from June through November.

Bamboo: The bamboo plant is actually a grass with a sweet root that is edible and a long stem frequently used for making furniture. Often exceeding eight feet in height, the most common bamboo is green until picked, when it turns a golden brown.

Banana: Polynesians use banana trees, which are not trees at all but a *pseudostem* (or false stem), not only for food but also for clothing, medicines, dyes and even alcohol; culturally, it represents man. The fruit, which grows upside down on broad-leaved plants, can be harvested as soon as the first banana in the bunch turns yellow.

Breadfruit: This large round fruit grows on trees that reach up to 60 feet in height. Breadfruit must be boiled, baked or fried. Historically, the tree's wood was used for surfboards and canoes, and the sticky sap of the breadfruit tree once served as a glue and as a method to catch birds for their colorful plumage.

Coconut: The coconut tree is probably the most important plant in the entire Pacific. Every part of the towering palm is used. The fronds were combined with *pili* grass to thatch roofs, the hollowed trunks are made into *pahu*, or drums, and the fiber can be dried for fuel. It was also fashioned into ropey sandals that allowed Hawaiians to walk across razor-sharp lava. Nutritionally, the water inside is sterile and full of healthful enzymes, and the meat can be eaten or pressed into cream and oil. Most importantly, coconuts grow well close to the ocean, offering welcome shade from the harsh tropical sun. Most people are concerned only with the hard brown nut, which yields delicious water as well as a tasty meat. If the coconut is still green, the meat is a succulent jellylike substance. Otherwise, it's a hard but delicious white rind.

Guava: A roundish yellow fruit that grows on a small shrub or tree, guavas are extremely abundant in the wild. They ripen between June and October.

Lychee: Found hanging in bunches from the lychee tree, this popular summer fruit is encased in red, prickly skin that peels off to reveal the sweet-tasting, translucent flesh.

Mango: Known as the king of fruits, the mango grows on tall shade trees. There are hundreds of varieties that come in varying colors and shapes; the most common in Hawaii are Haden, but I love the Ah Pin. The fruit ripens in the spring and summer.

Mountain apple: This sweet fruit grows in damp, shaded valleys at an elevation of about 1800 feet. The flowers resemble fluffy crimson balls; the fruit, which ripens from July to December, is also a rich red color.

Papaya: This delicious fruit, which is picked as it begins to turn yellow, grows on unbranched trees. The sweet flesh can be bright orange or coral pink in color. Summer is the peak harvesting season.

Passion fruit: Known as *lilikoi* on the islands, this tasty yellow fruit is oval in shape and grows to a length of about two or three inches. It's produced on a vine and ripens in summer or fall.

Taro: The tuberous root of this Hawaiian staple is pounded into a grayish purple paste known as poi. One of the most nutritious foods, it has a rather bland taste. Taro is also served in other forms, such as chips and bread. The plant has wide, shiny, thick leaves with reddish stems; the root is white with purple veins.

FAUNA

On Oahu, it seems there is more wildlife in the water and air than on land. A scuba diver's paradise, the ocean is also a promised land for many other creatures. Coral, colorful fish and migrating whales are only part of this underwater community. Sadly, many of the island's coral reefs have been dying mysteriously in the last several years. No one is sure why, but many believe this is partially due to runoff from pesticides used in agriculture.

FISH   It'll come as no surprise to anyone that Oahu's waters literally brim with an extraordinary assortment of fish—over 400 different species, in fact.

The goatfish, with more than 50 species in its family worldwide, boasts at least ten in Oahu waters. This bottom dweller is recognized by a pair of whiskers, used as feelers for searching out food, that are attached to its lower jaw. The *moano* sports two stripes across its back and has shorter whiskers. The red-and-black banded goatfish has a multihued color scheme that also includes yellow and white markings; its light yellow whiskers are quite long. The head of the goatfish is considered poisonous and is not eaten.

Occasionally found on the sharper end of your line is the bonefish, or *oio*. One of the best game fish in the area, its head extends past its mouth to form a somewhat transparent snout. The *awa*, or milkfish, is another common catch. This silvery, fork-tailed fish can grow longer than three feet and puts up a good fight.

A kaleidoscope of brilliantly colored specimens can be viewed around the reefs of Oahu; you'll feel like you're in a technicolor movie when snorkeling. Over 20 known species of butterfly fish are found in this area. Highlighted in yellow, orange, red, blue, black and white, they swim in groups of two and three. The long, tubular body of the needle-fish, or *aha*, can reach up to 40 inches in length; this greenish, silvery species is nearly translucent. The parrotfish, or *uhu*, gets its name from its fused teeth, which form a beaklike mouth. The masked an-gelfish flits around in deeper waters on the outer edge of reefs. The im-perial angelfish is distinguishable by fantastic color patterns of dark blue hues. The colorful *humuhumunukunukuapuaa* (Hawaiian trig-gerfish) is found in the shallow waters along the outer fringes of reefs. Although it is commonly known as the fish with the longest name, the distinction actually belongs to the *lauwiliwilinukunukuoioi* (long-nosed butterflyfish).

Sharks, unlike fish, have skeletons made of cartilage; the hardest parts of their bodies are their teeth (once used as tools by the Hawaiians). If you spend a lot of time in the water, you may spot a shark. But not to worry; Hawaiian waters are just about the safest around. The harmless, commonly seen blacktipped and whitetipped reef sharks (named for the color of their fins) are as concerned about your activities as you are about theirs. The gray reef shark (gray back, white belly with a black tail) and tiger shark, however, are predatory and aggressive, but they are rarely encountered.

Another cartilaginous creature you might see in shallow water near the shoreline is the manta ray, a "winged" plankton feeder with two ap-pendages on either side of its head that work to direct food into its mouth. The eagle ray, a bottom dweller featuring "wings" and a tail longer than its body, feeds in shallow coastal waters. When it's not feed-ing, it lies on the ocean floor and covers itself with a light layer of sand. Since some eagle rays have stingers, take precautions by shuffling the sand as you walk. Not only will you not be impaled, you will also be less likely to squash smaller, unsuspecting sea creatures.

While on Oahu, you'll inevitably see fish out of water as well—on your plate. The purple-blue-green-hued mahimahi, or dolphin fish, can reach six feet and 70 pounds. The *opakapaka* is another common dish and resides in the deeper, offshore waters beyond the reef. This small-scaled snapper is a reddish-olive color and can grow up to four feet long. Elongated with a sharply pointed head, the *ono* (also known as the wahoo) is a carnivorous, savage striped fish with dark blue and silver coloring. Perhaps the most ubiquitous fish is the *ahi*, or tuna, often used for sashimi.

WHALES & DOLPHINS   Every year, humpback whales converge in the warm waters off the island to give birth to their calves. Beginning their migration in Alaska, they can be spotted in Hawaiian waters from November through May. The humpback, named for its practice of show-ing its dorsal fin when diving, is quite easy to spy. They feed in shallow waters, usually diving for periods of no longer than 15 minutes. They of-ten sleep on the surface and breathe fairly frequently. Unlike other whales, humpbacks have the ability to sing. Loud and powerful, their songs carry above and below the water for miles. The songs change every year, yet, incredibly, all the whales always seem to know the current one. Quite playful, they can be seen leaping, splashing and flapping their 15-foot tails over their backs.

Spinner dolphins are also favorites among visitors. Named for their "spinning" habit, they can revolve as many as six times during one leap. They resemble the spotted dolphin, another frequenter of Hawaiian waters, but are more likely to venture closer to the shore. Dolphins have clocked in with speeds ranging from 9 to 25 mph, a feat they often achieve by propelling themselves out of the water (or even riding the bow wave of a ship). Their thick, glandless skin also contributes to this agility. The skin is kept smooth by constant renewal and sloughing (bottlenoses replace their epidermis every two hours). Playful and intelligent, dolphins are a joy to watch. Many research centers are investigating the mammals' ability to imitate, learn and communicate; some believe that dolphin intelligence may be comparable to that of humans.

GREEN SEA TURTLES   Green sea turtles are commonly seen in Hawaiian waters, popping their heads up for a breath of air or sliding along rocky reefs to feed on the seaweed, or *limu*, that gives their flesh its distinctive green tint. Measuring three to four feet in diameter, these large reptiles frolic in saltwater only, and are often visible from the shore. The Hawaiians frequently ate *honu*, which was considered a delicacy. These creatures are an amazing 150 million years old, yet in the past century they were hunted so heavily by fishing crews that their population nearly crashed. Since being federally designated as a protected, threatened species, their numbers are rising. But their newest threat is a puzzling disease that causes large tumors to grow on their flesh.

BIRDS   The island is also home to many rare and endangered birds. Like the flora, the birds in the Hawaiian Islands are highly specialized. The state bird, the nene, or Hawaiian goose, is a cousin to the Canadian goose and mates for life. Unless you visit the Big Island, Kauai or Haleakala, the only place you'll find a nene is at the Honolulu Zoo.

Known in Hawaiian mythology for its protective powers, the *pueo*, or Hawaiian owl, a brown-and-white-feathered bird, is considered an endangered species on Oahu, and may be spotted in the mountainous areas of the island.

There *are* a few birds native to Hawaii that have thus far avoided the endangered species list. One of the most common birds is the yellow-green *amakihi*, but the red *iiwi*, more common on the neighbor islands is near extinction on Oahu.

Other native birds that make Oahu their home are the Hawaiian stilt and the Hawaiian coot—both water birds—along with the black noddy, American plover and wedge-tailed shearwater.

One common seabird is the *iwa*, or frigate, a very large creature measuring three to four feet in length, with a wing span averaging seven feet. The males are solid black, while the females have a large white patch on their chest and tail. A predatory bird, they're easy to spot raiding the nesting colonies of other birds along the offshore rocks. If you see one, you may want to seek cover; legend says they portend a storm.

No doubt you will encounter the boisterous black myna birds with their beady yellow eyes and shiny black feathers. They seem to be as numerous and sassy as the tourists on Waikiki's beach.

That cooing sound you'll hear, especially in the early morning when you're trying to sleep, emanates from the ubiquitous tiger dove. Brought to the islands in 1922, these newcomers have flourished. However, oftentimes you'll see these charming birds with mangled feet. The crippling is a result of avian pox, a danger to many of Hawaii's native birds.

An even more recent newcomer is the red-vented bulbul, which arrived in the 1950s from India. This black- or brown-breasted bird has a red area under its tail and a small black crest on its head. Found only on Oahu, this noisy garden pest has caused considerable damage to the island's orchid industry.

OTHER ANIMALS Not many wild four-footed creatures roam Oahu. Deer, feral goats and pigs were brought here early on and have found a home in the forests. Some good news for people fearful of snakes: There is nary a serpent (or a sea serpent) in the state, although lizards such as skinks and geckos abound.

One can only hope that with the renewed interest in Hawaiian culture, and growing environmental awareness, Oahu's plants and animals will continue to exist as they have for centuries.

OUTDOOR ADVENTURES

CAMPING

Camping on Oahu usually means pitching a tent. There are a few secluded spots and hidden beaches, plus numerous county, state and federal parks where you can set up camp. However, before you set out on your camping trip, there are a few very important matters that I want to explain more fully. First, bring a campstove: firewood is scarce in most areas and soaking wet in others. You should also be careful to purify all of your drinking water. And be extremely cautious near streambeds as flash-flooding sometimes occurs, particularly on the windward coast. This is particularly true during the winter months, when heavy storms from the northeast lash the island.

Another problem that you're actually more likely to encounter are those nasty varmints that buzz your ear just as you're falling asleep—mosquitoes. Oahu contains neither snakes nor poison ivy, but it has plenty of these dive-bombing pests. Like me, you probably consider that it's always open season on the little bastards.

With most of the archipelago's other species, however, you'll have to be a careful conservationist. You'll be sharing the wilderness with boars, goats, tropical birds, deer and mongooses, as well as a spectacular array of exotic and indigenous plants. They exist in one of the world's most delicate ecological balances. There are more endangered species in Hawaii than in all the rest of the United States. So keep in mind the maxim that the Hawaiians try to follow. *Ua mau ke ea o ka aina i ka pono:* The life of the land is perpetual in righteousness.

Along with its traffic and crowds, Oahu has numerous parks with campsites. Unfortunately, these disparate elements overlap, and you may sometimes find you've escaped from Honolulu's urban jungle and landed in a swamp of weekend beachgoers. So it's best to plan outdoor adventures far in advance and to schedule them for weekdays when possible.

Remember when planning your trip, rainfall is heaviest on the Windward Coast, a little lighter on the North Shore and lightest of all on the Leeward Coast.

HAWAII GEOGRAPHIC MAPS & BOOKS ✉ *49 South Hotel Street #215, Honolulu, HI 96806* ✆ *808-538-3952, 800-538-3950* You might want to obtain some hiking maps at this store.

COUNTY PARKS ✉ *Department of Parks and Recreation, Honolulu Municipal Building, 650 South King Street, ground floor, Honolulu, HI 96813* ✆ *808-523-4527* ✎ *www.co.honolulu.hi.us/parks* Currently, camping is allowed at 15 beach parks operated by the City and County of Honolulu. Seven of these parks are on the island's windward side and five on the leeward side. Another two are on the North Shore. **Bellows Field Beach Park** at Waimanalo on the Windward Coast, only allows camping at its 50 campsites on the weekends. **Swanzy Beach Park** at Kaaawa, **Maili** and **Kualoa** are also weekend-only campgrounds (Kualoa is closed in summer). The others permit tent camping every night except Wednesday and Thursday. There are no trailer hookups. Camping at county parks requires a permit. The free permits can be obtained from the Department of Parks and Recreation in the Honolulu Municipal Building or from any of the satellite city halls around the island.

STATE PARKS ✉ *1151 Punchbowl Street, Room 310, Honolulu, HI 96813* ✆ *808-587-0300* ✎ *www.hawaiistateparks.org/parks, dlnr@hawaii.gov* There are four state parks on Oahu with camping facilities. **Malaekahana State Recreation Area** on the Windward Coast between Laie and Kahuku offers both tent camping and housekeeping cabins. Also on the Windward Coast, Oahu's largest state park **Kahana Valley State Park**, located between Kaaawa and Punaluu, has campsites. Tent camping is available at **Sand Island State Recreation Area** on Sand Island in Honolulu, as well as at **Keaiwa Heiau State Recreation Area** in the hills above Honolulu. State parks allow camping for up to five days, depending on the park. It's first-come, first-served on the first day, but after that visitors may reserve spaces. The Division of State Parks issues permits Monday through Friday, or you can also write for one in advance. All campsites on Oahu are $5 per night per campsite.

HOOMALUHIA BOTANICAL GARDEN ✉ *45-680 Luluku Road, Kaneohe*
✆ *808-233-7323* This garden allows camping on the grounds Friday
through Sunday. There is no fee, but a permit is required and no hookups are available. Gates lock at 4 p.m.—no in-and-out privileges after-
ward except between 5:30 and 6:30 p.m. Reservations recommended.

FISHING

Fishing on Oahu is good year-round, and the offshore waters are
crowded with many varieties of edible fish. The ancient Hawaiians
used pearl shells to attract the fish, and hooks, some made from human
bones, to snare them. Your friends will probably be quite content to see
you angling with store-bought artificial lures. The easiest, most eco-
nomical way to fish is to surf-cast with a hand-held line—you won't
need to have a license or charter a boat. Just get a 50- to 100-foot line,
and attach a hook and a ten-ounce sinker. Wind the line loosely around a
smooth block of wood, then remove the wood from the center. If your
coil is free from snags, you'll be able to throw-cast it easily. You can either hold the line in your hand, feeling for a strike, or tie it to the frail
end of a bamboo pole.

Beaches and rocky points are generally good places to surf-cast; the
best times are during the incoming and outgoing tides. Popular baits include octopus, eel, lobster, crab, frozen shrimp and sea worms.

For freshwater angling head up into the Koolau Mountains to fish the
Nuuanu Reservoir (open to the public by lottery). Another possibility is
the **Wahiawa Public Fishing Area**, also known as Lake Wilson. Both of
these reservoirs are good places to catch Chinese catfish. Call the Division of Aquatic Resources, Department of Land & Resources at 808-
587-0110 for information on permits and seasons.

Many visitors to Hawaii don't think of Oahu as a place to deep-sea fish
and instead wait until they get to the Neighbor Islands, but that may be
a mistake. Oahu is the cheapest place in Hawaii to fish, with rates about
25 percent lower than, say, Maui.

The fish caught vary depending on the time of year, although it's mostly
mahimahi, especially during the winter months. In the fall and summer
you are likely to catch marlin, and in summer, *ahi* as well. Although
you're not guaranteed a catch, some record-breaking fish have been
caught on boats operating out of Oahu. In 1970, an 1805-pound Pacific
blue marlin, the largest fish ever caught anywhere in the world with a
rod and reel, was the result of an Oahu-based fishing charter.

Although the boats are all charters, share charters are the norm, with a
minimum of four passengers required. If there are not enough for a
particular boat, the skipper may recommend a different boat or another day to go out. Keeping the fish you catch is not always part of the
deal. If you would like to do so, negotiate with the boat owner or skipper beforehand.

Most of the island's fishing fleet dock at Kewalo Basin (Fisherman's
Wharf) on Ala Moana Drive between Waikiki and downtown Honolulu.

Street A315 ☎ *808-396-2607, 877-388-1376* 🖰 *www.sportfishhawaii.com* This out-fitter books deep-sea fishing trips that go out for blue marlin, yellowfin tuna and mahimahi. Charters leave from Kewalo Basin, and reservations are required (all equipment provided).

MAGGIE JOE SPORTFISHING ☎ *808-591-8888, 877-806-3474* 🖰 *www.fish-hawaii.com* Offering half-, three-quarter- or full-day trips, Maggie Joe's inter-island company has four boats.

KUU HUAPALA 🖂 *P.O. Box 6040, Honolulu, HI 96818* ☎ *808-596-0918* 🖰 *www.sportfishing-hawaii.com* The *Kuu Huapala* catches mahimahi, marlin and tuna year-round on half- and full-day excursions out of Kewalo Basin.

AIKANE SPORTFISHING 🖂 *808-356-1800, 888-349-7888* 🖰 *www.oahufishing.com* Aikane's 40-foot *Kekahi* trolls the water for Pacific blue marlin, *ahi* and mahimahi. Charters leave from Hickam Air Force Base near the airport (transportation from Waikiki is available for a fee).

TORCHFISHING & SPEARFISHING

The old Hawaiians also fished at night by torchlight. They fashioned torches by inserting nuts from the *kukui* tree into the hollow end of a bamboo pole, then lighting the flammable nuts. When fish swam like moths to the flame, the Hawaiians speared, clubbed or netted them.

Today, it's easier to use a lantern and spear. (In fact, it's all *too* easy and tempting to take advantage of this willing prey: Take only edible fish and only what you will eat, and follow state rules on size and season limits for some species.) It's also handy to bring a facemask or a glass-bottomed box to aid in seeing underwater. The best time for torchfishing is a dark night when the sea is calm and the tide low.

During daylight hours, the best place to spearfish is along coral reefs and in areas where the bottom is a mixture of sand and rock. Equipped with speargun, mask, fins and snorkel, you can explore underwater grottoes and spectacular coral formations while seeking your evening meal. Spearguns can be purchased inexpensively throughout the island.

Aquaculture the Ancient Way

KUALOA RANCH & ACTIVITY CLUB 🖂 *Kualoa Ranch, Kaneohe* ☎ *800-231-7321* 🖰 *www.kualoa.com* Ancient Hawaiians would have fared well on the television series *Survivor;* they had fishtrapping down pat. Using enclosed brackish water off the coast, fish were bred and maintained in fishponds through ingenious use of *makaha,* sluice gates that controlled the in- and outflow of water. Designed to allow young fish in and keep the ready-to-eat fish from escaping, the gates also helped control the growth of algae, the lowest but most vital rung on the pond food ladder. This ancient technique is still practiced in Kaneohe Bay, where the Kualoa Ranch & Activity Club maintains an operational pond and sells its produce.

CRABBING

For the hungry adventurer, there are several crab species in Hawaii. The most sought after are the Kona and Samoan varieties. Kona crabs are found in relatively deep water, and can usually be caught only from a boat. Samoan crabs inhabit sandy and muddy areas in bays and near river mouths. All you need to catch them are a boat and a net fastened to a round wire hoop secured by a string. The net is lowered to the bottom; then, after a crab has gone for the bait, the entire contraption is raised to the surface.

SQUIDDING

Between June and December, squidding is another popular sport. Actually, the term is a misnomer: Squid inhabit deep water and are not usually hunted. What you'll really be after are octopuses. There are two varieties here, both of which are commonly found in water three or four feet deep: the *hee*, a grayish-brown animal that changes color like a chameleon, and the *puloa*, a red-colored mollusk with white stripes on its head.

Both are nocturnal and live in holes along coral reefs. At night by torchlight you can spot them sitting exposed on the bottom. During the day, they crawl inside the holes, covering the entrances with shells and loose coral.

The Hawaiians used to pick the octopus up, letting it cling to their chest and shoulders. When they were ready to bag their prize, they'd dispatch the creature by biting it between the eyes. You'll probably feel more comfortable spearing the critter.

SHELLFISH GATHERING

Other excellent food sources are the shellfish that inhabit coastal waters. Oysters and clams, which use their muscular feet to burrow into sand and soft mud, can be collected along the bottom of Oahu's bays. Spiny lobsters, rarely found in Hawaii waters, are illegal to spear, but can be taken in season with short poles to which cable leaders and baited hooks are attached. You can also just grab them with a gloved hand but be careful—spiny lobsters live up to their name! You can also gather limpets, though I don't recommend it. These tiny black shellfish, locally known as *opihi*, cling tenaciously to rocks in the tidal zone. In areas of very rough surf, the Hawaiians gather them by leaping into the water after one set of waves breaks, then jumping out before the next set arrives. Being a coward myself, I simply order them in Hawaiian restaurants.

SEAWEED GATHERING

There are still some people who don't think of seaweed as food, but it's very popular in Japanese cuisine, and it once served as an integral

Ocean Safety

For swimming, surfing and scuba diving, there's no place quite like Oahu. With endless miles of white-sand beach, the island attracts aquatic enthusiasts worldwide. They come to enjoy Oahu's colorful coral reefs and matchless surf conditions. Many water lovers, however, don't realize how dangerous the sea can be. Particularly on Oahu, where waves can reach 30-foot heights and currents flow unobstructed for thousands of miles, the ocean is sometimes as treacherous as it is spectacular. Dozens of people drown every year in Hawaii, many others are dragged from the crushing surf with broken backs, and countless numbers sustain minor cuts and bruises.

These accidents can be avoided if you approach the ocean with a respect for its power as well as an appreciation of its beauty. Just heed a few simple guidelines. First, never turn your back on the sea. Waves come in sets: One group may be small and quite harmless, but the next could be large enough to sweep you away. Never swim alone.

Don't try to surf, or bodysurf, until you're familiar with the sports' techniques and precautionary measures. Be careful when the surf is high.

If you get caught in a rip current, don't swim *against* it: swim *across* it, parallel to the shore. These currents, running from the shore out to sea, can often be spotted by their ragged-looking surface water and foamy edges.

Around coral reefs, wear something to protect your feet against cuts. Recommended are inexpensive Japanese *tabis*, or reef slippers. If you do get a coral cut, clean it with hydrogen peroxide, then apply an antiseptic or antibiotic substance.

When stung by a Portuguese man-of-war or a jellyfish, rinse the affected area with sea water to remove any tentacles. Use gloves or towels—not your bare fingers—to remove remaining tentacles. Human urine, once considered an effective remedy, is no longer a recommended treatment. With jellyfish stings only, you might also try vinegar or isopropyl alcohol.

If you step on the sharp, painful spines of a sea urchin, be sure the entire spine is removed. Soaking the wound in vinegar helps to dissolve the spine; for pain, soak the affected area in very hot water for 30 to 90 minutes. If the pain persists for more than a day, or you notice swelling or other signs of infection, consult a doctor.

Oh, one last thing. The chances of encountering a shark are about as likely as sighting a UFO. But should you meet one of these ominous creatures, stay calm. Simply swim quietly to shore. By the time you make it back to terra firma, you'll have one hell of a story to tell.

part of the Hawaiian diet. It's extremely nutritious, easy to gather and very plentiful.

Rocky shores are the best places to find the edible species of seaweed. Some of them float in to shore and can be picked up; other species cling stubbornly to rocks and must be freed with a knife; still others grow in sand or mud. Low tide is the best time to collect seaweed: More plants are exposed, and some can be taken without even getting wet.

SNORKELING & SCUBA DIVING

One of the great myths about Oahu is that you need to go far off the beaten track to discover its secret treasures. The fact is that within half an hour of Waikiki are excellent snorkeling and diving opportunities. From popular Hanauma Bay, just a short ride from the heart of Honolulu, to Kaena Point on the Leeward Coast, there are snorkeling and diving opportunities for beginners and certified pros alike. Or you can snorkel at Makua Beach, located between Makaha and Yokohama Bay on the Leeward Coast, and swim with the dolphins. Because conditions vary, I strongly recommend seeking instruction and advice from local diving experts before setting out.

Exploring underwater in Oahu is one of the most wonderful experiences available on the island. But it's up to us to protect that environment while we enjoy it. Coral reefs are actually animals that live in large colonies. They are also home to hundreds of creatures, including colorful reef fish. It takes years and years for coral reefs to regenerate themselves when damaged, and if they are badly damaged they die. We can help protect the reefs by not touching them (they are protected by Hawaiian law—it is illegal to take live coral from their beds); not walking or standing on them; and not feeding the fish that inhabit them, which upsets the eco-balance.

Waikiki

WAIKIKI DIVING CENTER ✉*424 Nahua Street, Honolulu* 📞*808-922-2121* ⌨*www.waikikidiving.com* This dive center takes divers to different sites around Oahu, depending on the time of year and the weather. The company offers two- to three-day PADI and NAUI courses and sells, rents and repairs diving equipment. It will also take nondivers out on an inexpensive introductory scuba charter so they can see what the sport is all about.

Snorkeling Safety Tips

Don't miss out on an opportunity to explore the depths of Oahu's busy ocean life. You're apt to find fish and coral in a dazzling array of colors, sizes and shapes. But take the following precautions before you dip into the water:

- Always snorkel with someone else

- Avoid big waves, surfers and windy conditions

- Bring a flotation device like an inner tube, noodle or life jacket, especially if you are with kids or are a novice swimmer

- Don't poke your hands into crevices or cracks in a reef (an eel hangout)

- Look up now and again to watch the weather conditions—if you're having trouble getting back to shore because the waves are too high, wait for the set to break

- Wear lots of waterproof sunscreen (and perhaps a T-shirt) because your back will be lobster red if you don't!

ATLANTIS ADVENTURES ☎ 808-973-9811, 800-548-6262 ✎ www.atlantis adventures.com If you are not interested in Snuba or scuba diving but do want to see what's down under, try a submarine excursion in Waikiki with Atlantis Adventures. You'll descend to 100 feet in air-conditioned hi-tech subs and explore an artificial reef complete with sunken ships and airplanes, created to bring back marine life to the area. It's not cheap, though.

Downtown Honolulu
SEE IN SEA ✉ 866 Iwilei Road ☎ 808-354-0405 ✎ www.seeinsea.com Excursions with this company visit the *Mahi* shipwreck, Fantasy Reef, Turtles Canyon, Airplanes and Makaha Caverns, to name a few. Rentals and instruction are also available.

Southeast Oahu
ALOHA DIVE SHOP ✉ Hawaii Kai Shopping Center, 377 Keahole Street, Hawaii Kai ☎ 808-395-5922 ✎ www.hawaiiweb.com/html/aloha_dive_shop.htm This shop runs day trips for certified divers and lesson packages for students at Maunalua Bay in the southeast corner of the island.

CAPTAIN BRUCE ✉ Waianae Boat Harbor ☎ 808-373-3590, 800-535-2487 ✎ www.captainbruce.com Featuring trips all around the island, including the *Mahi* shipwreck and Makaha Caverns, this dive company is a great option. Waikiki pick-up is available.

Windward Coast
AARON'S DIVE SHOP ✉ 307 Hahani Street, Kailua ☎ 808-262-2333, 888-847-2822 ✎ www.hawaii-scuba.com Choose between beach and boat dives, as well as special night trips at Aaron's.

North Shore
HALEIWA SURF CENTER ✉ Haleiwa Alii Beach Park, Haleiwa ☎ 808-637-5051 Depending on the season, the surf center teaches such sports as snorkeling, surfing, swimming, lifesaving and sailing. This county agency is also an excellent source of information on the island's water sports and facilities.

SURF N' SEA ✉ 62-595 Kamehameha Highway, Haleiwa ☎ 808-637-9887 ✎ www. surfnsea.com Specializing in small groups, this company offers half-day beach dives in the summer months on the North Shore and Leeward Coast including the *Mahi* shipwreck.

SNUBA

Somewhere between snorkeling and scuba diving is Snuba, created for those who would like to take snorkeling a step further but may not be quite ready for scuba diving. It's a shallow-water dive system that allows underwater breathing. Basically this is how it works. Swimmers wear a breathing device (the same one used in scuba diving) that is connected to a built-in scuba tank that floats on a raft. They also wear a weight belt, mask and fins. The air comes through a 20-foot tube connected to the raft, which follows the swimmer. Groups of six participants are taken out with a guide. They can dive up to 20 feet.

BREEZE HAWAII ✉3014 *Kaimuki Avenue* ✆808-735-1857 ✐*www.breeze hawaiidiving.com* This group offers Snuba tours at Hanauma Bay. Common sightings include an array of fish, eels, dolphins and turtles.

SURFING, WINDSURFING & KITESURFING

Surfing, a sport pioneered centuries ago by Hawaiian royalty, is synonymous with Oahu. Stars bring their boards from all over the world to join international competitions that take advantage of ideal surf and wind conditions. From the 30-foot winter rollers on the North Shore to beginner lessons off Waikiki, this is beach boy and girl territory. Windsurfing is equally popular in areas like the North Shore and Kailua Bay, which is also an especially good spot for kitesurfing.

If you plan to surf Oahu (or any of the other Hawaiian islands), check out www.globalsurfers.com. This online surf community maintained by surfers offers valuable information on surf spots on Oahu—from beginner breaks like "Canoes," "Point Panics" and "Secrets," to intermediate breaks like "Monster Mush," "Pyramid Rock" and "Hauula Bowls," to expert-only breaks like "Off-the-Wall," "Pinballs" and "Pipeline." Not only do they inform you about the break, the type of wave, and the length of the ride, they give you the rap on what to wear (board shorts or wet suits), the crowd level, the best board to use, and the ever-important "localism" of the locale. Remember when surfing in Hawaii, give the locals proper respect.

Waikiki
PRIME TIME SPORTS ✉Kalia Road ✆808-949-8952 For everything "on the water, in the water and under the water" check out Prime Time Sports near Fort DeRussy Beach. They offer beach accessories, equipment sales and rentals, lessons and plenty of friendly advice. Private and group surfing lessons have a "stand and surf" guarantee.

THE ALOHA BEACH SERVICE ✆808-922-3111 The Aloha Beach Service, in front of the Sheraton Moana Surfrider Hotel, offers lessons and rents long boards.

Greater Honolulu
DOWNING HAWAII ✉3021 *Waialae Avenue* ✆808-737-9696 In the Diamond Head area, this shop rents boards. Closed Sunday.

Windward Coast
KAILUA SAILBOARD AND KAYAK COMPANY ✉130 *Kailua Road, Kailua* ✆808-262-2555 ✐*www.kailuasailboards.com, info@kailuasailboards.com* This adventure company will teach you the tricks of the trade or help you brush up on your technique. You can also rent sailboards, boogieboards, long boards, kayaks, snorkeling and kitesurfing equipment here.

NAISH HAWAII ✉155-A *Hamakua Drive, Kailua* ✆808-261-6067 ✐*www.naish. com* In the same area as Kailua Sailboards, Naish offers lessons and rentals. This company manufactures its own boards and also operates

Ride the Wind

There's no better place to learn windsurfing than on Oahu. The water is warm and the conditions are near perfect. Although not a particularly easy sport to learn, in a week or two you could be holding your own as you glide over the waves.

Windsurfing, also known as boardsailing, is a technique sport rather than a muscle sport, no doubt one of the reasons women can learn to do it faster than men. At the beginning you will use a 12-foot board, known as a learner board, or in sailboard slang, an aircraft carrier. These have a dagger board for stabilization and a small soft sail that flutters in the wind as you move slowly across the water. Most people spend just a few days learning on one of these boards, before progressing to a shorter or "fun board."

The shorter the board, the more wind you need. For an eight-and-a-half-foot board, 15 to 20 knots of wind are required. Because these boards don't usually have a dagger board, sailors use the wind to steer by tipping their board in the direction they want to go.

In order to sail, you have to be balanced. And in order to be balanced, you have to position yourself properly on the board. The faster you go, the more the board is out of the water. Your feet should be in the center of the "wetted" surface, the part of the board that's in the water. Advanced sailors wear a harness around their waists. The harness has a hook that fits into loops hanging from the boom. It helps sailors hold the sail without effort.

If you would like to learn how to windsurf, Kailua, a bedroom community on Oahu, is the top choice. It is the state's best spot for those who are at beginning and intermediate levels in the sport. A protective reef and no breakers mean the waters aren't too rough, and the local community has established scores of low-key B&Bs to cater to the windsurfing crowd.

a shop filled with the latest in sailboarding and kitesurfing apparel and accessories, as well as long boards.

North Shore

HALEIWA SURF CENTER ✉️ *Haleiwa Alii Beach Park, Haleiwa* 📞 *808-637-5051* A resource for both the participatory and spectator aspects of surfing and windsurfing is found here. Surf lessons normally run September to April.

SURF N' SEA HALEIWA ✉️ *62-595 Kamehameha Highway, Haleiwa* 📞 *808-637-9887* ✎ *www.surfnsea.com* Surfing lessons and rentals are available at this facility. Lessons last two to three hours; price includes all gear.

SAILING

One of the best ways to enjoy Oahu's shoreline is aboard a sailboat. From brief cruises off Honolulu to a day-long charter along the North Shore, this is the perfect antidote to the tourist crowds. It's also surprisingly affordable.

HONOLULU SAILING COMPANY ✉ *47-335 Lulani Street, Honolulu* 📞 *808-239-3900, 800-829-0114* 🖥 *www.honsail.com* Ever dream of sailing off into the sunset, wind blowing in your hair? Snorkeling trips, swimming in the ocean off Diamond Head, a sunset cruise or a whale-watching venture can all be arranged here. You can even get married at sea by your licensed and uniformed captain. This personable outfit will sail to meet your needs.

NORTH SHORE CATAMARAN CHARTERS ✉ *Haleiwa Harbor, Haleiwa* 📞 *808-351-9371* 📠 *808-637-9757* 🖥 *www.sailingcat.com, info@sailingcat.com* Away from the hustle and bustle of Waikiki, the waters of the North Shore are ideal for whale watching. Aboard this outfitter's 25-passenger catamaran, you can get up close with humpback whales during their migration season from December to May—from January through mid-March, you're guaranteed a sighting. North Shore Catamaran also offers daily sunset cruises with *pupus* as well as seasonal snorkeling tours and private charters. Reservations recommended.

HAWAII YACHTS 📞 *800-908-5250* 🖥 *www.hawaiiyachts.com* If you're eager to charter your own yacht, contact this company, which charters all sizes of vessels ranging from fishing boats to luxury yachts.

KAYAKING

A sport well-suited for Oahu, kayaking is an ideal way to explore the island's protected bays, offshore islands and inland rivers. Waikiki's San Souci Beach offers paddlers a chance to surf the waves. On the Windward Coast, just off Lanikai beach, kayakers can enjoy the bird sanctuaries of the Mokulua Islands. Another kayaking spot is Kahana Bay and the mile-long Kahana stream. The North Shore offers Waimea Bay in the summer and the short but sweet Waimea River affords those who love birding and kayaking a chance to do both sports at one time.

GO BANANAS ✉ *799 Kapahulu Avenue* 📞 *808-737-9514* 🖥 *www.gobananas kayaks.com* To rent or purchase kayaks and equipment consider this shop just outside Waikiki.

KAILUA SAILBOARD AND KAYAK COMPANY ✉ *130 Kailua Road, Kailua* 📞 *808-262-2555* On the Windward Coast, stop here to rent or purchase kayaks and sign up for lessons.

PARASAILING

For a bird's-eye view of Southeastern Oahu, there's nothing quite like soaring over the water attached to a parasail.

SEABREEZE PARASAIL ✉ *Koko Marina Shopping Center, 7192 Kalanianaole Highway, Hawaii Kai* 📞 *808-396-0100* 🖥 *www.seabreezewatersports.com* Seabreeze provides Waikiki pick-ups for a flight above tropically blue Moanalua Bay. Minimum weight is 60 pounds. You can also tie in a scuba dive to your excursion as well.

WAKEBOARDING & WATERSKIING

Snowboarders with the summertime blues gave rise to wakeboarding. If the thrill of waterskiing is a little *too* thrilling, wakeboarding may be the sport to try. A relatively easy-to-control board is pulled slowly (well, 20–35 mph) behind a boat, while the rider skims the wake. The equipment is much easier to maneuver than waterskis, and when your skills are up to par, you can venture into the fancy stuff: jumps, backrolls and zig-zags.

Waterskiing is more physically demanding than wakeboarding, using every muscle in your body, requiring a higher speed and employing narrower, less agile skis.

HAWAII WATER SPORTS CENTER ✉️Koko Marina Shopping Center, 7192 Kalanianaole Highway, Hawaii Kai ☎808-395-3773 🖰www.hawaiiwatersportscenter. com Near Koko Head, this center offers instruction every day. Lessons are between 20 and 30 minutes long. Reservations required.

SKYDIVING & HANG GLIDING

For those with daring, opportunities to jump out of a plane or soar over cliffs and sea blue ocean are available from the following companies.

BIRDSEYE VIEW OF OAHU ✉️328 Ilihau Street, Kailua ☎808-381-4296 Birdseye View of Oahu offers daily ultralight airplane and tandem hang-gliding instruction at Kaneohe Marine Base. Call the company, and they'll also give you information on hang gliding in the area.

SKYDIVE HAWAII ✉️68-760 Farrington Highway ☎808-637-9700 🖰www.sky divehawaii.com You can learn to skydive and participate in a tandem dive with this company at Dillingham Airfield on the North Shore.

PACIFIC SKYDIVING CENTER ✉️68-760 Farrington Highway ☎808-637-7472 🖰www.pacific-skydiving.com Another skydiving option at Dillingham Field is this operation.

JOGGING

Jogging is very big on Oahu. There are several popular spots, and though they are never quite deserted, the crowds rarely become unmanageable. **Ala Moana Regional Park** is a good area for a run; the paved road fronts the beach, and the cool ocean breezes are welcome. **Kapiolani Park** is another mecca for jogger's. **Ala Wai Canal** is a less-recommended road; it's along a main drag and can get chaotic. Oahu also hosts endless races and marathons. For information on participation, pick up a free copy of *Hawaii Race Magazine*, available at most newsstands. Another source for where to run is **Running Room** (808-737-2442). There is also the *Runner's Guide to Oahu* (University of Hawaii Press) for serious folks.

RIDING STABLES

It's not the Wild West, but Oahu is *paniolo* country. To explore its beaches, valleys and pasturelands, contact the following listings.

KUALOA RANCH HAWAII ✉ *49-560 Kamehameha Highway, Kaaawa* ☎ *808-237-8515* ✑ *www.kualoa.com, activityinfo@kualoa.com* Located on the Windward Coast across from Chinaman's Hat, Kualoa Ranch leads one- and two-hour rides that provide startling views of the ocean and surrounding mountains. Guided rides for kids ages three through seven are available. They also offer many other activities including movie site tours, a jungle expedition and an ocean voyaging tour.

GUNSTOCK RANCH ✉ *56-250 Kamehameha Highway, Laie* ☎ *808-293-2060, 808-341-3995* ✑ *www.gunstockranch.com, gunstockranch@gunstockranch.com* At the base of the Koolau Mountains, this friendly ranch offers scenic trail rides for all ages and abilities. Options include 30-minute "horse experiences" for *keiki* ages two to seven; twice-daily 90-minute guided rides through the verdant mountains; and even a 90-minute moonlight ride offered twice a month. Reservations required.

TURTLE BAY RESORT ☎ *808-293-8811* ✑ *www.turtlebayresort.com* This resort on the North Shore has riding programs for the general public. They offer 45-minute guided tours, or you can enjoy a 60-minute private ride or lesson. All take place on the grounds of the hotel, with trails along the beach and through a lovely wooded area.

HAPPY TRAILS RANCH ✉ *59-231 Pupukea Road, Pupukea* ☎ *808-638-7433* ✑ *www.happytrailshawaii.com* On the North Shore, this ranch conducts one-and-a-half and two-hour trail rides through a rainforest valley and pastureland. The ranch has peacocks, chickens, a wild boar and six species of ducks. Children will love this place, and they can ride if they are six years or older.

GOLF

Even before Tiger Woods, golf has been a very popular sport among visitors in Hawaii, and no other island has more golf courses than Oahu. With so many to choose from, there's one to suit every level of play. And the scenery is spectacular.

Greater Honolulu

ALA WAI GOLF COURSE ✉ *404 Kapahulu Avenue* ☎ *808-733-7387* For a round of golf in Honolulu, try Hawaii's first municipal course. The *Guinness Book of World Records* once named it the busiest course in the world.

Southeast Oahu

HAWAII KAI GOLF COURSE ✉ *8902 Kalanianaole Highway* ☎ *808-395-2358* 🖷 *808-395-7726* ✑ *www.hawaiikaigolf.com* This is a popular spot with both tourists and *kamaaina* and features two 18-hole courses—one executive and one championship.

Windward Coast

WAIMANALO OLOMANA GOLF LINKS ✉ *41-1801 Kalanianaole Highway, Waimanalo* ☎ *808-259-7926* 🖥 *www.olomanagolflinks.com* A lush setting is offered at this 18-hole course.

BAY VIEW GOLF PARK ✉ *45-285 Kaneohe Bay Drive, Kaneohe* ☎ *808-247-0451* Stop at this 18-hole course for an inexpensive round of golf.

PALI GOLF COURSE ✉ *45-050 Kamehameha Highway, Kaneohe* ☎ *808-266-7612* Located below the Nuuanu Pali Lookout, these 18 holes afford sweeping views of the rugged Koolaus and the Windward coastline.

North Shore

KAHUKU GOLF COURSE ✉ *56-501 Kamehameha Highway, Kahuku* ☎ *808-293-5842* If you want to play a casual game, try this nine-hole course.

TURTLE BAY GOLF ✉ *Kahuku* ☎ *808-293-8574* The links at this resort were created around an existing 100-acre wetland preserve, which serves as home to several endangered Hawaiian birds. One of the two 18-hole courses was designed by Arnold Palmer.

Leeward Coast and Central Oahu

HAWAII COUNTRY CLUB ✉ *94-1211 Kunia Road, Wahiawa* ☎ *808-621-5654* Set amid fields of sugarcane and pineapple along the Leilehua Plateau in the center of Oahu, this 18-hole, par-72 course is a bit rundown, but offers some challenging holes.

THE MILILANI GOLF CLUB ✉ *95-176 Kuahelani Avenue, Mililani* ☎ *808-623-2222* 🖥 *www.mililanigolf.com* Though not particularly demanding, this 18-hole course provides lovely views of the Koolau and Waianae ranges.

TED MAKALENA GOLF COURSE ✉ *93-059 Waipio Point Access Road, Waipahu* ☎ *808-675-6052* This flat public course is not well-maintained, but its 18 holes are still popular with local duffers.

KO OLINA GOLF CLUB ✉ *92-1220 Aliinui Drive, Kapolei* ☎ *808-676-5309* 🖥 *www.koolinagolf.com* Golfers must drive their carts under a waterfall to get to the twelfth hole of this championship course. They will also enjoy the series of lakes, brooks and waterfalls that meanders through the 18-hole course.

MAKAHA GOLF CLUB ✉ *84-626 Makaha Valley Road, Makaha* ☎ *808-695-9544* Especially beautiful is this 18-hole course in the Makaha Valley, where sheer volcanic cliffs tower 1500 feet above lush greens, and golfers share the course with birds and peacocks.

TENNIS

Many Oahu resorts offer complete tennis facilities. But don't despair if your hotel lacks nets. There are dozens of public tennis courts in locations around the island. Following is a partial listing.

COUNTY DEPARTMENT OF PARKS AND RECREATION ✉ *1000 Uluohia Street, Suite 309, Kapolei* ☎ *808-768-3033* 📠 *808-768-3053* 🖥 *www.honolulu.gov/parks/programs/tennis/index.htm, parks@honolulu.gov* Contact this office for more information on public courts throughout the island.

Waikiki

KAPIOLANI PARK ✉*2740 Kalakaua Avenue* Four lighted courts.

DIAMOND HEAD TENNIS CENTER ✉*3908 Paki Avenue* Ten courts.

Greater Honolulu

ALA MOANA TENNIS CENTER ✉*Ala Moana Regional Park, Ala Moana Boulevard* Ten lighted courts.

KEEHI LAGOON ✉*405 Lagoon Drive; Off the Nimitz Highway* Twelve courts (four lighted).

MANOA VALLEY DISTRICT PARK ✉*2721 Kaaipu Street* Four lighted courts.

Windward Coast

KAILUA DISTRICT PARK ✉*21 South Kainalu Drive, Kailua* Eight lighted courts.

KANEOHE DISTRICT PARK ✉*45-660 Keaahala Road, Kaneohe* Six lighted courts.

North Shore

SUNSET BEACH NEIGHBORHOOD PARK ✉*59-360 Kamehameha Highway, Haleiwa* Two lighted courts.

Leeward Coast

WAIANAE DISTRICT PARK ✉*85-601 Farrington Highway, Waianae* Eight courts (two lighted).

BIKING

Oahu is blessed with excellent roads, well-paved and usually flat, and cursed with heavy traffic. About three-quarters of Hawaii's population lives here, and it sometimes seems like every person owns a car.

Honolulu can be a cyclist's nightmare, but outside the city the traffic is somewhat lighter. And Oahu drivers, accustomed to tourists driving mopeds, are relatively conscious of bicyclists. It's certainly possible to bike through Central Oahu. Kamehameha Highway is an option, although it is dotted with steep grades and sections that aren't too bike-friendly. Riders may cruise the Kalanianaole Highway, past Kapiolani Park and around Diamond Head to Hanauma Bay, pedal along the Waianae Coast or zip across the interior from Waialua to Pearl City. Other rides cover the area between Haleiwa and Kahuku and the stretch between Waimanalo Beach and Kaaawa.

If you'd really like to get away from it all, try mountain biking. One of Oahu's most popular mountain bike trails is **Maunawili** on the windward side. It starts from the Pali lookout and goes all the way to Waimanalo. Just past Waimea Bay is the **Ke Ala Pupukea** bike path, which goes through Sunset Beach Park and Waimea Bay Beach Park. It also conveniently passes a supermarket.

Keep in mind that the Windward Coast and the North Shore are the wet sides, and the south and west coasts are the driest of all. And remember, rip-offs are a frequent fact of life on Oahu. Leaving your bike unlocked is asking for a long walk back.

THE DEPARTMENT OF TRANSPORTATION ✐ www.state.hi.us/dot/ highways/bike/oahu These folks offer a free "Bike Oahu" map that lists detailed routes, road grades and where along the way you can find water and food. The entire brochure is available on their website.

HAWAII BICYCLING LEAGUE ✉ 3442 Waialae Avenue #1, Honolulu ✆ 808-735-5756 808-735-7989 ✐ www.hbl.org, bicycle@hbl.org If you'd like a little two-wheeled company, check out the Hawaii Bicycling League, which regularly sponsors weekend bike rides and free annual events.

Bike Rentals
COCONUT CRUISERS ✉ 305 Royal Hawaiian Avenue, Waikiki ✆ 808-392-1174 ✐ www.coconutcruisers.com This company offers beach cruisers and mountain bikes for daily or weekly rentals.

THE BIKE SHOP ✉ 1149 South King Street, Honolulu ✆ 808-596-0588 ✐ www. bikeshophawaii.com This store rents mountain bikes, road bikes and even bike racks so you can cruise anywhere on the island.

Bike Repairs
EKI CYCLERY ✉ 1603 Dillingham Boulevard, Honolulu ✆ 808-847-200 ✐ www. ekicyclery.com In addition to doing repair work, this shop sells accessories and mountain bikes although, watch out, their employees can be a bit unhelpful. With mountain, road and triathlon bikes for sale.

THE BIKE SHOP ✉ 1149 South King Street, Honolulu ✆ 808-596-0588 ✐ www. bikeshophawaii.com You can get repair work done here.

ISLAND TRIATHLON & BIKE ✉ 569 Kapahulu Avenue, Honolulu ✆ 808-732-7227 ✐ www.itbhawaii.com This shop does repairs and sells bikes.

HIKING

There are numerous hiking trails within easy driving distance of Honolulu. I have listed these as well as trails in the Windward Coast and North Shore areas. Unfortunately, many Oahu treks require special permission from the state, the armed services or private owners. But you should find that the hikes suggested here, none of which require official sanction, will provide you with ample adventure.

Many of the trails you'll be hiking on Oahu are composed of volcanic rock. Since this is a very crumbly substance, be cautious when climbing any rock faces. It's advisable to wear long pants when hiking in order to protect your legs from rock outcroppings, insects and spiny plants. Stay on the trails: Oahu's dense undergrowth makes it very easy to get lost. If you get lost at night, stay where you are. Because of the low latitude, night descends rapidly here; there's practically no twilight. Once darkness falls, it can be very dangerous to move around.

All distances listed for hiking trails are one way unless otherwise noted, so remember to leave time for the return trip.

Greater Honolulu

DIAMOND HEAD   If you're staying in Waikiki, the most easily accessible hike is the .6-mile jaunt up Diamond Head crater. There's a sweeping view of Honolulu from atop this famous landmark. The trail begins inside the crater, so take Diamond Head Road around to the inland side of Diamond Head, then follow the tunnel leading into the crater.

LANIPO TRAIL   In the Koolau Mountains above Diamond Head there is a challenging trail that climbs almost 2000 feet and affords excellent panoramas of the Windward Coast. To get to the Lanipo Trail (3 miles), take Waialae Avenue off of Route H-1. Then turn up Wilhelmina Rise and follow until it reaches Maunalani Circle and the trailhead.

WAAHILA RIDGE TRAIL   For spectacular vistas overlooking the lush Palolo and Manoa valleys, you can hike Waahila Ridge Trail (2 miles). To get there, take St. Louis Heights Drive (near the University of Hawaii campus) and then follow connecting roads up to Waahila Ridge State Recreation Area.

The following trails can be combined for longer hikes.

MANOA FALLS TRAIL   A pleasant jaunt that follows Waihi Stream through a densely vegetated area to a charming waterfall, this trail goes 0.8 mile through Manoa Valley. From Honolulu, take Kapiolani Boulevard to University Avenue, then turn right on Manoa Road, which ends at the trailhead.

MANOA CLIFF TRAIL   This 3.4-mile trail is well-maintained and makes for a pleasant family hike, following a precipice along the west side of Manoa Valley. The trailhead is at a parking lot at the end of Round Top Toad near the top of Tantalus in the hills above Honolulu.

PUU OHIA TRAIL   For splendid views of the Manoa and Nuuanu valleys, take this .75-mile trail, which crosses Manoa Cliff Trail.

MAKIKI VALLEY LOOP TRAIL   A 2.5-mile loop at the entrance to Makiki Recreation Area on Makiki Heights Drive begins near Tantalus and is composed of three interlinking trails. This loop passes stands of eucalyptus and bamboo trees and offers some postcard views of Honolulu.

JUDD MEMORIAL   Another loop trail, this .75-mile path crosses Nuuanu Stream and traverses bamboo, eucalyptus and Norfolk pine groves en route to the Jackass Ginger Pool. To get there, take the Pali Highway (Route 61) several miles north from Honolulu. Turn onto Nuuanu Pali Drive and follow it about a mile to Reservoir Number Two spillway and look for the trailhead.

OLD PALI ROAD   You can access a two-mile-long portion of this road directly to the right of the Pali Lookout. The narrow paved roadway provides easy hikes that are perfect for family excursions and reward with sweeping panoramas of the Windward Coast.

KOOLAUPOKO TRAIL   For those with a more strenuous hike in mind, this 9-mile trail departs from the Pali Lookout parking lot for magnificent rainforest, valley and ocean views. In places the trail is quite steep and occasionally demanding.

AIEA LOOP TRAIL   In the mountains above Pearl Harbor, at Keaiwa Heiau State Recreation Area, you will find this 4.8-mile loop trail. Set in a heavily forested area, the hike passes the wreckage of a World War II cargo plane. It provides an excellent chance to see some of the native Hawaiian trees—*lehua*, *ohia* and *koa*—used by local woodworkers. (For directions to Keaiwa Heiau State Recreation Area, see the "Greater Honolulu Beaches & Parks" section in this book.)

WAIMANO TRAIL   Another hike is along this 7-mile trail, which climbs 1600 feet to an astonishing vista point above Oahu's Windward Coast. There are swimming holes en route to the vista point. To get there, take Kamehameha Highway (Route 90) west to Waimano Home Road (Route 730). Turn right and go two and a half miles to a point along the road where you'll see a building on the right and an irrigation ditch on the left. The trail follows the ditch.

Southeast Oahu

There are several excellent hikes along this shore. The first few are within ten miles of Waikiki, near Hanauma Bay. From the beach at Hanauma you can hike two miles along the coast and cliffs to the Halona Blowhole. This trek passes the Toilet Bowl, a unique tidepool with a hole in the bottom that causes it to fill and then flush with the wave action. Waves sometimes wash the rocks along this path, so be prepared to get wet (and be careful!).

At the intersection where the short road leading down toward Hanauma Bay branches from Kalanianaole Highway (Route 72), there are two other trails.

KOKO HEAD TRAIL   A steep 1-mile hike to the top of a volcanic cone, this trail starts on the ocean side of the highway. This trek features some startling views of Hanauma Bay, Diamond Head and the Koolau Range.

KOKO CRATER TRAIL   This 1-mile trail leads from the highway up to a 1208-foot peak. The views from this crow's nest are just as spectacular as from Koko Head Trail.

Windward Coast

There are several other particularly pretty hikes much farther north, near the village of Hauula. In Hauula, if you turn off of Kamehameha Highway and head inland for about a quarter-mile up Hauula Homestead Road, you'll come to Maakua Road. Walk up Maakua Road, which leads into the woods. About 300 yards after entering the woods, the road forks. If you continue straight ahead you'll be on Hauula Trail, but if you veer left you'll encounter yet another trail branching off to the left in about 150 yards. This is Papali Trail (also known as Maakua Trail).

HAUULA TRAIL   This trail ascends 2.5-miles along two ridges and provides fine vistas of the Koolau Range and the Windward Coast.

PAPALI TRAIL This 2.5-mile hike drops into Papali Gulch, then climbs high along a ridge from which you can view the surrounding countryside.

North Shore and Leeward Coast

KAENA POINT You can approach the trail to the point either from the North Shore or the Leeward Coast. It's a dry, rock-strewn path that leads to Oahu's westernmost tip. There are tidepools and swimming spots en route, plus spectacular views of a rugged, uninhabited coastline; it's a great place to spot porpoises, and is the legendary home of Nanue the Shark Man. If you're lucky, you may sight nesting albatross or rare Hawaiian Monk seals. Keep your distance as both are protected species and a portion of the point is a wildlife preserve. In ancient times, this was sacred land; it was believed the souls of the dead departed from Kaena to the afterworld, called *Po*, the realm of the spirits. To get to the trailhead, just drive to the end of the paved portion of Route 930 on the North Shore or Route 93 on the Leeward Coast. Then follow the trail out to Kaena Point. It's about two miles via the Leeward Coast, and a half-mile via the North Shore.

For those hikers looking to see new parts of the island and gain a deeper respect for its beauty—or for nature lovers who want to help preserve and enrich Oahu's wilderness areas—several organizations offer guided treks throughout the island. Led by knowledgeable naturalists and experts on the complex systems that make up this dazzling landscape, organized hikes and nature walks provide opportunities to learn the storied history of the island's natural beauty.

NATURE CONSERVANCY OF HAWAII ✉ *923 Nuuanu Avenue, Honolulu, HI 96817* ✆ *808-537-4508* 🖷 *808-545-2019* 🖉 *www.tnc.org/hawaii* This nonprofit conservation organization conducts several hikes and work trips each month for members at the Honouliuli Preserve in the southern Waianae Mountains of western Oahu. Check their website for upcoming excursions.

HAWAII NATURE CENTER ✉ *2131 Makiki Heights Drive, Honolulu, HI 96822* ✆ *808-955-0100, 888-955-0104* 🖉 *www.hawaiinaturecenter.org* This group offers hikes throughout Oahu two or three times a month. It also offers talks by naturalists on such subjects as geology, birdlife, native flora and taro cultivation. There are hikes and activities for the little ones, too, with activities aimed for explorers as young as three years old.

SIERRA CLUB ✉ *1040 Richards Street #306, Honolulu, HI 96803* ✆ *808-538-6616* 🖉 *www.hi.sierraclub.org* The Sierra Club sponsors weekly hikes on Oahu, as well as trail building and other projects aimed at helping to preserve the island's natural heritage. The club has a recorded message line that lists weekly weekend outings.

HAWAIIAN TRAIL AND MOUNTAIN CLUB ✉ *808-674-1459, 808-377-5442* 🖉 *www.aditl.com/htmc* In existence since 1910, the Hawaiian Trail and Mountain Club maintains a clubhouse for members in Waimanalo and sponsors hikes every weekend. Unlike the other environmental organizations listed here, this one is run entirely by volunteers and does not have an office. To become a member you must go on three hikes. Call ahead since some of the hikes are members only.

HISTORY & CULTURE

POLYNESIAN ARRIVAL The island of Hawaii, the Big Island, was the last land mass created in the ongoing dramatic geologic upheaval that formed the Hawaiian islands. But it was most likely the first Hawaiian island to be inhabited by humans. Perhaps as early as the third century, Polynesians sailing from the Marquesas Islands, and then later from Tahiti, landed on Hawaii's southern tip. In Europe, mariners were rarely venturing outside the Mediterranean Sea, and it would be centuries before Columbus happened upon the New World. Yet, in the Pacific, entire families were crossing 2500 miles of untracked ocean in hand-carved canoes with sails woven from coconut fibers. The boats were formidable structures, catamaran-like vessels with a cabin built on the platform between the wooden hulls. The sails were woven from *hala* (pandanus) leaves. Some of the vessels were a hundred feet long and could do 20 knots, making the trip to Hawaii in a month.

The Polynesians had originally come from the coast of Asia about 3000 years before. They had migrated through Indonesia, then pressed inexorably eastward, leapfrogging across archipelagoes until they finally reached the last chain, the most remote—Hawaii.

These Pacific migrants were undoubtedly the greatest sailors of their day, and stand among the finest in history. When close to land they could smell it, taste it in the seawater, see it in a lagoon's turquoise reflection on the clouds above an island. They navigated by the stars and carried the plants and animals they would need to start a new life. From the color of the water they determined ocean depths and current directions. They had no charts, no compasses, no sextants; sailing directions were simply recorded in legends and chants. Yet Polynesians discovered the Pacific, from Indonesia to Easter Island, from New Zealand to Hawaii. They made the Vikings and Phoenicians look like landlubbers.

CAPTAIN COOK They were high islands, rising in the northeast as the sun broke across the Pacific. First one, then a second and, finally, as the tall-masted ships drifted west, a third island loomed before them. Landfall! The British crew was ecstatic. It meant fresh water, tropical fruits, solid ground on which to set their boots and a chance to carouse with the native women. For their captain, James Cook, it was another in an amazing career of discoveries. The man whom many call history's greatest explorer was about to land in one of the last spots on earth to be discovered by the West.

He would name the place for his patron, the British earl who became famous by pressing a meal between two crusts of bread: the Sandwich Islands. Later they would be called Owhyhee, and eventually, as the Western tongue glided around the uncharted edges of a foreign language, Hawaii.

It was January 1778, a time when the British Empire was still basking in a sun that never set. The Pacific had been opened to Western powers over two centuries before, when a Portuguese sailor named Magellan crossed it. Since that time, the British, French, Dutch and Spanish had tracked through in search of future colonies.

They happened upon Samoa, Fiji, Tahiti and the other islands that spread across this third of the globe, but somehow they had never sighted Hawaii. Even when Cook finally spied it, he little realized how important a find he had made. Hawaii, quite literally, was a jewel in the ocean, rich in fragrant sandalwood, ripe for agricultural exploitation and crowded with sea life. But it was the archipelago's isolation that would prove to be its greatest resource. Strategically situated between Asia and North America, it was the only place for thousands of miles to which whalers, merchants and bluejackets could repair for provisions and rest.

Cook was 49 years old when he shattered Hawaii's quiescence. The Englishman hadn't expected to find islands north of Tahiti. Quite frankly, he wasn't even trying. It was his third Pacific voyage and Cook was hunting bigger game, the fabled Northwest Passage that would link this ocean with the Atlantic.

But these mountainous islands were still an interesting find. He could see by the canoes venturing out to meet his ships that the lands were inhabited; when he finally put ashore in Waimea on Kauai, on January 20, 1778, Cook discovered a Polynesian society. He saw irrigated fields, domestic animals and high-towered temples. The women were bare-breasted, the men wore loincloths. As his crew bartered for pigs, fowls and bananas, he learned that the natives knew about metal and coveted iron like gold.

If iron was gold to these "Indians," then Cook was a god. He soon realized that his arrival had somehow been miraculously timed, coinciding with the Makahiki festival, a months-long celebration highlighted by sporting competitions, feasting, hula and exaltation of the ruling chiefs. Even war ceased during this gala affair. Makahiki honored the roving deity Lono, whose return to Hawaii on "trees that would move over seas" was foretold in ancient legend. Cook was a strange white man sailing tall-masted ships—obviously he was Lono. The Hawaiians gave him gifts, fell in his path and rose only at his insistence.

But even among religious crowds, fame is often fickle. After leaving Kauai, Cook sailed north to the Arctic Sea, where he failed to discover the Northwest Passage. He returned the next year to Kealakekua Bay on the Big Island, arriving at the tail end of another exhausting Makahiki festival. By then the Hawaiians had tired of his constant demands for provisions and were suffering from a new disease that was obviously carried by Lono's archangelic crew—syphilis. This Lono was proving something of a freeloader.

Tensions ran high. The Hawaiians stole a boat. Cook retaliated with gunfire. A scuffle broke out on the beach and in a sudden violent outburst, which surprised the islanders as much as the interlopers, the Hawaiians discovered that their god could bleed. The world's finest mariner lay face down in foot-deep water, stabbed and bludgeoned to death.

Cook's end marked the beginning of an era. He had put the Pacific on the map, his map, probing its expanses and defining its fringes. In Hawaii he ended a thousand years of solitude. The archipelago's geographic isolation, which has always played a crucial role in Hawaii's development, had finally failed to protect it, and a second theme had come into play—the islands' vulnerability. Together with the region's "backwardness," these conditions would now mold Hawaii's history. All in

KAMEHAMEHA AND KAAHUMANU The next man whose star would rise
above Hawaii was present at Cook's death. Some say he struck the Englishman,
others that he took a lock of the great leader's hair and used its residual power, its
mana, to become king of all Hawaii.

Kamehameha was a tall, muscular, unattractive man with a furrowed face, a
lesser chief on the powerful island of Hawaii. When he began his career of con-
quest a few years after Cook's death, he was a mere upstart, an ambitious, arro-
gant young chief. But he fought with a general's skill and a warrior's cunning, often plunging into the midst of a melee. He had an astute sense of technology, an
intuition that these new Western metals and firearms could make him a king.

In Kamehameha's early years, the Hawaiian islands were composed of many fief-
doms. Several kings or great chiefs, continually warring among themselves, ruled
individual islands. At times, a few kings would carve up one island or a lone king
might seize several. Never had one monarch controlled all the islands.

But fresh players had entered the field: Westerners with ample firepower and awesome ships. During the decade following Cook, only a handful had arrived, mostly
Englishmen and Americans, and they had not yet won the influence they soon
would wield. However, even a few foreigners were enough to upset the balance of
power. They sold weapons and hardware to the great chiefs, making several of
them more powerful than any of the others had ever been. War was imminent.

Kamehameha stood in the center of the hurricane. Like any leader suddenly
caught up in the terrible momentum of history, he never quite realized where he
was going or how fast he was moving. And he cared little that he was being carried
in part by Westerners who would eventually want something for the ride. Kamehameha was no fool. If political expedience meant Western intrusion, then so be
it. He had enemies among chiefs on the other islands; he needed the guns.

When two white men came into his camp in 1790, he had the military advisers to
complement a fast expanding arsenal. Within months he cannoned Maui. In
1792, Kamehameha seized the Big Island by inviting his main rival to a peaceful
parley, then slaying the hapless chief. By 1795, he had consolidated his control of
Maui, grasped Molokai and Lanai, and begun reaching greedily toward Oahu.
Kamehameha began a decisive battle in his campaign to unite the Hawaiian islands, defeating the forces of Kalanikupule. He struck rapidly, landing near Waikiki and sweeping inland, forcing his enemies to their deaths over the precipitous
cliffs of the Nuuanu Pali.

The warrior had become a conqueror, controlling all the islands except Kauai,
which he finally gained in 1810 by peaceful negotiation. Kamehameha proved to
be as able a bureaucrat as he had been a general. He became a benevolent despot
who, with the aid of an ever-increasing number of Western advisers, expanded
Hawaii's commerce, brought peace to the islands and moved his people inexorably toward the modern age.

He came to be called Kamehameha the Great, and history first cast him as the
George Washington of Hawaii, a wise and resolute leader who gathered a war-
torn archipelago into a kingdom—Kamehameha I. But with the revisionist history of the 1960s and 1970s, as Third World people questioned both the Western

version of events and the virtues of progress, Kamehameha began to resemble Benedict Arnold. He was seen as an opportunist, a megalomaniac who permitted the Western powers their initial foothold in Hawaii. He used their technology and then, in the manner of great men who depend on stronger allies, was eventually used by them.

As long a shadow as Kamehameha cast across the islands, the event that most dramatically transformed Hawaiian society occurred after his death in 1819. The kingdom had passed to Kamehameha's son Liholiho, but Kamehameha's favorite wife, Kaahumanu, usurped the power. Liholiho was a prodigal son, dissolute, lacking self-certainty, a drunk. Kaahumanu was a woman for all seasons, a canny politician who combined brilliance with boldness, the feminist of her day. She had infuriated Kamehameha by eating forbidden foods and sleeping with other chiefs, even when he placed a taboo on her body and executed her lovers. She drank liquor, ran away, proved completely uncontrollable and won Kamehameha's love.

It was only natural that when he died, she would take his *mana*, or so she reckoned. Kaahumanu gravitated toward power with the drive of someone whom fate has unwisely denied. She carved her own destiny, announcing that Kamehameha's wish had been to give her a governmental voice. There would be a new post and she would fill it, becoming in a sense Hawaii's first prime minister.

And if the power, then the motion. Kaahumanu immediately marched against Hawaii's belief system, trying to topple the old idols. For years she had bristled under a polytheistic religion regulated by taboos, or *kapus*, which severely restricted women's rights. Now Kaahumanu urged the new king, Liholiho, to break a very strict *kapu* by sharing a meal with women.

Since the act might help consolidate Liholiho's position, it had a certain appeal to the king. Anyway, the *kapus* were weakening: These white men, coming now in ever greater numbers, defied them with impunity. Liholiho vacillated, went on a two-day drunk before gaining courage, then finally sat down to eat. It was a last supper, shattering an ancient creed and opening the way for a radically new divinity. As Kaahumanu had willed, the old order collapsed, taking away a vital part of island life and leaving the Hawaiians more exposed than ever to foreign influence.

Already Western practices were gaining hold. Commerce from Honolulu, Lahaina and other ports was booming. There was a fortune to be made dealing sandalwood to China-bound merchants, and the chiefs were forcing the common people to strip Hawaii's forests. The grueling labor might make the chiefs rich, but it gained the commoners little more than a barren landscape. Western diseases struck virulently. The Polynesians in Hawaii, who numbered 300,000 in Cook's time, were extremely susceptible. By 1866, their population had dwindled to less than 60,000. It was a difficult time for the Hawaiian people.

MISSIONARIES AND MERCHANTS   Hawaii was not long without religion. The same year that Kaahumanu shattered tradition, a group of New England missionaries boarded the brig *Thaddeus* for a voyage around Cape Horn. It was a young company—many were in their twenties or thirties—and included a doctor, a printer and several teachers. They were all strict Calvinists, fearful that the second coming was at hand and possessed of a mission. They were bound for a strange land called Hawaii, 18,000 miles away.

A Brief, Brief History of Honolulu

When Captain Brown sailed into Honolulu Harbor in 1794, he was the first known foreigner to arrive in the paradise. He named the area Fair Harbor. Eventually the name Honolulu (meaning "sheltered harbor") gained precedence. King Kamehameha I settled here in 1809 after conquering Oahu, and Honolulu gained financial status when it flourished as a major shipping port. Although the town traded extensively in pineapple and sugar, and served as a supply port for whalers, its main claim to fame was sandalwood. Honolulu's sandalwood trade enjoyed a brief but brilliant boom. The islanders exported the wood to China in exchange for silk and porcelain, which was then shipped to New England. The ships returned to Honolulu with New England goods. Environmental protection policies were not in place at this time in history, and the forests were soon depleted. Nonetheless, Honolulu remained an important port; in 1850, King Kamehameha III declared the area the capital of his kingdom.

From their perspective, Hawaii was a lost paradise, a hellhole of sin and savagery where men slept with several wives and women neglected to wear dresses. To the missionaries, it mattered little that the Hawaiians had lived this way for centuries. The churchmen would save these heathens from hell's everlasting fire whether they liked it or not.

The delegation arrived in Kailua on the Big Island in 1820 and then spread out, establishing important missions in Honolulu and Lahaina. Soon they were building schools and churches, conducting services in Hawaiian and converting the natives to Christianity.

The missionaries rapidly became an integral part of Hawaii, despite the fact that they were a walking contradiction to everything Hawaiian. They were a contentious, self-righteous, fanatical people whose arrogance toward the Hawaiians blinded them to the beauty and wisdom of island lifestyles. Where the natives lived in thatch homes open to the soothing trade winds, the missionaries built airless clapboard houses with New England–style fireplaces. While the Polynesians swam and surfed frequently, the new arrivals, living near the world's finest beaches, stank from not bathing. In a region where the thermometer rarely drops much below 70°, they wore long-sleeved woolens, ankle-length dresses and clawhammer coats. At dinner they preferred salt pork to fresh beef, dried meat to fresh fish. They considered coconuts an abomination and were loath to eat bananas.

And yet the missionaries were a brave people, selfless and God-fearing. Their dangerous voyage from the Atlantic had brought them into a very alien land. Many would die from disease and overwork; most would never see their homeland again. Bigoted though they were, the Calvinists committed their lives to the Hawaiian people. They developed the Hawaiian alphabet, rendered Hawaiian into a written language and, of course, translated the Bible. Theirs was the first printing press west of the Rockies. They introduced Western medicine throughout the islands and created such an effective school system that, by the mid-19th century, 80 percent of the Hawaiian population was literate. Unlike almost all the other white people who came to Hawaii, they not only took from the islanders, they also gave.

But to these missionaries, *giving* meant ripping away everything repugnant to God and substituting it with Christianity. They would have to destroy Hawaiian culture in order to save it. Though instructed by their church elders not to meddle in island politics, the missionaries soon realized that heavenly wars had to be fought on earthly battlefields. Politics it would be. After all, wasn't government just another expression of God's bounty?

They allied with Kaahumanu and found it increasingly difficult to separate church from state. Kaahumanu converted to Christianity, while the missionaries became government advisers and helped pass laws protecting the sanctity of the Sabbath. Disgusting practices such as hula dancing were prohibited.

Politics can be a dangerous world for a man of the cloth. The missionaries were soon pitted against other foreigners who were quite willing to let the clerics sing hymns, but were damned opposed to permitting them a voice in government. Hawaii in the 1820s had become a favorite way station for the whaling fleet. As the sandalwood forests were decimated, the island merchants began looking for other industries. By the 1840s, when over 500 ships a year anchored in Hawaiian ports, whaling had become the islands' economic lifeblood. During the heyday of the whaling industry, more American whaling ships visited Hawaii than any other port in the world.

Like the missionaries, the whalers were Yankees, shipping out from bustling New England ports. But they were a hell of a different cut of Yankee. These were rough, crude, boisterous men who loved rum and music, and thought a lot more of fornicating with island women than saving them. After the churchmen forced the passage of laws prohibiting prostitution, the sailors rioted along the waterfront and fired cannons at the mission homes. When the smoke cleared, the whalers still had their women.

Religion simply could not compete with commerce, and other Westerners were continuously stimulating more business in the islands. By the 1840s, as Hawaii adopted a parliamentary form of government, American and British fortune hunters were replacing missionaries as government advisers. It was a time when anyone, regardless of ability or morality, could travel to the islands and become a political powerhouse literally overnight. A consumptive American, fleeing the mainland for reasons of health, became chief justice of the Hawaiian Supreme Court while still in his twenties. Another lawyer, shadowed from the East Coast by a checkered past, became attorney general two weeks after arriving.

The situation was no different internationally. Hawaii was subject to the whims and terrors of gunboat diplomacy. The archipelago was solitary and exposed, and Western powers were beginning to eye it covetously. In 1843, a maverick British naval officer actually annexed Hawaii to the Crown, but the London government later countermanded his actions. Then, in the early 1850s, the threat of American annexation arose. Restless Californians, fresh from the gold fields and hungry for revolution, plotted unsuccessfully in Honolulu. Even the French periodically sent gunboats in to protect their small Catholic minority.

Finally, the three powers officially stated that they wanted to maintain Hawaii's national integrity. But independence seemed increasingly unlikely. European countries had already begun claiming other Pacific islands, and with the influx of Yankee missionaries and whalers, Hawaii was being steadily drawn into the American orbit.

THE SUGAR PLANTERS There is an old Hawaiian saying that describes the 19th century: The missionaries came to do good, and they did very well. Actually

This second generation, quite willing to sacrifice glory for gain, fit neatly into the commercial society that had rendered their fathers irrelevant. They were shrewd, farsighted young Christians who had grown up in Hawaii and knew both the islands' pitfalls and potentials. They realized that the missionaries had never quite found Hawaii's pulse, and they watched uneasily as whaling became the lifeblood of the islands. Certainly it brought wealth, but whaling was too tenuous—there was always a threat that it might dry up entirely. A one-industry economy would never do; the mission boys wanted more. Agriculture was the obvious answer, and eventually they determined to bind their providence to a plant that grew wild in the islands—sugar cane.

The first sugar plantation, the Koloa Sugar Company, was started on Kauai in 1835, but not until the 1870s did the new industry blossom. By then, the Civil War had wreaked havoc with the whaling fleet, and a devastating winter in the Arctic whaling grounds practically destroyed it. The mission boys, who had prophesied the storm, weathered it quite comfortably. They had already begun fomenting an agricultural revolution.

THE GREAT MAHELE Agriculture, of course, means land, and until the 19th century all Hawaii's acreage was held by chiefs. So in 1848, the mission sons, together with other white entrepreneurs, pushed through the Great Mahele, one of the slickest real estate laws in history. Before the Great Mahele, Hawaiians flourished because they had the rights of access and were able to use the resources of both land and sea. Their traditions were based on common use. Rationalizing that it would grant chiefs the liberty to sell land to Hawaiian commoners and white men, the mission sons established a Western system of private property.

The Hawaiians, who had shared their chiefs' lands communally for centuries, had absolutely no concept of deeds and leases. What resulted was the old $24-worth-of-beads story. The benevolent Westerners wound up with the land, while the lucky Hawaiians got practically nothing. Large tracts were purchased for cases of whiskey; others went for the cost of a hollow promise. The entire island of Niihau, which is still owned by the same family, sold for $10,000. It was a bloodless coup, staged more than 40 years before the revolution that would topple Hawaii's monarchy. In a sense it made the 1893 uprising anticlimactic. By then Hawaii's future would already be determined: White interlopers would own four times as much land as Hawaiian commoners.

Following the Great Mahele, the mission boys, along with other businessmen, were ready to become sugar planters. The *mana* once again was passing into new hands. Obviously, there was money to be made in cane, a lot of it, and now that they had land, all they needed was labor. The Hawaiians would never do. Cook might have recognized them as industrious, hardworking people, but the sugar planters considered them shiftless. Disease was killing them off anyway, and the Hawaiians who survived seemed to lose the will to live. Many made appointments with death, stating that in a week they would die; seven days later they were dead.

Foreign labor was the only answer. In 1850, the Masters and Servants Act was passed, establishing an immigration board to import plantation workers. Cheap Asian labor would be brought over. It was a crucial decision, one that would ramify forever through Hawaiian history and change the very substance of island so-

56   ciety. Between 1850 and 1930, 180,000 Japanese, 125,000 Filipinos, 50,000 Chinese and 20,000 Portuguese immigrated. Eventually these foreign workers transformed Hawaii from a chain of Polynesian islands into one of the world's most varied and dynamic locales, a meeting place of East and West.

The Chinese were the first to come, arriving in 1852 and soon outnumbering the white population. Initially, with their long pigtails and uncommon habits, the Chinese were a joke around the islands. They were poor people from southern China whose lives were directed by clan loyalty. They built schools and worked hard so that one day they could return to their native villages in glory. They were ambitious, industrious and—ultimately—successful.

Too successful, according to the sugar planters, who found it almost impossible to keep the coolies down on the farm. The Chinese came to Hawaii under labor contracts, which forced them to work for five years. After their indentureship, rather than reenlisting as the sugar bosses had planned, the Chinese moved to the city and became merchants. Worse yet, they married Hawaiian women and were assimilated into the society.

These coolies, the planters decided, were too uppity, too ready to fill social roles that were really the business of white men. So in the 1880s, they began importing Portuguese, over 20,000 of them. But the Portuguese thought they already *were* white men, while any self-respecting American or Englishman of the time knew they weren't.

The Portuguese spelled trouble, and in 1886 the sugar planters turned to Japan, with its restricted land mass and burgeoning population. The new immigrants were peasants from Japan's southern islands, raised in an authoritarian, hierarchical culture in which the father was a family dictator and the family was strictly defined by its social status. Like the Chinese, they built schools to protect their heritage and dreamed of returning home someday; but unlike their Asian neighbors, they only married other Japanese. They sent home for "picture brides," worshipped their ancestors and Emperor and paid ultimate loyalty to Japan, not Hawaii.

The Japanese, it soon became evident, were too proud to work long hours for low pay. Plantation conditions were atrocious; workers were housed in hovels and frequently beaten. The Japanese simply did not adapt. Worst of all, they not only bitched, they organized, striking in 1909.

So in 1910, the sugar planters turned to the Philippines for labor. For two decades the Filipinos arrived, seeking their fortunes and leaving their wives behind. They worked not only with sugar cane but also with pineapples, which were becoming a big business in the 20th century. They were a boisterous, fun-loving people, hated by the immigrants who preceded them and used by the whites who hired them. The Filipinos were given the most menial jobs, the worst working conditions and the shoddiest housing. In time, another side of their character began to show—a despondency, a hopeless sense of their own plight, their inability to raise passage money back home. They became the untouchables of Hawaii.

REVOLUTIONARIES AND ROYALISTS   Sugar, by the late 19th century, was king. It had become the center of island economy, the principal fact of life for most islanders. Like the earlier whaling industry, it was drawing Hawaii ever closer to the American sphere. The sugar planters were selling the bulk of their crops in California; having already signed several tariff treaties to protect their

American market, they were eager to further strengthen mainland ties. Besides,
many sugar planters were second-, third- and fourth-generation descendants of
the New England missionaries; they had a natural affinity for the United States.

There was, however, one group that shared neither their love for sugar nor their
ties to America. To the Hawaiian people, David Kalakaua was king, and America
was the nemesis that had long threatened their independence. The whites might
own the land, but the Hawaiians, through their monarch, still held substantial
political power. During Kalakaua's rule in the 1870s and 1880s, anticolonialism
was rampant.

The sugar planters were growing impatient. Kalakaua was proving very antago-
nistic; his nationalist drumbeating was becoming louder in their ears. How could
the sugar merchants convince the United States to annex Hawaii when all these
silly Hawaiian royalists were running around pretending to be the Pacific's answer to the British Isles? They had tolerated this long enough. The Hawaiians were
obviously unfit to rule, and the planters soon joined with other businessmen to
form a secret revolutionary organization. Backed by a force of well-armed followers, they pushed through the "Bayonet Constitution" of 1887, a self-serving docu-
ment that weakened the king and strengthened the white landowners. If Hawaii
was to remain a monarchy, it would have a Magna Carta.

But Hawaii would not be a monarchy long. Once revolution is in the air, it's often
difficult to clear the smoke. By 1891, Kalakaua was dead and his sister, Liliuokalani, had succeeded to the throne. She was an audacious leader, proud of her
heritage, quick to defend it and prone to let immediate passions carry her onto
dangerous ground. At a time when she should have hung fire, she charged, pro-
claiming publicly that she would abrogate the new constitution and reestablish a
strong monarchy. The revolutionaries had the excuse they needed. They struck in
January 1895, seized government buildings and, with four boatloads of American
marines and the support of the American minister, secured Honolulu. Liliuokalani surrendered.

It was a highly illegal coup; legitimate government had been stolen from the Hawaiian people. But given an island chain as isolated and vulnerable as Hawaii, the
revolutionaries reasoned, how much did it really matter? It would be weeks before
word reached Washington of what a few Americans had done without official sanction, then several more months before a new American president, Grover Cleve-
land, denounced the renegade action. By then the revolutionaries would already
be forming a republic. They chose as their first president Sanford Dole, a missionary's son whose name would eventually become synonymous with pineapples.

Not even revolution could rock Hawaii into the modern age. For years, an unsta-
ble monarchy had reigned; now an oligarchy composed of the revolution's leaders would rule. Officially, Hawaii was a democracy; in truth, the Chinese and
Japanese were hindered from voting, and the Hawaiians were encouraged not to
bother. Hawaii, reckoned its new leaders, was simply not ready for democracy.
Even when the islands were finally annexed by the United States in 1898 and
granted territorial status, they remained a colony.

More than ever before, the sugar planters, alias revolutionaries, held sway. By the
early 20th century, they had linked their plantations into a cartel, the Big Five. It
was a tidy monopoly composed of five companies that owned not only the sugar

and pineapple industries, but the docks, shipping companies and many of the stores, as well. Most of these holdings, happily, were the property of a few interlocking, intermarrying mission families—the Doles, Thurstons, Alexanders, Baldwins, Castles, Cookes and others—who had found heaven right here on earth. They golfed together and dined together, sent their daughters to Wellesley and their sons to Yale. All were proud of their roots, and as blindly paternalistic as their forefathers. It was their destiny to control Hawaii, and they made very certain, by refusing to sell land or provide services, that mainland firms did not gain a foothold in their domain.

What was good for the Big Five was good for Hawaii. Competition was obviously not good for Hawaii. Although the Chinese and Japanese were establishing successful businesses in Honolulu and some Chinese were even growing rich, they posed no immediate threat to the Big Five. And the Hawaiians had never been good at capitalism. By the early 20th century, they had become one of the world's most urbanized groups. But rather than competing with white businessmen in Honolulu, unemployed Hawaiians were forced to live in hovels and packing crates, cooking their poi on stoves fashioned from empty oil cans.

Political competition was also unhealthy. Hawaii was ruled by the Big Five, so naturally it should be run by the Republican Party. After all, the mission families were Republicans. Back on the mainland, the Democrats had always been cool to the sugar planters, and it was a Republican president, William McKinley, who eventually annexed Hawaii. The Republicans, quite simply, were good for business.

The Big Five set out very deliberately to overwhelm any political opposition. When the Hawaiians created a home-rule party around the turn of the century, the Big Five shrewdly co-opted it by running a beloved descendant of Hawaii's royal family as the Republican candidate. On the plantations they pitted one ethnic group against another to prevent the Asian workers from organizing. Then, when labor unions finally formed, the Big Five attacked them savagely. In 1924, police killed 16 strikers on Kauai. Fourteen years later, in an incident known as the "Hilo massacre," the police wounded 50 picketers.

The Big Five crushed the Democratic Party by intimidation. Polling booths were rigged. It was dangerous to vote Democratic—workers could lose their jobs, and if they were plantation workers, that meant losing their houses as well. Conducting Democratic meetings on the plantations was about as easy as holding a hula dance in an old missionary church. The Democrats went underground.

Those were halcyon days for both the Big Five and the Republican Party. In 1900, only five percent of Hawaii's population was white. The rest was composed of races that rarely benefitted from Republican policies. But for the next several decades, even during the Depression, the Big Five kept the Republicans in power.

While the New Deal swept the mainland, Hawaii clung to its colonial heritage. The islands were still a generation behind the rest of the United States—the Big Five enjoyed it that way. There was nothing like the status quo when you were already in power. Other factors that had long shaped Hawaii's history also played into the hands of the Big Five. The islands' vulnerability, which had always favored the rule of a small elite, permitted the Big Five to establish an awesome cartel. Hawaii's isolation, its distance from the mainland, helped protect their monopoly.

7, 1941. On what would afterwards be known as the "Day of Infamy," a flotilla of six aircraft carriers carrying over 400 planes unleashed a devastating assault on Pearl Harbor. Attacking the Pacific Fleet on a Sunday morning, when most of the American ships were unwisely anchored side by side, the Japanese sank or badly damaged six battleships, three destroyers and several other vessels. Over 2400 Americans were killed.

The Japanese bombers that attacked Pearl Harbor sent shock waves through Hawaii that are still rumbling today. World War II changed all the rules of the game, upsetting the conditions that had determined island history for centuries.

Ironically, no group in Hawaii would feel the shift more thoroughly than the Japanese. On the mainland, Japanese-Americans were rounded up and herded into relocation camps. But in Hawaii that was impossible; there were simply too many (160,000—fully one-third of the island's population), and they comprised too large a part of the labor force. Instead, the community's business, religious and civic leaders, about 1200 to 1800, were sent to internment camps on Oahu or on the mainland.

Many Japanese were second-generation, *nisei*, who had been educated in American schools and assimilated into Western society. Unlike their immigrant parents, the *issei*, they felt few ties to Japan. Their loyalties lay with America, and when war broke out they determined to prove it. They joined the U.S. armed forces and formed a regiment, the 442nd, which became the most frequently decorated outfit of the war. The Japanese were heroes, and when the war ended many heroes came home to the United States and ran for political office. Men like Daniel Inouye and Spark Matsunaga began winning elections and would eventually become United States senators.

By the time the 442nd returned to the home front, Hawaii was changing dramatically. The Democrats were coming to power. Leftist labor unions won crucial strikes in 1941 and 1946. Jack Burns, an ex-cop who dressed in tattered clothes and drove around Honolulu in a beat-up car, was creating a new Democratic coalition.

Burns, who would eventually become governor, recognized the potential power of Hawaii's ethnic groups. Money was flowing into the islands—first military expenditures and then tourist dollars, and non-whites were rapidly becoming a new middle class. The Filipinos still constituted a large part of the plantation force, and the Hawaiians remained disenchanted, but the Japanese and Chinese were moving up fast. Together they formed a majority of Hawaii's voters.

Burns organized them, creating a multiracial movement and thrusting the Japanese forward as candidates. By 1954, the Democrats controlled the legislature, with the Japanese filling one out of every two seats in the capital. Then, when Hawaii attained statehood five years later, the voters elected the first Japanese ever to serve in Congress. (Today one of the state's U.S. senators and a congresswoman are Japanese.) On every level of government, from municipal to federal, the Japanese predominated. They had arrived. The *mana*, that legendary power coveted by the Hawaiian chiefs and then lost to the sugar barons, had passed once again—to a people who came as immigrant farm-workers and stayed to become the leaders of the 50th state.

60   The Japanese and the Democrats were on the move, but in the period from World War II until the present day, everything was in motion. Hawaii was in upheaval. Jet travel and a population boom shattered the islands' solitude. While in 1939 about 500 people flew to Hawaii, now about seven million visitors land every year. The military population escalated as Oahu became a key base not only during World War II but throughout the Cold War and the Vietnam War, as well. Hawaii's overall population exploded from about a half-million just after World War II to over one million at the present time.

No longer did the islands lag behind the mainland; they rapidly acquired the dubious quality of modernity. Hawaii became America's 50th state in 1959, Honolulu grew into a bustling highrise city, and hotels and condominiums mushroomed along the beaches of Maui, a neighboring island. Outside investors swallowed up two of the Big Five corporations, and several partners in the old monopoly began conducting most of their business outside Hawaii. Everything became too big and moved too fast for Hawaii to be entirely vulnerable to a small interest group. Now, like the rest of the world, it would be prey to multinational corporations.

By the 1980s, it would also be of significant interest to investors from Japan. In a few short years they succeeded in buying up a majority of the state's luxury resorts, including every major beachfront hotel in Waikiki, sending real estate prices into an upward spiral that did not level off until the early 1990s. During the rest of the decade, the economy was stagnant, with real estate prices dropping, agriculture declining and tourism leveling off at seven million visitors annually.

HAWAIIAN SOVEREIGNTY   One element that has not plateaued during the last several years is the Native Hawaiian movement. Nativist sentiments were spurred in January 1993 by the 100th anniversary of the American overthrow of the Hawaiian monarchy. Over 15,000 people turned out to mark the illegal coup. Later that year, President Clinton signed a statement issued by Congress formally apologizing to the Hawaiian people.

In 1994, the United States Navy returned the island of Kahoolawe to the state of Hawaii. Long a rallying symbol for the Native Hawaiian movement, the unoccupied island had been used for decades as a naval bombing target. By 1996, efforts to clean away bomb debris and make the island habitable were well under way, although completion of the clean-up is still years off.

Then in 1998, the issue of Hawaii's monarchy arose again when demonstrators marched around the entire island of Oahu and staged rallies to protest the 100th anniversary of the United States' annexation of Hawaii. In 2003 Kahoolawe was officially returned to the state of Hawaii, to be held in trust for a sovereign Hawaiian nation.

Today, numerous perspectives remain to be reconciled, with grassroots movements working to secure a degree of autonomy for Hawaii's native people. The most common goal seems to be a status similar to that accorded the American Indians by the federal government, although there are still those who seek a return to an independent Hawaii, either as a restored monarchy or along democratic lines. Also pending resolution is the distribution of land to Native Hawaiians with documented claims, as well as a financial settlement with the state government. It's a complex situation involving the setting right of injustices of a century past.

HAWAIIAN CULTURE

Hawaii, according to Polynesian legend, was discovered by Hawaii-loa, an adventurous sailor who often disappeared on long fishing trips. On one voyage, urged along by his navigator, Hawaii-loa sailed toward the planet Jupiter. He crossed the "many-colored ocean," passed over the "deep-colored sea," and eventually came upon "flaming Hawaii," a mountainous island chain that spewed smoke and lava.

History is less romantic. The Polynesians who found Hawaii were probably driven from their home islands by war, famine or some similar calamity. They traveled in groups, not as lone rangers, and shared their canoes with dogs, pigs and chickens, with which they planned to stock new lands. Agricultural plants such as coconuts, yams, taro, sugar cane, bananas and breadfruit were also stowed on board.

Most important, they transported their culture, an intricate system of beliefs and practices developed in the South Seas. After undergoing the stresses and demands of pioneer life, this traditional lifestyle was transformed into a new and uniquely Hawaiian culture.

It was based on a caste system that placed the *alii* or chiefs at the top and the slaves, *kauwa*, on the bottom. Between these two groups were the priests, *kahuna* and the common people or *makaainana*. The chiefs, much like feudal lords, controlled all the land and collected taxes from the commoners who farmed it. They used an *ahupuaa* system to divide and manage the islands. The pie-shaped wedges of land varied in size, depending on a chief's status, but each ran from the mountains to the sea, providing the residents with all the resources they needed to exist. Those who lived in the uplands traded food they raised with their *ohana* (family) that resided by the sea. People rarely ventured beyond their own *ahupuaa*, and while they might trade with neighboring *ahupuaa*, they would never hunt or harvest outside their own boundaries. Even today, folks in Hawaii tend to stick close to home in deference to the old system.

Life centered around the *kapu*, a complex group of regulations that dictated what was sacred or profane. For example, women were not permitted to eat pork or bananas; commoners had to prostrate themselves in the presence of a chief. These strictures were vital to Hawaiian religion; *kapu* breakers were directly violating the will of the gods and could be executed for their actions. And there were a lot of gods to watch out for, many quite vindictive. The four central gods were *Kane*, the creator; *Lono*, the god of agriculture and peace; *Ku*, the war god; and *Kanaloa*, lord of the underworld. They had been born from the sky father and earth mother, and had in turn created many lesser gods and demigods who controlled various aspects of nature.

It was, in the uncompromising terminology of the West, a stone-age civilization. Though the Hawaiians lacked metal tools, the wheel and a writing system, they managed to include within their inventory of cultural goods everything necessary to sustain a large population on a chain of small islands. They fashioned fish nets from native *olona* fiber, made hooks out of bone, shell and ivory, and raised fish in rock-bound ponds. The men used irrigation in their farming. The women made clothing by pounding mulberry bark into a soft cloth called tapa, dyeing elaborate patterns into the fabric. They built peak-roofed thatch huts from native *pili* grass and *hala* leaves. The men fought wars with spears, slings, clubs and daggers. The women used mortars and pestles to pound the roots of the taro plant into poi, the islanders' staple food. Bread, fruit, yams and coconut were other menu standards.

The West labeled these early Hawaiians "noble savages." Actually, they often lacked nobility. The Hawaiians were cannibals who practiced human sacrifice during religious ceremonies and often used human bone to fashion fish hooks. They constantly warred among themselves and would mercilessly pursue a retreating army, murdering as many of the vanquished soldiers as possible.

But they weren't savages either. The Hawaiians developed a rich oral tradition of genealogical chants and created beautiful lilting songs to accompany their hula dancing. Their musicians mastered several instruments including the *ukeke* (a single-stringed device resembling a bow), an *ohe hano ihu* or nose flute, rattles and drums made from gourds, coconut shells or logs. Their craftsmen produced the world's finest featherwork, tying thousands of tiny feathers onto netting to produce golden cloaks and ceremonial helmets. (Conscious of the fragility of their resources, Hawaiians used to trap birds by smearing branches with sticky sap. Once the birds were caught, they would pluck only the choicest feathers, clean the bird's claws and then release them.)

The Hawaiians helped develop the sport of surfing. They also swam, boxed, bowled and devised an intriguing game called *konane*, a cross between checkers and the Japanese game of go. They built networks of trails across lava flows, and created an elemental art form in the images—petroglyphs—that they carved into lava rock along the trails.

They also achieved something far more outstanding than their varied arts and crafts, something that the West, with its awesome knowledge and advanced technology, has never duplicated. The Hawaiians created a balance with nature. They practiced conservation, establishing closed seasons on certain fish species and carefully guarding their plant and animal resources. The Hawaiians sustained themselves by primarily eating vegetables and poi, while supplementing their diet with fish and several varieties of seafood or *limu*. Further, they used nature's herbs such as *noni* and *kukui* to treat ailments. But what they took from nature they also gave back.

They led a simple life, without the complexities the outside world would eventually thrust upon them. It was a good life: Food was plentiful, people were healthy and the population increased. For a thousand years, the Hawaiians lived in delicate harmony with the elements. It wasn't until the West entered the realm, transforming everything, that the fragile balance was destroyed. But that is another story entirely.

The most isolated population center on earth, Hawaii is 2390 miles from the mainland United States and 4900 miles from China. Because of its unique history and isolated geography, Hawaii is truly a cultural melting pot. It's one of the few states in the union in which caucasians are a minority group. Whites, or *haole* as they're called in the islands, comprise only about 27 percent of Hawaii's 1.2 million population. Asians (including Japanese, Korean, Filipino, Chinese and "other Asian") 41 percent, Hawaiians and part-Hawaiians account for 29 percent, and other racial groups 3 percent. It's a very vital society, with nearly 19 percent of the people born of racially mixed parents.

One trait characterizing many of these people is Hawaii's famous spirit of aloha, a genuine friendliness, an openness to strangers, a willingness to give freely. For example, those beautiful Hawaiian quilts you see are not generally used for snuggling under. Instead, they serve as an expression of historical events and are used as gifts of aloha. Undoubtedly, this openness is one of the finest qualities any people has ever demonstrated. Aloha originated with the Polynesians and played an important role in ancient Hawaiian civilization.

The aloha spirit is alive and well on Oahu, although bad attitudes toward *haole*, are not unknown. All parties, however, seem to understand the crucial role tourism has come to play in Oahu's economy, which means you're not likely to experience unpleasantness from the locals you'll meet—unless you behave unpleasantly. A smile goes a long way.

ECONOMY

For years, sugar was king in Hawaii, the most lucrative part of the island economy. Today, tourism is number one. About four million Americans, and almost seven million travelers worldwide visit the Aloha State every year. It's now a $10 billion business that expanded exponentially during the 1970s and 1980s, leveled off in the 1990s.

The U.S. military is another large industry, with some 17 percent of the state's population either on active duty or retired personnel—Hawaii has a greater percentage of its population in the military than any other state. With 161 installations in the state, the military controls nearly 6 percent of Hawaii's land mass, including 22 percent of Oahu. The armed forces pump more than $3 billion into the local economy annually, and it is pursuing plans to expand and step up its training, research, development and testing activities on all islands.

Because it is almost entirely dependent upon tourism and construction, Oahu's economy is fragile and subject to frequent boom and bust cycles. The cost of living is at least 30 percent higher than the rest of the nation, due to the expense of importing fuel, food and other necessities. Although unemployment is low, most jobs are in the low-paying service industry, requiring many residents to hold more than one job. Meanwhile, housing prices have skyrocketed beyond the reach of most local families, resulting in widespread homelessness, especially among native Hawaiians.

CUISINE

Nowhere is the influence of Oahu's melting pot population stronger than in the kitchen. While in the islands, you'll probably eat not only with a fork, but with chopsticks and fingers as well. You'll sample a wonderfully varied cuisine. In addition to standard American fare, hundreds of restaurants serve Hawaiian, Japanese, Chinese, Korean, Portuguese and Filipino dishes. There are also fresh fruits aplenty—pineapples, papayas, mangoes, bananas and tangerines—plus local fish such as mahimahi, marlin and snapper.

A quick translation will help you when choosing a seafood platter from Hawaiian waters. Firm-textured with a light taste, the most popular fish is mahimahi, or dolphin fish (no, it's not one of those amazing creatures that do fancy tricks on the waves); its English equivalent is dorado. *Ahi* is yellowfin tuna and is especially delicious as sashimi (raw) or blackened. *Opakapaka* is pink snapper and is a staple of Pacific Rim cuisine. Other snappers include *uku* (gray snapper), *onaga* (ruby snapper) and *ehu* (red snapper). *Ono* (which means delicious in Hawaiian) is king mackerel or *wahoo*, a white fish that lives up to its name.

The mainstay of the traditional Hawaiian diet is poi, a purplish paste pounded from baked or steamed taro tubers. It's pretty bland fare, but it does make a good side dish with *imu*-cooked pork or tripe stew. You should also try *laulau*, a combination of fish, pork and taro leaves wrapped in a *ti* leaf and steamed. And don't neglect to taste baked *ulu* (breadfruit) and *opihi* (limpets). Among the other Hawaiian culinary traditions are *kalua* pig, a shredded pork dish baked in an *imu* (underground oven); *lomilomi* salmon, which is salted and mixed with onions and tomatoes; and chicken *luau*, prepared in taro leaves and coconut milk.

A visit to Hawaii isn't complete without attending a luau, although the tourist versions bear little resemblance to the real thing. Still, they're entertaining and a chance to try foods cooked in a traditional underground oven, or *imu*. The feast centers around a whole pig, and you'll also likely be served poi, *lomi* salmon, *laulau*, chicken and fish, along with modern salads and rice. The music and hula dancing is usually the energetic Tahitian style, and be prepared for corny jokes and the chance to try hula yourself. The mai tais are usually free and strong, so go easy or you may end up with your head in the *haupia* (coconut pudding) by night's end.

Japanese dishes include sushi, sukiyaki, teriyaki and tempura, plus an island favorite—sashimi, or raw fish. On most any menu, including McDonald's, you'll find *saimin*, a noodle soup filled with meat, vegetables and *kamaboko* (fishcake).

You can count on the Koreans for kim chi, a spicy salad of pickled cabbage and *kalbi*, barbecued beef short ribs prepared with soy sauce and sesame oil. The Portuguese serve up some delicious sweets including *malasadas* (donuts minus the holes) and *pao doce*, or sweet bread. For Filipino fare, I recommend *adobo*, a pork or chicken dish spiced with garlic and vinegar, and *pochero*, a meat entrée cooked with bananas and several vegetables. In addition to a host of dinner dishes, the Chinese have contributed treats such as *manapua* (a steamed bun filled with barbecued pork) and oxtail soup. They also introduced crack seed to the islands. Made from dried and preserved fruit, it provides a treat as sweet as candy.

As the Hawaiians say, *"Hele mai ai."* Come and eat!

LANGUAGE

The language common to all Hawaii is English, but because of its diverse cultural heritage, the archipelago also supports several other tongues. Foremost among these are Hawaiian and pidgin. Hawaiian, closely related to other Polynesian languages, is one of the most fluid and melodious languages in the world. It's composed of only twelve letters: five vowels—*a, e, i, o, u* and seven consonants—*h, k, l, m, n, p, w.* The *okina* ('), also called a glottal stop, when used, counts as a thirteenth letter.

At first glance, the language appears formidable: How the hell do you pronounce *humuhumunukunukuapuaa*? But actually it's quite simple. After you've mastered a few rules of pronunciation, you can take on any word in the language.

The first thing to remember is that every syllable ends with a vowel, and the next to last syllable usually receives the accent.

The next rule to keep in mind is that all the letters in Hawaiian are pronounced. Consonants are pronounced the same as in English (except for the *w*, which is pronounced as a *v* when it introduces the last syllable of a word—as in *ewa* or *awa.* Vowels are pronounced the same as in Spanish: *a* as in *among, e* as in *they, i* as in *machine, o* as in *no* and *u* as in *too.* Hawaiian has four vowel combinations or diphthongs: *au*, pronounced *ow; ae* and *ai*, which sound like *eye*; and *ei*, pronounced *ay.* As noted above, the glottal stop (') occasionally provides a thirteenth letter.

By now, you're probably wondering what I could possibly have meant when I said Hawaiian was simple. I think the glossary that follows will simplify everything while helping you pronounce common words and place names. Just go through the list, starting with words like aloha and luau that you already know. After you've practiced pronouncing familiar words, the rules will become second nature; you'll no longer be a *malihini* (newcomer).

Just when you start to speak with a swagger, cocky about having learned a new language, some young Hawaiian will start talking at you in a tongue that breaks all the rules you've so carefully mastered. That's pidgin. It started in the 19th century as a lingua franca among Hawaii's many races. Pidgin speakers mix English and Hawaiian with several other tongues to produce a spicy creole. It's a fascinating language with its own vocabulary, a unique syntax and a rising inflection that's hard to mimic.

Pidgin is definitely the hip way to talk in Hawaii. A lot of young Hawaiians use it among themselves as a private language. At times they may start talking pidgin to you, acting as though they don't speak English; then if they decide you're okay, they'll break into English. When that happens, you be one *da kine brah.*

So *brah*, I take *da kine* pidgin words, put 'em together with Hawaiian, make one big list. Savvy?

aa (ah-**ah**)—a type of rough lava

ae (eye)—yes

aikane (eye-**kah**-nay)—friend, close companion

akamai (ah-kah-**my**)—wise

alii (ah-**lee**-ee)—chief

aloha (ah-**lo**-ha)—hello; greetings; love

aole (ah-**oh**-lay)—no

auwe (ow-**way**)—ouch!; oh no!

brah (bra)—friend; brother; bro'

bumby (**bum**-bye)—after a while; by and by

da kine (da kyne)—whatdyacallit; thingamajig; the best

dah makule guys (da mah-**kuh**-lay guys)—senior citizens

diamond head—in an easterly direction (Oahu only)

duh uddah time (duh **uh**-duh time)—once before

ewa (**eh**-vah)—in a westerly direction (Oahu only)

e komo mai (eh kohmoh mai)—welcome, come in

hale (**hah**-lay)—house

haole (**how**-lee)—Caucasian; white person

hano hou (hah nah hou)—encore

hapa (**hah**-pa)—half

hapa-haole (**hah**-pa **how**-lee)—half-Caucasian

heiau (hey-**yow**)—temple

hele on (**hey**-lay on)—go, move, outta here

hoaloha (ho-ah-**lo**-ha)—friend

holo holo (**ho**-low **ho**-low)—to visit

howzit? (hows-it)—how you doing? what's happening?

huhu (hoo-hoo)—angry

hukilau (**who**-key-lau)—community fishing party

hula (**who**-la)—Hawaiian dance

imu (**ee**-moo)—underground oven

ipo (**ee**-po)—sweetheart

kahuna (kah-**who**-nah)—priest; specialist or expert in any field

kai (kye)—ocean

kaka-roach (**kah**-kah roach)—ripoff; theft

kamaaina (kah-mah-**eye**-nah)—one born and raised in Hawaii; a long-time island resident

kane (**kah**-nay)—man

kapu (**kah**-poo)—taboo; forbidden

kaukau (cow-cow)—food

keiki (**kay**-key)—child

kiawe (key-**ah**-vay)—mesquite tree

kokua (ko-**coo**-ah)—help

kona winds (**ko**-nah winds)—winds that blow against the trades

kuli kuli (koo-lee koo-lee)—be quiet, be still

lanai (lah-**nye**)—porch; also island name

lauhala (lau-**hah**-lah) or *hala* (**hah**-lah)—a pandanus tree whose leaves are used in weaving

lei (lay)—flower garland

lolo (low-low)—stupid

lomilomi (**low**-me-**low**-me)—massage; salted raw salmon

luau (**loo**-ow)—Hawaiian meal

mahalo (mah-**hah**-low)—thank you

mahalo nui loa (mah-**ha**-low **new**-ee **low**-ah)—thank you very much

mahu (**mah**-who)—gay; homosexual

makai (mah-**kye**)—toward the sea

malihini (mah-lee-**hee**-nee)—newcomer; stranger

mauka (**mau**-kah)—toward the mountains

nani (**nah**-nee)—beautiful

ohana (oh-**hah**-nah)—family

okole (oh-**ko**-lay)—rear; ass

okolemaluna (oh-ko-lay-mah-**loo**-nah)—a toast: bottoms up!

ono (**oh**-no)—tastes good

pahoehoe (pah-**hoy**-hoy)—smooth or ropy lava

pakalolo (pah-kah-**low**-low)—marijuana

popakiki (poh-poh-**key**-key)—stubborn; hard head

pali (**pah**-lee)—cliff

paniolo (pah-nee-**oh**-low)—cowboy

pau (pow)—finished; done

pilikia (pee-lee-**key**-ah)—trouble

puka (**poo**-kah)—hole

pupus (**poo**-poos)—hors d'oeuvres

shaka (**shah**-kah)—hand greeting

swell head—"big head"; egotistical

tapa (**tah**-pah)—also *kapa*; fabric made from the beaten bark of mulberry trees

wahine (wah-**hee**-nay)—woman

wikiwiki (**wee**-key-**wee**-key)—quickly; in a hurry

you get stink ear—you don't listen well

MUSIC

Music has long been an integral part of Hawaiian life. Most families keep musical instruments in their homes, gathering to play at impromptu living room or backyard jam sessions. Hawaiian folk tunes are passed down from generation to generation. In the earliest days, it was the sound of rhythm instruments and chants that filled the air. Drums, including the *pahu hula*, were fashioned from hollowed-out gourds, coconut shells or hollowed sections of coconut palm trunks, then covered with sharkskin. Gourds and coconuts, *uliuli*, adorned with tapa cloth and feathers, were also filled with shells or pebbles to produce a rattling sound. Other instruments included the nose flute, or *ohe*, a piece of bamboo similar to a mouth flute, but played by exhaling through the nostril; the bamboo organ; and *puili*, sections of bamboo split into strips, which were struck rhythmically against the body. Stone castanets, *iliili*, and *ke laau* sticks are also used as hula musical instruments.

Western musical scales and instruments were introduced by explorers and missionaries. As ancient Hawaiian music involved a radically different musical system, Hawaiians had to completely re-adapt. Actually, Western music caught on quickly, and the hymns brought by missionaries fostered a popular musical style—the *himeni*, or Hawaiian church music.

Strangely enough, a Prussian bandmaster named Henry Berger had a major influence on contemporary Hawaiian music. Brought over in the

19th century by King Kalakaua to lead the Royal Hawaiian Band, Berger helped Hawaiians make the transition to Western instruments.

69

3 HISTORY & CULTURE MUSIC

Hawaii has been the birthplace of several different musical instruments and styles. The "leaping flea," better known as the ukulele, was introduced to the islands by the Portuguese in 1879, and it quickly became the most popular Hawaiian instrument. Its small size made it easy to carry, and with just four strings, it was simple to play. Legend has it that the ukulele was introduced to the islands in 1879 when the *Ravenscrag* arrived in Honolulu from the island of Madeira, bringing a boatload of Portuguese to work the sugar cane fields. Known as a *braguinha* by the Portuguese, the Hawaiians named it the ukulele, or "jumping flea," for the way one's fingers dance across the instrument. King David Kalakaua was purported to design and play his own instruments after he was taught by Augusto Dias, whose shop he visited frequently. Other notable Hawaiian royalty ukulele players included Queen Emma, Queen Liliuokalani, Prince Leleiohoku and Princess Likelike. In fact, Queen Liliuokalani authored a number of songs, the best known being "Aloha Oe." The words to the song are preserved on a plaque set in a boulder at Washington Place, where she resided after her overthrow.

The slack-key style of guitar playing also comes from Hawaii, where it's called *ki ho'alu*. When the guitar was first brought to Hawaii in the 1830s by Mexican and Spanish cowboys, the Hawaiians adapted the instrument to their own special breed of music. In tuning, the six (or twelve) strings are loosened so that they sound a chord when strummed and match the vocal range of the singer. Slack-key is played in a variety of ways, from plucking or slapping the strings to sliding along them. A number of different tunings exist, and many have been passed down orally through families for generations. Some of the more renowned guitarists playing today include Keola Beamer and Cyril Pahinui.

During the late 19th century, *"hapa*-haole" songs became the rage. The ukulele was instrumental in contributing to this Hawaiian fad. Written primarily in English with pseudo-Hawaiian themes, songs like "Tiny Bubbles" and "Lovely Hula Hands" were later introduced to the world via Hollywood. The Hawaiian craze continued on the mainland with radio and television shows such as "Hawaii Calls" and "The Harry Owens

Hawaiian Melodies

Waikiki is the nightlife hotspot in the islands. Performing Thursday nights on the breezy Moana Terrace at the Waikiki Beach Resort is **Pomaika'i Keawe Lyman**, whose voice sounds just like her late grandmother Aunty Genoa Keawe, the first lady of Hawaiian falsetto music. Slack key masters **George Kuo**, **Martin Pahinui** and **Aaron Mahi** play at the Moana Terrace on Sunday nights. **Olomana** is a must-see on Friday and Saturday nights at the Hilton Hawaiian Village Resort's Paradise Lounge. **Henry Kapopno** plays regularly at Duke's Canoe Club in the Outrigger Waikiki Hotel. Outside of Waikiki **Makana**, **Jerry Santos**, or **Robert and Roland Cazimero** perform for lucky diners at Chai's Island Bistro in the Aloha Tower Mareketplace.

Show." In the 1950s, little mainland girls donned plastic hula skirts and danced along with Hilo Hattie and Ray Kinney.

It was not until the 1970s that both the hula and music of old Hawaii made a comeback. Groups such as the Sons of Hawaii and the Makaha Sons of Niihau, along with the late Aunty Genoa Keawe and Gabby Pahinui, became popular. Before long, a new form of Hawaiian music was being heard, a combination of ancient chants and contemporary sounds, performed by such islanders as Henry Kapono, Kalapana, Olomana, the Beamer Brothers, Bla Pahinui, the Peter Moon Band, Kealii Reichel, Kapena and the Brothers Cazimero.

An entire new category of music was also established in Hawaii: dubbed "Jawaiian," the sound incorporates Jamaican reggae and contemporary Hawaiian music, and is especially popular among the state's younger population. Pro-sovereignty groups like Sudden Rush have taken this trend one step further, laying down their message-imbued rap lyrics on reggae tunes and Hawaiian classics to create a unique genre.

Today many of these groups, along with other notables such as Hapa, the Kaau Crater Boys, Brother Noland, Willie K., Del Beazley, Butch Helemano, Obrien Eselu and Jake Shimabukuro, bring both innovation to the Hawaiian music scene and contribute to the preservation of an ancient tradition.

In addition, now-deceased masters of Hawaiian song like Gabby Pahinui and Iz (Israel Kamakawiwo'ole) have gained renewed popularity and respect for the links they created between old and contemporary Hawaiian music.

For both classic and contemporary Hawaiian music, tune your radio dial to KONG (93.5 FM), KSRF (95.9 FM), KUAI (720 AM) and KTOH (99.9 FM).

HULA

Along with palm trees, the hula—swaying hips, grass skirts, colorful leis—is linked forever in people's minds with the Hawaiian Islands. This western idea of hula is very different from what the dance has traditionally meant to native Hawaiians.

Hula is an old dance form, its origin shrouded in mystery. The ancient hula, *hula kahiko*, was more concerned with religion and spirituality than entertainment. Originally performed only by men, it was used in rituals to communicate with a deity—a connection to nature and the gods. Accompanied by drums and chants, *hula kahiko* expressed the islands' culture, mythology and history in hand and body movements. It later evolved from a strictly religious rite to a method of communicating stories and legends. Over the years, women were allowed to study the rituals and eventually became the primary dancers.

When Westerners arrived, the *hula kahiko* began another transformation. Explorers and sailors were more interested in its erotic element, ignoring the cultural significance. Missionaries simply found it scandalous and set out to destroy the tradition. They dressed Hawaiians in western garb and outlawed the *hula kahiko*.

The hula tradition was resurrected by King David Kalakaua, who said, "Hula is the language of the heart, and therefore the heart beat of the Hawaiian people." Known by the moniker "Merrie Monarch," Kalakaua loved music and dance. For his coronation in 1883, he called together the kingdom's best dancers to perform the chants and hulas once again. He was also instrumental in the development of the contemporary hula, the *hula auwana*, which added new steps and movements and was accompanied by ukuleles and guitars rather than drums.

By the 1920s, modern hula had been popularized by Hollywood, westernized and introduced as kitschy tropicana. Real grass skirts gave way to cellophane versions, plastic leis replaced fragrant island garlands, and exaggerated gyrations supplanted the hypnotic movements of the traditional dance.

Fortunately, with the resurgence of Hawaiian pride in recent decades, Polynesian culture has been reclaimed and *hula kahiko* and traditional chants have made a welcome comeback. Hula *halau* (schools) are serious business throughout the islands (and even on the mainland). Competitions bring together *halau* throughout the islands. On Oahu, the major event is the Prince Lot Hula Festival held in Moanalua Gardens every July. Another is "E Ho I Mai Ika Piko Hula," a world invitiational festival at the Waikiki Shell.

WAIKIKI

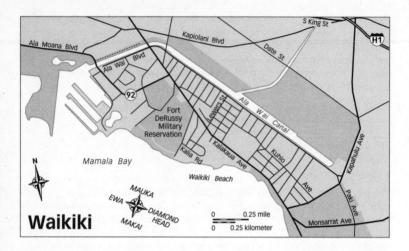

Waikiki

To understand the geography of Waikiki, you need only know about Waikiki Beach. And to understand Waikiki Beach, you must know two things. The first is that major hotels line the beach, practically from one end to the other, and are used as landmarks by visitors and local residents alike. The other fact to remember is that to visitors, Waikiki Beach is a single sandy ribbon two miles long, but to local folks, it represents many beaches in one. When you park your beach towel here, consider that every few strides will carry you into another realm of Waikiki's culture and history.

Waikiki is where Hawaiian tourism began, and its reputation as a retreat dates back centuries. It is believed that the area was a favorite recreation site for the long-ago kings of Oahu and Maui, and a holy place as well. The site of the Royal Hawaiian Hotel was previously a *heiau pookanaka*, or sacrificial temple, and strictly off-limits to the common people.

When Hawaii's royalty established Honolulu as their capital in the mid-1800s, Waikiki continued as a getaway, thanks to sunny shores and well-formed waves, just right for their favorite sport of surfing. The royal family would often invite well-known visitors such as Robert Louis Stevenson (who purportedly wrote several novels here) and Jack London to join them at their Waikiki retreat. And it gradually gained a reputation with not-so-well-known haoles as well. By the late 1800s, guesthouses were springing up along the strand. The first hotel, the Moana, was built at the turn of the 20th century, as was a tram line from downtown Honolulu that brought visitors and townspeople to enjoy the beach and surf at Waikiki. Their taste for "country life" did not extend to embrace the mosquitoes (deemed unsanitary and dangerous) that thrived in the wetlands; a struggle between the burgeoning tourist industry and Waikiki's farmers ensued over the local "swamps."

Although *Waikiki* translates into "spouting waters," there's little evidence nowadays of those natural springs. The area might have remained an isolated getaway
surrounded by wetlands, taro patches and duck ponds if it weren't for the dredg-
ing of the Ala Wai canal in the 1920s. The wetlands were drained and filled with
coral from the canal, laying the foundation for what would someday be one of the
world's most famous resort areas. But not quite yet.

First there had to be more tourists—and a way to bring them to Honolulu. Matson
Navigation built the 650-passenger *Mololo* in 1925, and the glory days of Hawaiian
tourism began. Matson also developed the Royal Hawaiian Hotel to the tune of $2
million, an astronomical sum at the time. But the investment paid off, and Waikiki began to compete with Europe as a vacation destination for the well-heeled.

More hotels were built, and during World War II, GIs on leave soaked up the sun
on Waikiki's shores, further establishing its reputation. Then in the jet age that
followed, it became a highrise resort area. A motley collection of hotels, squeezed
together in the small space that is Waikiki, stands as an architectural monument
to the neighborhood's history and gives each section of Waikiki a different flavor.

This fabled peninsula extends two miles from the Ala Wai Yacht Harbor to Diamond Head and measures a half-mile in width from the Ala Wai Canal to the
Pacific. Kalakaua Avenue, the main drag, is packed elbow to elbow with throngs of
visitors. Paralleling the ocean, this broad boulevard is all at once noisy, annoying,
exciting, cosmopolitan and fascinating. Today, visitors from Japan, Korea and
Australia add to the international atmosphere.

But the main appeal is still the district's white-sand corridor. Dotting the beach
are picnic areas, restrooms, showers, concession stands and beach equipment
rentals. Most of the beach is protected by coral reefs and sea walls, so the swimming is excellent, the snorkeling fair. This is also a prime area for surfing. Two- to
four-foot waves, good for beginners and still challenging to experienced surfers,
are common here. That makes it a suitable spot for a statue of the legendary late
Duke Kahanamoku, widely considered the ambassador of modern surfing and
still revered by the current generation of wave riders. You can see his statue at
Kuhio Beach Park, facing Kalakaua Avenue. The hotels disappear at popular Kapiolani Beach Park, which has undergone a freshening up of its public facilities
while retaining its broad oceanfront lawns and shady trees.

SIGHTS

WAIKIKI HISTORIC TRAIL

 hidden

www.waikikihistorictrail.com With the glut of high-rise resorts and
upscale boutiques, it may be hard to believe that Waikiki had a
noteworthy history at all. You can explore the hidden past of
Hawaii's most popular tourist destination by following this historic walking tour. You'll learn about the transition from
swamp to exotic destination. You'll also pick up some intriguing facts along the way: For instance, Kalanianaole, the main
drag through town, was named for Prince Jonah Kuhio Kalanianaole, a delegate from Hawaii to Congress who was best
known for his support of the Hawaiian Homestead Act; surfer

Duke Paoa Kahanamoku was also the world's fastest swimmer; the "Wizard Stones of Kapaemahu" were placed in their location to honor four Tahitian soothsayers who purportedly left their powers in the stones before disappearing; King David Kalakaua once had a residence near King's Alley while King William Lunalilo, known as the kind chief, lived a quieter life in his Waikiki residence. Be sure to download the information from the Historic Trail website before you embark on the tour. Follow the surfboard-shaped markers beginning at Kapiolani Beach. You'll end up at the Hilton's Rainbow Towers and lagoon. If you don't have a computer, you'll need to head to the Hawaii Tourism Authority in Honolulu's Hawaii Convention Center (1801 Kalakaua Avenue, first floor; 808-973-2255).

HILTON HAWAIIAN VILLAGE ✉2005 Kalia Road It's difficult to visit Waikiki and not spot this colorful "village." Even if you're staying somewhere else on the island, be sure to wander through the shops and gardens of the complex; the landscaped grounds include 22 acres of indigenous flora sprinkled with koi ponds, penguin and flamingo habitats, and a number of squawking cockatoos. Two rainbow-patterned mosaics flank both sides of the 31-story Rainbow Tower.

KAHANAMOKU BEACH The western flank of Waikiki Beach sits near the Hilton Hawaiian Village. Here you will find a pretty lagoon fringed by palm trees. The curving strand nearby, fronting the resort, is called Kahanamoku Beach, named for Hawaii's great surfer, Duke Kahanamoku. Kahanamoku, the gold medalist swimmer of the 1912 and 1920 Olympics, popularized the sport of surfing by traveling with his ten-foot-long hardwood board. The beach features numerous facilities. Beach stands rent everything from towels, chairs and air mattresses to snorkel sets, surfboards and Hobie-cat sailboats.

ATLANTIS ADVENTURES ☏808-973-9811, 800-548-6262 ☏808-973-2499 ☐www.atlantisadventures.com, ores@atlantisadventures.com Also near the Hilton Hawaiian Village is Port Hilton, the pier from which the resort complex launches catamaran cruises. One of these boats will take you to what may be one of the few truly hidden attractions around Waikiki. The Atlantis Adventures' 64-passenger submarine carries visitors to the bottom of the ocean for a close-up look at an artificial reef, complete with sunken ships and airplanes, created to bring back marine life to the area. In fact, the submarine experience is likely to be better than the sea life, which is often limited. Above the water, Atlantis also offers a sunset dinner cruise along Waikiki Beach and the Kahala coastline. Steep admission.

FORT DERUSSY BEACH Owned by the military but open to the public, this strand features the area's widest swath of white sand. It is also beautifully backdropped by a grove of palm trees. There are restrooms, picnic tables and barbecues, plus tennis, squash and volleyball courts on the property.

U.S. ARMY MUSEUM OF HAWAII ✉On the grounds of the Hale Koa Hotel, 2055 Kalia Road, Fort DeRussy ☏808-955-9552 ☏808-941-3617 ☐www.hiarmy museumsoc.org, info@hiarmymuseumsoc.org Showcasing every weapon from

FATTY'S CHINESE KITCHEN

PAGE 90

Locally loved diner for delicious fried fish and sticky rice plate lunches

DUKE'S CANOE CLUB

PAGE 96

Beachside, surf-style venue boasting live island music by Hawaiian greats

QUEEN KAPIOLANI HIBISCUS GARDEN

PAGE 80

Lush, hibiscus-filled flowerbeds in a secluded park—said to be enchanted

DIAMOND HEAD BEACH HOTEL

PAGE 86

Elegant, Balinese-themed waterfront suites located near the fabled crater

Hawaiian shark teeth blades to Vietnam-era instruments of destruction, this museum near Fort DeRussy Beach features a rotating gallery and theater. You can also trace the United States' unending series of military campaigns from the uniforms and equipment (ours and theirs) on exhibit here. Closed Monday.

TEA CEREMONIES ✉*Urasenke Hawaii Branch, 247 Saratoga Road* ✆*808-923-1057* 📠*808-923-3784* ✐*urasenkef001@hawaii.rr.com* Perhaps there's some truth in the idea that the way to the heart is through the stomach. The Japanese concept of *Chado* conveys its ideals (harmony, respect, purity and tranquility) through the practice of tea ceremonies. Followers of *Chado* preach that a world fraught with tension can be helped by the process of preparing the perfect cup of tea. All aspects of the preparation are important. The Way of Tea has been in existence since at least the 16th century, but only recently have the teachings gained wider acknowledgment. Hawaii hosts a branch of the Urasenke Foundation, the international society of *Chado*. They host tea ceremonies that are open to

Waikiki Sights

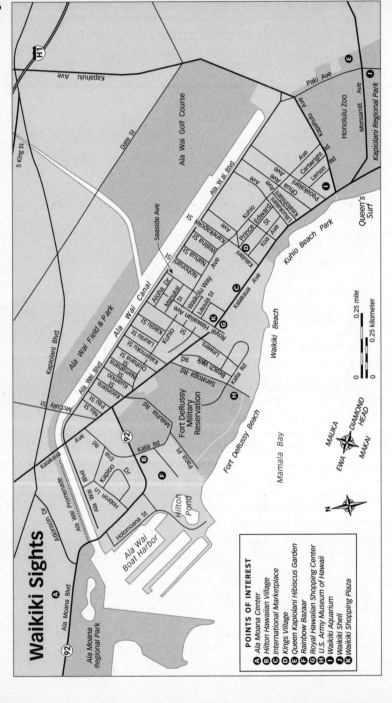

S King St
Kapahulu Ave
H1
Date St
Ala Wai Golf Course
Ala Wai Blvd
Kapiolani Blvd
Seaside Ave
Kanekapole St
Ala Wai Field & Park
Ala Wai Canal
Nohonani St
Nahua St
Walina St
Kaiulani Ave
Kapahulu Ave
Cartwright Rd
Ohua Ave
Paokalani Ave
Kealohilani Ave
Liliuokalani Ave
Lemon Rd
Paki Ave
Monsarrat
Kuhio Ave
Prince Edward St
Koa Ave
Honolulu Zoo
Kapiolani Regional Park
E
J
I
D
Aloha Dr
Makua St
Walina Way
Lauula Ave
Royal Hawaiian Ave
C
K
G
Kaiolu St
Kuhio Rd
Launiu St
Kaiulani Ave
Kalakaua Ave
Kuhio Beach Park
Queen's Surf
Waikiki Beach
McCully St
Ala Wai Blvd
Kaiolu St
Kalaimoku St
Olohana St
Namahana St
Koonana St
Kuamoo St
Pau St
Niu St
Kalia Rd
Beach Walk
Lewers
Saratoga Rd
Fort DeRussy Military Reservation
Maluhia Rd
H
92
Kalakaua Ave
Ena Rd
Kalia Rd
Paoa Rd
B
F
Fort DeRussy Beach
Mamala Bay
Ala Wai Promenade
Atkinson Dr
Ala Wai Blvd
Kapioo Dr
Hobron Ln
Ala Moana Blvd
A
92
Holomoana St
Hilton Pond
Ala Wai Boat Harbor
Ala Moana Regional Park

0.25 mile
0.25 kilometer
0

N

EWA / MAUKA / DIAMOND HEAD / MAKAI

POINTS OF INTEREST

- **A** Ala Moana Center
- **B** Hilton Hawaiian Village
- **C** International Marketplace
- **D** Kings Village
- **E** Queen Kapiolani Hibiscus Garden
- **F** Rainbow Bazaar
- **G** Royal Hawaiian Shopping Center
- **H** U.S. Army Museum of Hawaii
- **I** Waikiki Aquarium
- **J** Waikiki Shell
- **K** Waikiki Shopping Plaza

the public on Wednesday and Friday at 10 a.m. and 11 a.m. Stop by and give tea a chance.

HIGHRISE HOTELS Past Fort DeRussy Beach stretches a palisade of multistoried caravansaries. Lining the beachfront, they provide numerous facilities for thirsty sunbathers or adventuresome athletes. Continue on and you will pass "the strip," a lengthy stretch of Waikiki Beach fronted entirely by hotels. This section marks Waikiki's center of action. The first one is the **Outrigger Reef on the Beach**, followed by the **Halekulani**, a pricey property that many consider Waikiki's finest hotel. Next is the **Sheraton Waikiki**. A highrise structure built with two curving wings, it resembles a giant bird roosting on the beach.

ROYAL-MOANA BEACH The hotels along Waikiki Beach are so famous that the nearby strand is named after them. Stretching between the Royal Hawaiian and Moana hotels, this beach has been a sun-soaked gathering place for decades. That's because these two grand dames are Waikiki's oldest hostelries.

ROYAL HAWAIIAN HOTEL ✉2259 *Kalakaua Avenue* ☎808-923-7311 📠808-931-7098 ⌨*www.royal-hawaiian.com* A Spanish Moorish–style caravansary painted a distinctive pink, this historic gem is dubbed the "Pink Palace." Built in 1927, it is a labyrinth of gardens, colonnades and balconies; the place certainly captures Waikiki's bygone era. At one time, the back lawn of the hotel had nearly 10,000 coconut trees. Now you can find 10,000 stores.

MOANA SURFRIDER RESORT ✉2365 *Kalakaua Avenue* ☎808-922-3111, 866-716-8112 📠808-924-4799 ⌨*www.moana-surfrider.com* Built in 1901, the Moana was Waikiki's first resort. Its vaulted ceilings, tree-shaded courtyard and spacious accommodations reflect the days when Hawaii was a retreat for the rich. Further delving into the history of the place can be done in its **Historical Room**, containing interesting photographs and memorabilia dating from the hotel's conception. The **Moana Banyan tree**, planted on the grounds in 1904, stretches 150 feet across and 75 feet high. The Moana's beach is also the site of one of Waikiki's most renowned surfing spots, "**Canoe's Surf**."

OUTRIGGER CANOES Along Waikiki Beach, concessions offer rides on outrigger canoes, which are long, sleek fiberglass crafts resembling ancient Polynesian canoes. Each seats four to six passengers, plus a captain. For a fee, you can join the crew on a low-key wave-riding excursion that will have you paddling as hard and fast as you can to catch waves and ride them far into the shore.

KUHIO BEACH PARK ✉*Kalakaua Avenue* Just beyond the Moana is this popular park, which runs along Kalakaua Avenue from Kaiulani to Kapahulu avenues. In addition to a broad sandy beach and a creative layout that includes a **banyan tree,** traditional **healing stones** and a cascading fountain, there are numerous facilities here—picnic areas, beach equipment rentals, showers and restrooms, as well as lifeguards. The shady pavilions also attract local folks who come to play cards and chess. Needless to say, it's often quite crowded. Diners like it because of its proximity to many Waikiki budget restaurants; parents favor the beach for its protective sea wall, which provides a secure area where children can swim; and people-watchers find it an ideal place to check out the crowds of tourists and local residents. The park features broad walkways, grassy areas and artificial waterfalls and tidepools.

PACIFIC BEACH HOTEL OCEANARIUM

⊠*2490 Kalakaua Avenue* ☎*808-922-1233* 📠*808-922-0129* 🖱*www.pacific beachhotel.com* Most hotels welcome guests into a wide atrium decorated with tropical flowers or striking artwork. The Pacific Beach Hotel, however, boasts a unique centerpiece—a three-story-high, 280,000-gallon aquarium. The Oceanarium, as it's called, is home to more than 70 different marine species, including several different stingrays. Constructed in 1979, it is the largest hotel aquarium of its kind, and is viewable from three hotel restaurants. Several times a day (noon, 1 p.m., 6:15 p.m. and 8 p.m.), divers enter the tank to feed its inhabitants.

LUCORAL MUSEUM ⊠*2414 Kuhio Avenue* ☎*808-922-1999* 📠*808-924-6698*

🖱*www.lucoralmuseum.com* The Lucoral has a collection of corals, pearls and gemstones from around the world, in both raw and finished forms as well as carved into various artworks. A re-creation of a mining cave allows a glance at freshly unearthed jade, rose quartz and other gems. Self-guided tours are always available, or, for a small fee, guided tours include bracelet-making for *keiki*. Closed weekends.

QUEEN'S SURF

The strand just beyond Kuhio Beach Park is named after Queen Liliuokalani, who once had a beach home here. Something of a bohemian quarter, this pretty plot draws gays, local artists and a wide array of intriguing characters. On the weekends, conga drummers may be pounding out rhythms along the beach while others gather to soak in the scene. Usually one weekend a month, films mostly relating to Hawaiian history and culture are shown on a 30-foot screen. The **"Sunset on the Beach" festivities** start at 4 p.m. with a craft fair featuring the work of local artisans. Pick up some snacks or a plate lunch at one of the food booths and find a comfy spot on the sand or pier. Live music begins at about 5 p.m., followed by the movie just after sunset. There also are picnic areas, shady pavilions, restroom facilities and showers. Contact the Waikiki Improvement Association (808-923-1094) for the most up-to-date information and movie listings.

KAPIOLANI REGIONAL PARK ⊠*Kalakaua Avenue* Extending across

140 acres on both sides of Kalakaua Avenue, beautiful Kapiolani Park is just next door to Queen's Surf. Hawaii's oldest park, this tree-studded playland dates back to 1887 when it was dedicated by King Kalakaua in honor of his Queen Kapiolani. After Hawaii was annexed in 1898, the park was used by the American Army as an encampment. Nowadays, perhaps more than anything else, it has come to serve as a jogger's par-

Babes in Tow

Waikiki is the perfect place to vacation with your toddler. Was there ever a better sandbox for making sandcastles? For a gentle, no-wave swimming area head to **Kuhio Beach Park** (page 77) with its protected seawall. When you (or your little one) tire of the ocean, walk or take the number 4, 8, 19, 20 or 43 bus to the **Honolulu Zoo** (page 79) or the **Waikiki Aquarium** (page 79). **Kapiolani Regional Park** (page 78) also has oodles of space to run and play tag. In the evening, you can always hire a babysitter from a bonded service (see "Traveling with Children" in Chapter One) for a night on the town.

adise. From dawn 'til dark, runners of all ages, colors, sizes and shapes beat a path around its perimeter. But Kapiolani offers something to just about everyone. There are tennis courts, softball and soccer fields, an archery area, and much more. To fully explore the park, you must visit each of its features in turn.

WAIKIKI SHELL ✉ *Kapiolani Park, 2805 Monsarrat Avenue* ☎ *808-527-5400, 808-591-2211 (box office)* 📠 *808-527-5433* ✍ *www.blaisdellcenter.com* This is a great place for an evening under the stars with Diamond Head as a backdrop. General admission means lawn seating, which is the perfect way to enjoy the Honolulu Symphony backing up headliners like Jimmy Buffet, local favorites like Kalapana, or megastars like Bob Dylan. Check with the Blaisdell Center box office to see if anything is scheduled for the Shell while you're in town.

HONOLULU ZOO ✉ *Kapiolani Park* ☎ *808-971-7171* 📠 *808-971-7173* ✍ *www.honoluluzoo.org* Kapiolani Park's grandest feature is its vast zoo, teeming with fascinating species. Like city zoos everywhere, this tropical facility has a resident population of elephants, giraffes, ostriches, zebras, hippos, Sumatran tigers, lions, alligators and so on. But it also includes animals more common to the islands, creatures like the nene (a rare goose and the Hawaii state bird), Komodo dragons and Galápagos tortoises. Perhaps most interesting of all, there is an outstanding population of tropical birds. Admission.

WAIKIKI AQUARIUM ✉ *Kapiolani Park, 2777 Kalakaua Avenue* ☎ *808-923-9741* 📠 *808-923-1771* ✍ *www.waquarium.org, info@waquarium.org* The aquarium is the place where you can finally discover what a *humuhumunukunukuapuaa*, that impossibly named fish, really looks like. (Don't be surprised if the name proves to be longer than the fish.) Within the aquarium's glass walls, you'll see more than 420 different species of aquatic animals and plants originating from Hawaiian and South Pacific waters. Ranging from rainbow-hued tropical fish to staghorn coral, they constitute a broad range of underwater creatures. Then there are Hawaiian monk seals (an endangered species) and other intriguing wildlife. The jellyfish gallery features a variety of these mysterious and ethereal creatures. Admission.

SANS SOUCI BEACH In 1893, writer Robert Louis Stevenson spent five weeks convalescing near this stretch of beach in Kapiolani Park, a popular spot where residents and visitors share the sand and reef-sheltered waters. It's also an easy place to set out for a kayak paddle to the marine preserve off Diamond Head or to head toward Waikiki, which stands in highrise silhouette.

NATATORIUM ✐*www.natatorium.org* Sans Souci Beach is bordered to the west by this saltwater pool and grandstand built in the 1920s as a monument to the 179 islanders who lost their lives in World War I. Closed in 1979 due to slipshod maintenance and deterioration, there is much debate whether it will ever reopen.

QUEEN KAPIOLANI HIBISCUS GARDEN

✉*Monsarrat and Paki avenues* Across from Kapiolani Park, this garden, with its colorful hibiscus flowerbeds and shady pavilion, is a pretty place to stroll and picnic. Despite its proximity to the Waikiki waterfront and a busy shopping area, the little spot has maintained its peace—I'm almost hesitant to mention it here. Perhaps it has remained a secret because of its relatively small size (tour buses can't stop here). Or perhaps there are more mysterious reasons for it. According to legend, Tahitian *kahunas* (priests) visited the area in the 14th century and left behind more than spiritual healing. The story goes that they also imbued the stones in the garden with their powers, which now protect the park's blossoms against errant pickers.

DIAMOND HEAD More than any other place in the islands, Diamond Head is the trademark of Hawaii. A 760-foot crater, it is the work of a volcano that has been dead for about 100,000 years. To the Hawaiians it was known as *Leahi*. They saw in its sloping hillsides the face of an *ahi*, or yellowfin tuna. Then, in the 19th century, sailors mistook its volcanic glass rocks for rare gems and gave the promontory its present name. Formed 350,000 years ago, this natural landmark was a sacred place to the ancient Hawaiians. A *heiau* once graced its slopes and King Kamehameha is said to have worshiped here, offering a human sacrifice to the Polynesian war god.

It is possible to drive into the gaping maw of this old dragon. Just take Kalakaua Avenue until it meets Diamond Head Road, then follow the latter around to the inland site of the crater. From there a tunnel leads inside. Once within, there is a steep three-quarter-mile trail climbing to the rim of the crater. From here you can gaze along Oahu's southeast corner and back across the splendid little quarter called Waikiki.

LODGING

While it may no longer be the simple country retreat it was at the 20th century's turn, Waikiki does have one advantage: Believe it or not, it's a great place to find low-rent hotels. A lot of the cozy old hostelries have been torn down and replaced with highrises, but a few have escaped the urban assault. Some of those skyscrapers, too, are cheaper than you might think.

Waikiki is not exactly quiet. Early-morning garbage trucks and late-night party-goers make for considerable street noise. Streets on the outskirts are less noisy than those in the heart of things. Ask for rooms off the street or high in the sky!

HOLIDAY INN WAIKIKI

$$–$$$ 198 ROOMS   ✉1830 Ala Moana Boulevard   ☎808-955-1111, 888-465-4329
📠808-947-1799   ✑www.holiday-inn.com, holinnwk@pixi.com

A good bargain within easy walking distance from both Ala Moana Center and the beach, accommodations at this 17-story caravansary are "Holiday Inn" plush. Each room has air conditioning, television, telephone, decorations, carpeting, a shower-tub combination, as well as a small refrigerator. The room I saw was quite spacious and contained a king-sized bed. There's also a fitness center.

ISLAND HOSTEL/HOTEL

$ 20 ROOMS   ✉1946 Ala Moana Boulevard   ☎808-942-8748
📠808-942-8748

What better combination can you ask for than a place that is both a hotel *and* a hostel? At this unusual establishment, located inside the Hawaiian Colony building, you can book a room with private bath (though hard to get since reservations aren't accepted here) or join fellow travelers in a coed dorm room. The dorm includes kitchen privileges.

HILTON HAWAIIAN VILLAGE

$$$$ 3250 ROOMS   ✉2005 Kalia Road   ☎808-949-4321   📠808-951-5458
✑www.hiltonhawaiianvillage.com

Offering well over 3000 rooms, this deluxe Hilton is the largest resort in the islands and Waikiki's premier family hotel. The grounds provide a Disneyesque atmosphere that keeps children of all ages engaged—fireworks on Friday evening, shopping malls, restaurants and nightly entertainment, not to mention a penguin pool, flamingos, cockatoos and koi ponds. Seaside diversions include paddle boats and surfboards as well as numerous swimming pools to dip in, an acre of sand for sandcastle-making and an ocean of fun. Not to be overlooked, the rooms are attractively furnished and well-cared for and the service is friendly and welcoming.

AMBASSADOR HOTEL OF WAIKIKI

$$–$$ 301 ROOMS   ✉2040 Kuhio Avenue   ☎808-941-7777, 800-923-2620
📠808-951-3939   ✑www.ambassadorwaikiki.com, reservations@ambassadorwaikiki.com

The Ambassador is convenient and comfortable, with studios and one-to three-bedroom suites, most of which have full kitchens, although few other amenities. Off-season internet rates can be even cheaper.

KAI ALOHA APARTMENT HOTEL

$$–$$ 18 ROOMS   ✉235 Saratoga Road   ☎808-923-6723   📠808-922-7592
✑www.kaialoha.magictravel.com, kai.aloha@hawaiiantel.net

Offering intimacy combined with modern convenience, each guest room at the Kai Aloha has air conditioning, an all-electric kitchen, radio, telephone with voice mail, cable television and carpeting. Studio apartments feature lovely rattan furniture and are attractively decorated with old drawings and paintings. The one-bedroom apartments will comfortably sleep four people. Daily maid service is provided. Minimum three-night stay.

HAWAIIANA HOTEL

$$–$$$ 93 ROOMS   ✉*260 Beach Walk*   📞*808-923-3811, 800-367-5122*
📠*808-926-5728*   ✐*www.hawaiianahotelatwaikiki.com, hawaiana@lava.net*

The Hawaiiana is an intimate, lowrise facility that offers a garden courtyard arrangement with rooms surrounding either of the hotel's two pools. Some rooms have a private lanai; all have wicker armoires, kitchenettes and pastel decor.

THE BREAKERS

$$–$$$ 64 ROOMS   ✉*250 Beach Walk*   📞*808-923-3181, 800-426-0494*
📠*808-923-7174*   ✐*www.breakers-hawaii.com, breakers@aloha.net*

Tucked away in the shadow of vaulting condominiums, this lowrise hotel is truly a find. Dating to the 1950s, this Waikiki original consists of 64 rooms and 15 suites surrounding a pool and landscaped patio. Shoji doors provide an "Asian" ambiance while kitchenettes, air conditioning and wi-fi access in every room—plus a prime location just one block from the beach—round out the features.

EMBASSY SUITES WAIKIKI BEACH RESORT

$$$ 369 UNITS   ✉*201 Beach Walk*   📞*800-362-2779*   📠*808-921-2343*
✐*www.embassysuiteswaikiki.com*

The selling point of this deluxe, 21-story property is that it's adjacent to both the beach and the Waikiki Beach Walk open-air shopping complex. That means you won't have to walk far to top off your day with a cold scoop of gelato, a frosty microbrew or *pupus* at some of Waikiki's trendiest restaurants. Many of the rooms have ocean views and lanais that provide a perfect perch to watch the pedestrian activity on the sidewalks below. The complimentary cooked-to-order breakfast is another good reason to stay here.

HALEKULANI

$$$$ 455 ROOMS   ✉*2199 Kalia Road*   📞*808-923-2311, 800-367-2343*
📠*808-926-8004*   ✐*www.halekulani.com*

Exuding elegance and refinement, the Halekulani, whose name means "house befitting heaven," is where the elite come to get away from it all. If you want to splurge, you can, too. The guest rooms and facilities are luxurious and the personalized service radiates with Hawaiian hospitality. If you don't want to float in the oceanfront swimming pool (which boasts an orchid made of 1.2 million South African glass mosaic tiles that reflect the changing light), you can visit the spa, indulge in an in-room massage or dine in one of their award-winning dining rooms.

BEST WESTERN COCONUT WAIKIKI

$$–$$$ 80 ROOMS   ✉*450 Lewers Street*   📞*808-923-8828*   📠*808-923-3473*
✐*www.aquaresorts.com, reservations@aquaresorts.com*

A ten-story highrise, the Coconut Waikiki has accommodations with kitchenettes; all guest rooms have refrigerators, microwaves, flat-screen TVs and free wi-fi; most rooms have a wet bar. Decorated with a colorful, modern take on classically mod Hawaiian style, the rooms are attractively appointed; some have views of Diamond Head and the Koolau Mountains. Continental breakfast included.

ROYAL HAWAIIAN HOTEL

$$$$ 528 ROOMS   ✉ *2259 Kalakaua Avenue*   ✆ *808-923-7311, 866-716-8109*   📠 *808-931-7098*   ✎ *www.royal-hawaiian.com*

This grand dame of Hawaiian hotels captures the sense of Old Hawaii. Built in 1927 and affectionately known as the "Pink Palace," the Royal Hawaiian is an elegant, Spanish Moorish–style building complete with colonnaded walkways and manicured grounds. The fabulous Moroccan-style lobby is bedecked with chandeliers. Adjacent to the original building is a 17-story tower that brings the room count to over 500. It's worth visiting even if you never check in.

CELEBRITY RESORTS WAIKIKI

$$$ 80 ROOMS   ✉ *431 Nohonani Street*   ✆ *808-923-7336, 866-507-1428*   📠 *808-923-1622*   ✎ *www.celebrityresorts.com*

This modern, attractive complex of three low-slung buildings surrounds a garden and swimming pool. The rooms are decorated in a tropical theme with rattan furniture and come with all-electric kitchenette, telephone, TV and air conditioning.

AQUA WAIKIKI TIDES

$$$ 119 ROOMS   ✉ *415 Nahua Street*   ✆ *808-922-6223*   ✎ *www.aquaresorts.com, reservations@aquaresorts.com*

Once a college dormitory, today this ten-story hotel has gone from comfortable but bland to tasteful and modern. The standard rooms have simple wood furniture, serene muted-green and amber linens, and private lanais. Located about three blocks from the beach, this hotel also has one- and two-bedroom suites with full kitchens and sitting areas.

MOANA SURFRIDER RESORT

$$$$ 799 ROOMS   ✉ *2365 Kalakaua Avenue*   ✆ *808-922-3111, 800-782-9488*   📠 *808-924-4799*   ✎ *www.moana-surfrider.com*

Waikiki was little more than a thatched-hut village when its first deluxe hotel went up in 1901. Today the Moana retains the aura of those early days in its Colonial architecture. Downstairs are restaurants, bars, a lobby and an ancient banyan tree beneath which Robert Louis Stevenson once wrote. A throwback to Colonial times, tea (fee) is served every afternoon at the Veranda and the oceanfront spa is the ultimate indulgence. Be sure to ask for a room in the original section.

HOSTELLING INTERNATIONAL—WAIKIKI

$ 63 BEDS   ✉ *2417 Prince Edward Street*   ✆ *808-926-8313*   📠 *808-922-3798*   ✎ *www.hostelsaloha.com, ayhaloha@lava.net*

Budget travelers might consider a stay here. This helpful facility features single-sex dormitory-style accommodations and private studio units with private baths. Open to both men and women, the hostel provides bedding and a common kitchen and creates a family-style atmosphere conducive to meeting other travelers. High-speed internet access is available for a fee. Seven-day maximum stay.

WAIKIKI PRINCE HOTEL

$ 24 ROOMS   ✉2431 Prince Edward Street   📞808-922-1544   📠808-924-3712
🖥www.waikikiprince.com, info@waikikiprince.com

Some of the walls are still cinderblock, but the price is right here. All guest rooms have air conditioning and cable television; many of the units are equipped with kitchenettes (which are outfitted with mini-refrigerators, microwaves, stoves and utensils).

ROYAL GROVE HOTEL

$ 87 UNITS   ✉151 Uluniu Avenue   📞808-923-7691   📠808-922-7508
🖥www.royalgrovehotel.com, reservations@royagrovehotel.com

Rising high from the ground, while still keeping costs low, is this six-story establishment. If you can get past the garish pink exterior here, you'll find the rooms more tastefully designed. All accommodations are carpeted and comfortably furnished, and some are decorated in simple but appealing styles. There are TVs and phones in all of the rooms, plus an almond-shaped pool and spacious lobby. Rents vary according to which wing of this sprawling building your bags are parked in. Most rooms even have kitchenettes with microwaves, as well as air conditioning, so it's hard to go wrong here. Slightly less expensive weekly rates are available.

AQUA WAIKIKI BEACHSIDE HOTEL

$–$$ 65 ROOMS   ✉2452 Kalakaua Avenue   📞808-931-2100, 866-406-2782
📠808-931-2129   🖥www.aquaresorts.com, reservations@aquaresorts.com

A small hotel right across the street from the beach, this is the kind of place where the receptionist already knows your name when you first walk in the door. It's as if they were waiting for you. The rooms are small but attractively done in coordinated coral colors with Asian-inspired screen paintings and furnishings. The ocean-facing rooms in front have a balcony with two chairs and a table, so guests can watch the parade of surfers and sun worshippers below. A complimentary continental breakfast is served in the palm court.

ASTON WAIKIKI CIRCLE HOTEL

$$$ 104 ROOMS   ✉2464 Kalakaua Avenue   📞808-923-1571, 877-997-6667
📠808-926-8024   🖥www.astonhotel.com, res.cir@astonhotels.com

This 14-story hotel-in-the-round has air-conditioned rooms, many with an ocean view, which is the main advantage. Oh, and you just have to cross Kalakaua to throw a towel on the beach.

WAIKIKI BEACH MARRIOTT RESORT & SPA

$$$$ 1310 ROOMS   ✉2552 Kalakaua Avenue   📞808-922-6611, 800-848-8110
📠808-921-5255   🖥www.marriottwaikiki.com

Ho hum. Another big, luxurious hotel property in Waikiki. But the Marriott, with 1310 rooms, two swimming pools, five restaurants and tons of shops, has the ideal location, right on Waikiki Beach and within walking distance of several major attractions like Diamond Head and Kapiolani Park. It also offers cultural activities, nightly Hawaiian entertainment and a snazzy spa with unique Polynesian treatments.

EWA HOTEL WAIKIKI

$$–$$$ 90 ROOMS ✉ *2555 Cartwright Road* 📞 *808-922-1677* 📞 *800-359-8639*
📠 *808-923-8538* 🖥 *www.ewahotel.com, mail@ewahotel.com*

Tucked away on a back street one block from the beach, this pastel-and-rattan establishment has a 1980s aura about it. Close to Kapiolani Park and offering kitchenettes in many rooms, it is particularly convenient for families.

THE CABANA AT WAIKIKI

$$$ 15 ROOMS ✉ *2551 Cartwright Road* 📞 *808-926-5555, 877-902-2121*
📠 *808-926-5566* 🖥 *www.cabana-waikiki.com, jim@cabana-waikiki.com*

Catering to gay and lesbian visitors, the Cabana offers a piece of paradise just walking distance from Queen's Surf. The hotel has nicely decorated one-bedroom suites, with queen beds in the bedroom and a full-sized day bed in the living room. Rattan furnishings and Hawaiian prints convey a tropical feel. All suites have private lanais, television, stereos and microwave-equipped kitchenettes, complete with coffee-makers, toasters and blenders. There is an eight-person jacuzzi for guest use. Continental breakfast and cocktails are included.

THE POLYNESIAN BEACH CLUB HOSTEL

$ 69 BEDS ✉ *2584 Lemon Road* 📞 *808-922-1340, 877-504-2924* 📠 *808-262-2817*
🖥 *www.hostelhawaii.com, reservation@hostelhawaii.com*

This hostel offers private, semiprivate and dormitory accommodations in a converted apartment building. Studios have their own refrigerators and all have bathrooms and can sleep up to three people. Semiprivate single and double rooms have shared bathrooms. Dorm rooms can sleep four to six people. Laundry facilities and a full kitchen are available for guests, as well as a barbecue and outdoor deck area. It is the closest hostel to the beach, which is one block away.

WAIKIKI GRAND HOTEL

$$$ 61 ROOMS ✉ *134 Kapahulu Avenue* 📞 *808-923-1814, 888-336-4368*
📠 *808-923-5003* 🖥 *www.waikikigrand.com, res@waikikigrand.com*

Located right across the street from lush Kapiolani Park, the individually named and decorated rooms in this ten-story building are comfortable, pleasant places to park your bags. Downstairs there's a windswept lobby.

QUEEN KAPIOLANI HOTEL

$$–$$$ 315 ROOMS ✉ *150 Kapahulu Avenue* 📞 *808-922-1941, 800-367-2317*
📠 *808-922-2694* 🖥 *www.queenkapiolani.com, reservations@queenkapiolani.com*

Rising 19 stories above nearby Kapiolani Park, this sparkling hotel features a spacious lobby, three floors of public rooms, several shops and a swimming pool. The guest rooms are plainly decorated and modest in size. Located one block from the beach.

NEW OTANI KAIMANA BEACH HOTEL

$$$–$$$$ 125 ROOMS ✉ *2863 Kalakaua Avenue* 📞 *808-923-1555, 800-356-8264*
📠 *808-922-9494* 🖥 *www.kaimana.com, rooms@kaimana.com*

Located on the outskirts of Waikiki, away from the hustle and bustle of the crowds, is this modest caravansary. Resting beside beautiful Sans Souci Beach, across the street from Kapiolani Park and in the shadow of Diamond Head, the Otani offers ocean or mountain views in airy and contemporary guest rooms. It's been around for a long time, and despite modernization and other changes, it has retained its commitment to a Hawaiian feel. Two remarkable restaurants and an oceanside bar may give the sense of a bigger hotel, but the staff create a more welcoming environment.

THE LOTUS AT DIAMOND HEAD

$$$$ 50 ROOMS ✉2885 Kalakaua Avenue ☎808-922-1700 📠808-923-2249
🖥www.castleresorts.com/Home/accommodations/the-lotus-at-diamond-head

There's a personable feeling here. Located at the foot of Diamond Head and Kapiolani Park, this boutique hotel boasts bright, airy rooms in its 12 floors. If you tire of the stunning views of Diamond Head, board games are available in the lobby, where you can also engage a challenger to a Wii game on the 42-inch flat screen. With the award-winning Diamond Head Grill serving innovative Hawaii Regional cuisine onsite, you may never want to leave.

DIAMOND HEAD BEACH HOTEL

$$–$$$ 50 ROOMS ✉2947 Kalakaua Avenue ☎808-922-1928
📠808-924-8980 🖥www.dhbhotel.com, info@dhbhotel.com

This ultra-elegant hotel, secluded from the bustle of Waikiki, is a great place to stay. Located close to the fabled crater, it is a contemporary establishment. The standard rooms are nondescript but the suites are done in a tasteful, Balinese-themed style, and many come with a kitchen. Right next to the ocean, this 13-story facility is one of the most desirable resting places around. Continental breakfast is included.

CONDOS

OUTRIGGER WAIKIKI SHORE

29 UNITS ✉2161 Kalia Road ☎808-922-3871, 800-688-7444 📠808-922-3887
🖥www.outriggerwaikikishore.com, wsr@outrigger.com

There are studios and one- and two-bedroom units here. These condos feature complete kitchens, washer/dryers and great views. Studios are $250 while one-bedroom units start at $350, with a two-night minimum. Two-bedroom units accommodating up to six start at $400.

ROYAL KUHIO

385 UNITS ✉2240 Kuhio Avenue ☎808-923-0555 📠808-923-0720
🖥www.waikikicondos.com, info@waikikicondos.com

A good bet for families, this highrise is just two blocks from Waikiki Beach. All units here feature fully equipped kitchens and balconies, most with ocean or mountain views. Studios are $145; one-bedroom units are $150.

WINSTON'S WAIKIKI CONDOS

10 UNITS ✉417 Nohonani Street, Suite 409 ☎808-924-3332, 800-545-1948
🖥www.winstonswaikikicondos.com, patwinston@gmail.com

At Winston's, deluxe one-bedroom condos rent for $99 to $145 (single or double occupancy only depending on the length of your stay). All suites are comfortably furnished with rattan furniture and feature lanais and full kitchens. The units, just one block from the beach, are well-maintained and clean. Washers and dryers are available. Patrick Winston offers special deals for *Hidden Oahu* readers, so make sure you call ahead and mention this book. One-week minimum stay preferred.

ASTON PACIFIC MONARCH

140 UNITS ✉2427 Kuhio Avenue ☎808-923-9805, 877-997-6667 ✆808-924-3220 ✐www.astonhotels.com, res.pam@astonhotels.com

The Pacific Monarch has studio apartments with kitchenettes ($205 to $230) and one-bedroom units with fully equipped kitchens ($260 to $300) for up to four. All rooms have balconies. There is a rooftop pool, jacuzzi and sauna, and the beach is just two blocks away.

ASTON WAIKIKI BEACH TOWER

104 UNITS ✉2470 Kalakaua Avenue ☎808-926-6400, 877-997-6667 ✆808-926-7380 ✐www.astonhotels.com, res.awt@astonhotels.com

Across the street from the beach, this converted-hotel-now-condo-complex does have location going for it. All units here feature contemporary furniture, washers and dryers, high-speed internet access, kitchens and beautiful lanais. The kids will enjoy the pool. One-bedroom units for up to four guests begin at $560. Two-bedroom suites for up to six guests start at $660.

ASTON AT THE WAIKIKI BANYAN

267 UNITS ✉201 Ohua Avenue ☎808-922-0555, 877-997-6667 ✆808-924-7114 ✐www.astonhotels.com, res.ban@astonhotels.com

Just one block from the beach, this highrise has one-bedroom units ($215 to $285) for one to five people. These ocean and mountain view units have full kitchens, rattan furniture and lanais, along with many kid-friendly activities.

DINING

This tourist mecca is crowded with restaurants. Since the competition is so stiff, the cafés here are cheaper than elsewhere on the islands. There are numerous American restaurants serving moderately good food at modest prices, so diners looking for standard fare will have no problem. But as you're probably seeking something more exotic, I'll also list some interesting Asian, Hawaiian, health food and other offbeat restaurants.

PRINCE COURT

$$$–$$$$ HAWAII REGIONAL ✉Hawaii Prince Hotel Waikiki, 100 Holomoana Street ☎808-956-1111, 808-944-4494

Hawaii regional cuisine accented by island fruits is featured at the Hawaii Prince Hotel's harborside restaurant, a dining room known for dishes like sea scallops and lobster. An extensive wine list is another plus at this Polynesian-style dining room appointed with warm lighting and floor-to-ceiling windows overlooking the harbor. Seafood buffet only Friday through Sunday nights.

BALI BY THE SEA

$$$$ PACIFIC RIM   ✉*Hilton Hawaiian Village, 2005 Kalia Road*   📞*808-949-4321 ext. 43, 808-941-2254*   📠*808-947-7926*   ⌁*www.hiltonhwaiianvillage.com*

Dishes like scallion-crusted *ahi* tempura and oven-roasted rack of lamb make this place a special favorite. Plush seating, nautical lamps, fresh flowers and soft ocean breezes add to the charm of this elegant restaurant. Dress code. Dinner only. Closed Sunday.

WAIKIKI STARLIGHT LUAU

$$$ LOCAL-STYLE   ✉*Hilton Hawaiian Village Beach Resort, 2005 Kalia Road*   📞*808-941-5828*   ⌁*www.hiltonhawaiianvillage.com/luau*

At the Hilton's open-air, rooftop luau, guests have the chance to sample not only traditional Hawaiian foods like roast pig and poi, but also local island favorites including *huli huli* chicken, Portuguese sausage, rice noodles, *ahi poke* and Molokai sweet potatoes. A dessert bar offers passion fruit–mango tarts and guava chiffon cake, among other sweet treats. After the buffet dinner, Polynesian dancers put on a show that is mesmerizing, particularly the four-man Samoan fire-knife dance.

HARD ROCK CAFE

$$–$$$ AMERICAN   ✉*1837 Kapiolani Boulevard*   📞*808-955-7383*   ⌁*www.hardrock.com*

Even though it's part of a chain, die-hard rock-and-roll fans will want to know that Honolulu has a Hard Rock Cafe, with its traditional collection of guitars, clothes, concert posters and other memorabilia donated by rock stars decorating the walls. It's a spacious, airy place that tends to get noisy. The food is as all-American as the decor, with burgers, barbecued ribs and chicken.

KEO'S THAI CUISINE

$$–$$$ THAI   ✉*2028 Kuhio Avenue*   📞*808-951-9355*   ⌁*www.keosthaicuisine.com, keos@keosthaicuisine.com*

Keo's is one of the ethnic restaurants most popular with local folks. Fulfilling to all the senses, this intimate place is decorated with fresh flowers and tropical plants. The cuisine includes such Southeast Asian dishes as the "evil jungle prince," a sliced beef, shrimp or chicken entrée with coconut milk, fresh basil and red chili, or for breakfast, the Hawaiian Scramble—eggs with bacon, green onions and soy sauce. You can choose from dozens of fish, shellfish, fowl and meat dishes. The menu offers variety, and Keo's comes highly recommended.

NICK'S FISHMARKET

$$$$ SEAFOOD   ✉*Waikiki Gateway Hotel, 2070 Kalakaua Avenue*   📞*808-955-6333*   📠*808-946-0478*   ⌁*www.nicksfishmarket.com, nickwaikiki@aol.com*

If you decide to stop at Nick's, plan on eating seafood. You have never seen such a list of fresh fish dishes. Not that much of it will seem familiar, but there is mahimahi, *opakapaka* and *ahi*. Or if you prefer to dine on something you recognize, how about shrimp scampi, abalone, lobster or scallops? The service is attentive.

ARANCINO

$$ ITALIAN ✉ *255 Beach Walk* ☎ *808-923-5557* 📠 *808-922-0105*
🖥 *www.arancino.net, info@arancino.net*

Authentic Italian specialties at affordable prices draw nightly crowds here. The place has the feel of a New York–style bistro, with excellent, home-style standards like fettuccine *alla crema* and risotto that are worth the potential 20-minute wait. If you're looking for Italian with a twist, some of the dishes here have a Japanese influence, like the spaghetti with *tobiko*.

SHORE BIRD BEACH BROILER

$$–$$$ AMERICAN/JAPANESE ✉ *Reef Hotel, 2169 Kalia Road* ☎ *808-922-2887*
📠 *808-926-5372*

This beachfront dining room is a great place to enjoy a reasonably priced dinner and an ocean view. This is a cook-your-own-food facility that offers hand-carved steaks, fresh fish, teriyaki chicken and barbecued ribs for dinner. The all-you-can-eat breakfast buffet, with American standards and some Japanese dishes as well, is a good deal. One of the best bargains on Waikiki Beach, the Shore Bird is inevitably crowded, so try to dine early.

OCEAN TERRACE RESTAURANT

$$$$ AMERICAN ✉ *Sheraton Waikiki, 2255 Kalakaua Avenue* ☎ *808-921-4600,*
808-922-4422 📠 *808-931-8530*

The food is pretty standard fare here but the view deserves five stars. Set poolside next to the beach in one of the state's largest hotels, this open-air dining room provides a welcome means to dine on the water. Daily buffet available. Breakfast only.

LA MER

$$$$ FRENCH ✉ *Halekulani Hotel, 2199 Kalia Road* ☎ *808-923-2311*
📠 *808-926-8004* 🖥 *www.halekulani.com*

It's not surprising that Waikiki's most fashionable hotel, the Halekulani, contains one of the district's finest restaurants. Situated on an open-air balcony overlooking the ocean, La Mer has a reputation for elegant dining in intimate surroundings. French-inspired dishes include crispy-skin *onaga* fillet with pork confit and truffle *jus*, and rack of lamb with a dijon mustard crust, provençal-style vegetables and creamy potatoes. Add the filigree woodwork and sumptuous surroundings and La Mer is one of the island's most attractive waterfront dining rooms. Formal attire required. Reservations recommended. Dinner only.

ORCHIDS

$$$$ HAWAII REGIONAL/INTERNATIONAL ✉ *Halekulani Hotel, 2199 Kalia Road* ☎ *808-923-2311* 📠 *808-926-8004* 🖥 *www.halekulani.com*

Downstairs from La Mer is this classy yet casual restaurant, serving a mix of Hawaiian and international cuisine like steamed *onaga* with sesame oil and shiitake mushrooms, roasted pepper–

spiced duck breast and roasted lamb chops. Orchids is open for breakfast, lunch, dinner and a Sunday brunch buffet.

WAIKIKI SHOPPING PLAZA

$–$$ INTERNATIONAL   ✉ *2250 Kalakaua Avenue*

To find an affordable meal on Kalakaua Avenue, the oceanfront strip, try the bottom floor of this plaza. Here about a dozen ethnic and American restaurants, like **Aqua Café** (808-922-6888) and **Kiwami Ramen** (808-924-6744), offer takeout food, as well as full-course sit-down dinners.

RESTAURANT SUNTORY

$$–$$$ JAPANESE   ✉ *Royal Hawaiian Shopping Center, 2233 Kalakaua Avenue*
📞 *808-922-5511*   📠 *808-923-6267*

The sushi bar here is an excellent, often busy, choice for sushi lovers. Or order traditional Japanese dishes and enjoy tableside preparation in the *teppanyaki* dining room. This third-floor restaurant prides itself on serving fresh island fish and locally grown organic produce; the atmosphere is charmingly authentic and elegant, but still comfortable enough for casual dining.

CHA CHA CHA RESTAURANT

$–$$ CARIBBEAN-MEXICAN   ✉ *342 Seaside Avenue*   📞 *808-923-7797*
📠 *808-926-7007*

The blue skies and green palms of the Caribbean never seem far away in Hawaii, and they feel even closer here. With its tropical color scheme and festive decor, this eatery serves up Mexican dishes such as burritos, tacos and quesadillas prepared Caribbean-style with unusual spices and sauces.

SEASIDE BAR & GRILL

$–$$ AMERICAN   ✉ *2256 Kuhio Avenue*   📞 *808-922-8227*   📠 *808-922-8227*

Favored by both tourists and locals for its low prices, the Seaside has a budget-priced early-bird special of steak or mahimahi nightly until 7 p.m. Choose any two items—lobster tail, crab legs, mahimahi, fried shrimp or New York steak—and they'll throw in a house salad as well. The fish is frozen and the place is actually two blocks from the "seaside," but for low-rent dining it's worth considering.

FATTY'S CHINESE KITCHEN

$ CHINESE/PLATE LUNCHES   ✉ *Kuhio Mall, 2345 Kuhio Avenue*
📞 *808-922-9600*

An L-shaped counter with swivel chairs is the most decor you can expect here. The prices on plate lunches and dinners are a throwback, too. With dozens of choices, including many "noodle in soup" dishes, Fatty's aims to suit every palate.

PERRY'S SMORGY

$–$$ AMERICAN   ✉ *2380 Kuhio Avenue*   📞 *808-926-0184*   📠 *808-922-1907*

A Waikiki standby, Perry's has an inexpensive, prix-fixe buffet at breakfast, lunch and dinner. With an extensive salad bar, plus a host of meat and fish platters, this all-you-can-eat emporium is hard to beat if you're hungry.

$ INTERNATIONAL   ✉*International Marketplace, 2330 Kalakaua Avenue*
📞*808-971-2080* ⌕*www.internationalmarketplacewaikiki.com*

The International Marketplace's food court features roughly 20 stands where you can indulge your sweet tooth with shave ice, pastries or ice cream, pick up a quick sandwich or snack, or satisfy your hunger with a full meal. You can take your meal out, or enjoy outdoor dining on a banyan-shaded patio. As its name implies, you can choose from a range of ethnic cuisines, including Greek, French, Vietnamese, American and more. Here you will find **Bautista's Filipino Kitchen** (808-923-7220), where the specialties include noodles, beef stew, mixed vegetables and *menudo* with green fish. For a gourmet spin on Chicago-style hot dogs, look for **Hank's Haute Dogs** (808-532-4265) just outside the main food court. Choices like duck and foie gras sausage with honey mustard or kobe beef sausage with pickled daikon truly astonish the taste buds. **Peking Garden** (808-926-6060) has traditional Chinese dishes including beef and broccoli, chicken chop suey and eggplant with chicken. For Japanese and Korean food, go to **Choi's Kitchen** (808-923-5614), where *saimin* and chicken teriyaki are popular dishes.

COCONUT WILLY'S BAR & GRILL

$$ AMERICAN   ✉*International Marketplace, 2330 Kalakaua Avenue*   📞*808-923-9454*
📞*808-923-0581* ⌕*www.coconutwillyswaikiki.net*

Outside of the food court at the International Marketplace, Coconut Willy's has a dinner menu that includes a New York steak and shrimp platter, fish and chips, and mahimahi. There are also burgers, sandwiches, salads and a long list of colorful tropical cocktails. Set beside the banyan tree that dominates the market, the place has a funky appeal.

ODORIKO JAPANESE RESTAURANT

$$–$$$ JAPANESE   ✉*King's Village, 2400 Koa Avenue*   📞*808-923-7368*
⌕*www.odorikohawaii.com, aloha@odorikohawaii.com*

Fish ponds at the entrance to Odoriko set the tone for the calm, reserved atmosphere of the dining room and sushi bar. This sedate restaurant, where unruly children and loud conversation are out of place, is frequented by Japanese natives. There's an extensive menu that features over 100 choices, including traditional entrées like *shabu shabu*, *teishoku* and sukiyaki, along with tempura, seafood dishes, sushi, sashimi, steak and lobster. Early-bird specials help keep the prices down.

EZOGIKU

$ JAPANESE   ✉*2420 Koa Avenue and 2146 Kalakaua Avenue*
📞*808-922-2473, 808-926-8616* 📞*808-926-2207* ⌕*www.ezogiku.com*

For a just-before-midnight snack—they close at 11 p.m.—or to satisfy cravings for a hot bowl of noodle soup, you're never too far from an Ezogiku. Rub shoulders with Japanese tourists at the counter in one of these hole-in-the-wall eateries serving ramen in a variety of styles, including curry, pork and wonton. There are two locations to choose from in Waikiki.

CIAO MEIN

$$$ ITALIAN/CHINESE   ✉️*Hyatt Regency Waikiki, third floor, 2424 Kalakaua Avenue*
📞*808-923-1234, ext. 59* 📠*808-237-6152* 🖥️*www.waikiki.hyatt.com*

Italian *and* Chinese? Sounds like an odd pairing, but the hybrid menu here is nonetheless delicious on both sides. On the Chinese side try spicy *kung pao* chicken, Szechuan eggplant or the savory flavors of Mongolian sizzle. If you're craving Italian, start with the carpaccio followed by pasta in a light tomato basil sauce. If you're feeling adventurous try Italian/Chinese fusion, like the hot bean salmon *alla siciliana*. Everything is served family-style, which means shared dishes that make this a great place to go with kids or in a group. Ciao Mein's decor is Euro-chic. Dinner only.

CHEESEBURGER IN PARADISE

$–$$ AMERICAN   ✉️*2500 Kalakaua Avenue* 📞*808-923-3731* 📠*808-923-1070*
🖥️*www.cheeseburgerland.com*

Fans whir overhead and a bar sits in the back; sheet music covers and old Matson oceanliner menus stand framed along the walls. Hard to believe someone would create this ambience for their restaurant, then name the place Cheeseburger in Paradise. But burgers it is, plus a selection of breakfast dishes for the morning.

LULU'S WAIKIKI SURF CLUB

$$–$$$ AMERICAN   ✉️*2586 Kalakaua Avenue* 📞*808-926-5222*
🖥️*www.luluswaikiki.com, aloha@lulushawaii.com*

Although the food is nothing to write home about and it has aggressively kitschy decor, Lulu's is worth mentioning simply because it's open nearly 24 hours daily, from 7 a.m. to 2 a.m., making it the spot for late-night partying. Lulu's is as much a nightspot as an eatery, with a menu that is heavy on surf and turf and grilled items, and attracts a loud, boisterous crowd. With its prime location across from the beach, it's great for people-watching and has a good view of surf breaks and Diamond Head.

HAU TREE LANAI

$$$$ INTERNATIONAL   ✉️*New Otani Kaimana Beach Hotel, 2863 Kalakaua Avenue*
📞*808-921-7066* 🖥️*www.kaimana.com*

Apart from the bustle of Waikiki but still right on the beach is this island-style dining room. Here beneath the interwoven branches of twin *hau* trees you can enjoy patio dining with a view that extends across Waikiki to the distant mountains. I favor the place for its breakfast (the French toast is delicious), but they also have a lunch and dinner menu that ranges from steamed vegetables to curried chicken to fresh island fish. In the evening the place is illuminated by torches, and soft breezes wisp off the water, adding to the enchantment. Reservations recommended.

DIAMOND HEAD GRILL

$$$-$$$$ HAWAII REGIONAL   ✉️*The Lotus at Diamond Head, 2885
Kalakaua Avenue* 📞*808-922-3734* 📠*808-791-5164*
🖥️*www.w-dhg.com, info@w-dhg.com*

Innovative, high-quality cuisine and excellent service put this on the list of Hawaii's best. The pan-seared *ahi* is one of those oh-so-good dishes that makes you want to order it each time you visit. The refined and artful presentation is complemented by the eatery's clean and contemporary decor with deco highlights. There's entertainment Wednesday through Saturday nights. No lunch.

SHOPPING

This tourist mecca is a great place to look but not to buy. Browsing the busy shops is like studying a catalog of Hawaiian handicrafts. It's all here—you'll find everything but bargains. With a few noteworthy exceptions, the prices include the unofficial tourist surcharges that merchants worldwide levy against visitors. Windowshop Waikiki, but plan on spending your shopping dollars elsewhere.

RAINBOW BAZAAR ⊠*Hilton Hawaiian Village, 2005 Kalia Road* Designed in Asian style, with curving tile roofs and brilliantly painted roof beams, you can stroll along this lovely arcade, past lofty banyan trees and flowering gardens, to stores filled with rare art and Far Eastern antiquities. Worth window shopping.

LOCAL MOTION ⊠*1958 Kalakaua Avenue* ☎*808-979-7873* ⊘*www.localmotion hawaii.com* This island-based company has opened an architecturally distinguished flagship shop for its line of logowear and sporting gear, including surfboards, body boards and backpacks.

WAIKIKI SHOPPING PLAZA ⊠*2250 Kalakaua Avenue* The main shopping scene is in the malls and this one has five floors of stores and restaurants. Here are jewelers, sundries and boutiques, plus specialty shops like **Borders Express** (808-922-4154), with an excellent line of magazines as well as paperbacks and bestsellers.

THE UKULELE HOUSE

⊠*Waikiki Shopping Plaza* ☎*808-923-8587* If you're in the market for a ukulele, stop by this gem, which carries everything from children's souvenir ukes for $10 to musically playable instruments ranging from $80 all the way to $2000-plus for vintage models. This world-famous supplier of unique ukuleles is also home of the world's largest ukulele. If you would like to try playing a ukulele on your visit to Hawaii, you can take free 30-minute lessons here (by appointment only).

ROYAL HAWAIIAN SHOPPING CENTER ⊠*2233 Kalakaua Avenue* ☎*808-922-0588* ⊘*www.royalhawaiiancenter.com* A four-story complex that runs for two blocks along Kalakaua Avenue, from Lewers Street to the Outrigger Waikiki, this is a key shopping destination. On the *makai* side (facing the ocean), it fronts the grounds of the Royal Hawaiian and the Sheraton Waikiki. It is Waikiki's largest mall, with Euro-American designer boutiques, upscale shops, numerous restaurants and fast-food kiosks, as well as an indoor shooting gallery and showroom. A weekly schedule of Hawaiiana and other cultural performances provides an entertaining respite from the pressures of shopping.

LITTLE HAWAIIAN CRAFT SHOP

✉ *Royal Hawaiian Shopping Center* ☎ *808-926-2662* Here you'll find an interesting selection of traditional and contemporary Hawaiian crafts including carved koa wood bowls, Niihau shell leis, Hawaiian quilts, ceramics and glassware.

DUKE'S LANE ✉ *Kalakaua Avenue to Kuhio Avenue* One Waikiki shopping area I do recommend is Duke's Lane. This alleyway may be the best place in all Hawaii to buy jade jewelry. Either side of the lane is flanked by mobile stands selling rings, necklaces, earrings, stick pins, bracelets and more. It's a prime place to barter for tiger's eyes, opals and mother-of-pearl pieces.

WAIKIKI TRADE CENTER ✉ *2255 Kuhio Avenue* With an air of Milanese splendor about it, this glass-and-steel complex is a maze of mirrors. In addition to the stained-glass windows and twinkling lights, there are several worthwhile shops in this strikingly attractive mall.

ISLAND TREASURES ANTIQUE MALL ✉ *2301 Kuhio Avenue* ☎ *808-922-8223* You'll find Waikiki's best selection of Hawaiiana in this multi-level complex that's home to a number of individual vendors. Fun for browsing and a purchase if you find something priced right. The shops open in the afternoon and stay open late, which makes it a good tie-in with an evening stroll. Call for hours. Closed Monday.

INTERNATIONAL MARKETPLACE ✉ *2330 Kalakaua Avenue* ☎ *808-971-2080* A Waikiki institution since 1957, this is a centrally located, mixed-plate bazaar that makes a convenient stop for last-minute gifts or the bargain hunter's scenic route between Kalaukaua and Kuhio avenues. Navigate your way through the maze of 130 vendors, many that are simply free-standing carts selling jewelry, aloha wear, handicrafts, imported South Seas trinkets, T-shirts and more. If you didn't make it to the Aloha Stadium swap meet, this is your next-best bet for kitschy souvenirs.

KING'S VILLAGE ✉ *131 Kaiulani Avenue at Kalakaua Avenue* This mock Victorian town suggests how Britain might have looked had the 19th-century English invented polyethylene. The motif may be trying to appear antiquated, but the prices are unfortunately quite contemporary. Not sure what to wear to your luau? **Amy's Corner** (808-924-7090) sells matching women's and men's aloha-print outfits if you really want to play up the kitsch. If you're in the vicinity at sundown, stop by to witness the snap and precision of the King's Guard. The rifle-toting drill team performs a flag-lowering ceremony daily at 6:15 p.m.

HYATT REGENCY WAIKIKI ✉ *2424 Kalakaua Avenue* ☎ *808-923-1234* ☎ *808-926-3415* ✐ *www.waikiki.hyatt.com* A toney selection of shops are located in the Hyatt Regency Waikiki. This triple-tiered arcade is *the* place to look when you are seeking the very best. There are fine art shops,

designer apparel stores, gem shops and shops that feature made-in-Hawaii products. Women may find it hard to leave **Le Lotus Bleu** (808-923-1818) empty-handed. This spunky little boutique always has at least one must-have item in its stock of women's clothing, where the styles range from funky to feminine, with an emphasis on distinct and trendy. It's on the first floor, fronting Kalakaua Avenue.

BAILEY'S ANTIQUES AND ALOHA SHIRTS ✉*517 Kapahulu Avenue* ✆*808-734-7628* ✐*www.alohashirts.com, baileysalohashirts@yahoo.com* Looking for a vintage silk shirt? Those famous Hawaiian styles, like the one Montgomery Clift sported in *From Here to Eternity*, are among the alluring items at Bailey's. This place carries over 15,000 Hawaiian shirts, and is the world's largest vintage shirt store. If an original silky is beyond your means, they also have reproductions as well as collectibles like Zippo lighters.

PEGGY'S PICKS ✉*732 Kapahulu Avenue* ✆*808-737-3297* Peggy's sells everything from Hawaiiana to an eclectic array of collectibles at affordable prices. Closed Sunday.

NIGHTLIFE

Hawaii has a strong musical tradition, kept alive by excellent groups performing their own compositions as well as old Polynesian songs. I'm not talking about the "Blue Hawaii"–"Tiny Bubbles"–"Beyond the Reef" medleys that draw tourists in droves, but *real* Hawaiian music. Oahu is the ideal island to seek out Hawaiian sounds. Many of these musicians—Keola Beamer, Kealii Reichel, Henry Kapono, Olomana and the Brothers Cazimero to name a few—may be playing at a local club. Consult the daily newspapers, or tune in to KCCN at 100 on the radio dial. This all-Hawaiian station is the home of island soul.

HARD ROCK CAFE ✉*1837 Kapiolani Boulevard* ✆*808-955-7383* ✐*www.hardrock.com* At the edge of Waikiki, the Hard Rock Cafe is always a kick. Decorated with tons of rock-and-roll memorabilia, this restaurant/bar is a popular nightspot for those who like loud music and a big crowd.

PARADISE LOUNGE ✉*Hilton Hawaiian Village, 2005 Kalia Road* ✆*808-949-4321* ✆*808-951-5458* On Friday and Saturday nights, a contemporary Hawaiian group stars here. Other forms of live entertainment are offered the rest of the week. Choose between table or lounge seating in this carpeted club, which is decorated with Hawaiian landscapes painted by local artists.

NICK'S FISHMARKET ✉*Waikiki Gateway Hotel, 2070 Kalakaua Avenue* ✆*808-955-6333* ✐*www.nicksfishmarket.com, nickwaikiki@aol.com* Over at Nick's there's live entertainment nightly except Monday and Tuesday. Expect to hear light rock, jazz, soul or blues while munching on half-price *pupus*.

SHORE BIRD BEACH BROILER ✉*Outrigger Reef, 2169 Kalia Road* ✆*808-922-2887* A group performs mellow Hawaiian music nightly at this late-night *pupus* spot.

LEWERS LOUNGE ✉Halekulani Hotel, 2199 Kalia Road ☎808-923-2311, 808-926-8004 Chic sophistication describes the ambiance at this Waikiki institution. Mixologist Dale DeGroff, who rose to fame at New York City's Rainbow Room, created a menu of signature drinks that will delight even the most discerning cocktail aficionados. The elegant piano lounge has warm lighting and elegant decor and features live classical and contemporary jazz nightly. Evening attire required.

RUMFIRE ✉Sheraton Waikiki, 2255 Kalakaua Avenue ☎808-922-4422 After a visit here, you'll turn your nose up at the standard mai tai. This modern lounge presents an extensive list of innovative cocktails featuring vintage and exotic rums from around the world. Wok-fired specialties, grilled fish, and cold and hot tapas are also on offer. Start early with happy hour specials and live music from 5 to 7 p.m. daily. Open until 2 a.m. Friday and Saturday.

MOOSE MCGILLYCUDDY'S ✉310 Lewers Street ☎808-923-0751 ⌨www.mooserestaurantgroup.com With room for 300 of your closest friends, the dance floor upstairs here spins Top-40 music Tuesday through Sunday nights. Known for its weird pictures, this establishment is easily spotted. Just look for the only building on Lewers Street sporting a stuffed moose head. Occasional cover.

MAI TAI BAR

✉Royal Hawaiian Hotel, 2259 Kalakaua Avenue ☎808-923-7311 ⌨www.royal-hawaiian.com There's Hawaiian music nightly at this tropical haven. Grab an umbrella-topped table on the terrace for primo views of the sun setting over the ocean.

DUKE'S CANOE CLUB

✉Outrigger Waikiki, 2335 Kalakaua Avenue ☎808-922-2268 📠808-923-4204 ⌨www.dukeswaikiki.com The bar here offers a beachfront setting, a distant view of Diamond Head, and plenty of atmosphere. Duke refers to Duke Kahanamoku, the Olympic swimming champion and surfer who helped restore surfing to a position of cultural prominence. The decor documents his career with archival photography and memorabilia. It draws overflowing crowds, particularly on Sunday afternoons when Henry Kapono performs. There are also live concerts on the beach on Friday, Saturday and Sunday.

LOTUS SOUNDBAR ✉2301 Kuhio Avenue ☎808-924-688 ⌨www.myspace.com/lotusoundbar Most Waikiki clubs are filled with tourists, but Lotus is an exception to this rule. The swanky multilevel, multiroom lounge is a popular late-night (meaning after 1 a.m.) destination for Honolulu hipsters lured by its first-class sound system and regular rotation of deejays spinning mostly house and hip-hop. If you're looking for a place to get your groove on, Lotus is worth the cover charge. From Thursday through Saturday, the music pumps until 4 a.m. Dress code enforced.

COCONUT WILLY'S BAR & GRILL ✉International Marketplace, 2330 Kalakaua Avenue ✆808-923-9454 📠808-923-0581 🖫www.coconutwillyswaikiki.net
Live bands start in the afternoon and continue on into the night here. The 35-and-over crowd turns out to dance to '50s and '60s classics as well as Hawaiian and country tunes.

TIKI'S GRILL & BAR

✉2570 Kalakaua Avenue ✆808-923-8454 📠808-922-5883 🖫www.tikis grill.com Bustling until closing time, the bar at this hip spot is frequented by locals and visitors drawn to its casual, relaxed atmosphere, exotic drinks menu and live Hawaiian music. The bar is situated on the lanai and looks out on Waikiki's main drag, making it a great place to people-watch and have a drink or two either before or after dinner.

THE WONDERLOUNGE ✉The Lotus at Diamond Head, 2885 Kalakaua Avenue ✆808-922-1700 📠808-923-2249 This trendy lounge became a prominent player on the Honolulu club scene when The Lotus was a W Hotel, so don't be confused if everyone still refers to it as "The W." The name may have changed, but every Friday and Saturday night, the deejays continue to spin and the party rages on. Seductive lighting and a serpentine marble bar set the mood for the beautiful people who come to play.

GERMAINE'S LUAU ✆808-949-6626, 800-367-5655 🖫www.germainesluau. com, reservations@germainesluau.com For an authentic *tourist* experience accompanied by a genuine aloha spirit, join the busloads of Waikiki visitors who are caravanned to Barbers Point for the ultimate in Hawaiian kitsch. At Germaine's you'll get to witness the unearthing ceremony of a pig from its underground *imu* (oven), dine on Hawaiian-style food and watch Polynesian dancers (or join them on stage), all at a beachfront site as the sun sets on the Pacific. Reservations recommended.

Gay Scene
The gay scene is centered around several clubs on Waikiki's Kuhio Avenue and in Eaton Square, near the corner of Eaton and Hobron streets, not far away.

IN BETWEEN ✉2155 Lauula Street ✆808-926-7060 🖫www.inbetweenonline. com On a short street near Kuhio and Lewers, this is a great place to bend an elbow with island regulars.

FUSION WAIKIKI ✉Paradise Building, 2260 Kuhio Avenue ✆808-924-2422 A spicy gay club open until 4 a.m., this hot spot takes up the second and third floors of the Paradise Building and features dancing to house and underground deejay music. There are male strip shows and female impersonation performances on Friday and Saturday. Cover.

ANGLES WAIKIKI ✉2256 Kuhio Avenue ✆808-926-9766 🖫www.angles waikiki.com, angles.waikiki@juno.com Clubgoers hang in and out here, where a bar in the center of the room provides a place to socialize, as does the lanai outside. There are pool tables and videos, as well as a dancefloor.

Every Wednesday, crowds compete for cash prizes in the Best Chest/ Best Buns contest.

HULA'S BAR AND LEI STAND ✉ *Waikiki Grand Hotel, 134 Kapahulu Avenue* 📞 *808-923-0669* 🖱 *www.hulas.com* Across the street from the Honolulu Zoo, Hula's, with an ocean view and a disco complete with strobe-lit dance-floor and videos, rocks nightly until 2 a.m.

VENUS NIGHTCLUB ✉ *1349 Kapiolani Boulevard* 📞 *808-951-8671* 🖱 *www. venusnightclub.com* Dance any night of the week 'til 4 a.m. to deejay-spun house, disco and hip-hop mixes at Venus. They also feature a male revue. Dress code. Cover.

BEACHES & PARKS

WAIKIKI BEACH

🏊 🐟 ⛱ 🚣 Famous all over the world, the strand in Waikiki is actually several beaches in one. Kahanamoku Beach, Fort DeRussy Beach, Royal-Moana Beach, Kuhio Beach Park and Queen's Surf form an unbroken string that runs from the Ala Wai Canal to Diamond Head Crater. Together they comprise Waikiki Beach. Along that string of beaches are some of *the* surf spots that have made Waikiki famous, including "Canoes" and "Queens." Ask one of the local beach boys where to go for a spot that fits your level of expertise. Bottom fishing will net you *akule*, snapper, *moana*, weke, *ulua*, *menpachi* and bonefish. Snorkeling is so-so. Since going to the beach in this busy enclave also means exploring Waikiki itself, I have placed the beach descriptions in the sightseeing section on the preceding pages.

DOWNTOWN HONOLULU

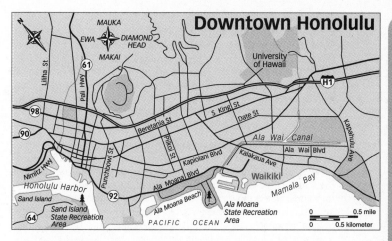

Downtown Honolulu

While the Neighbor Islands and rural Oahu still move at a leisurely, laidback pace, downtown Honolulu marches to a different drummer. As the political and commercial heart of Hawaii and the center of the only major metropolis in all of Polynesia, it plays a role far more vital than its compact size would seem to warrant.

The state, county and city government offices can all be found here, as can the headquarters of the companies that control Hawaii and whose influence reaches well beyond its shores to both the U.S. mainland and Asia. Honolulu's importance as a city has a long history, one that is partially told in its many historic buildings.

The development of Honolulu received a major boost when King Kamehameha III moved his capital from Lahaina to Honolulu in the 1840s. Although the missionaries had already established themselves in the area, it was at about this time that they began to build the church and houses that can still be seen today. As sugar developed as an agricultural industry and a cash economy took hold, the companies that were created to handle this business chose Honolulu as their headquarters.

A walk through the downtown area is a journey into the city's history. Begin at the old mission houses, now the Mission Houses Museum, and stroll past Kawaihao Church and Iolani Palace. Continue on to Merchant Street, with its 19th- and early-20th-century brick buildings, which once housed the city's financial district and headquarters for the "Big Five" companies that controlled Hawaii's economy. Wander through Chinatown, past crowded restaurants adorned with ducks hanging in the windows and herbal medicine shops lined with jars and drawers of leaves, twigs, bark and flowers.

Walk down by the waterfront, where Matson Line luxury steamers delivered the first tourists and gave birth to an industry that still keeps Hawaii's economy thriving. And finally, ride the elevator to the top of the Aloha Tower for a bird's-eye view of the highrise office buildings that define downtown Honolulu today.

SIGHTS

Downtown

MISSION HOUSES MUSEUM ✉*553 South King Street* ☎*808-531-0481* 📠*808-545-2280* ✎*www.missionhouses.org, info@missionhouses.org* A fitting place to begin your tour of downtown is among the oldest homes in the islands. The buildings here seem to be borrowed from a New England landscape, and in a sense they were. The Frame House, a trim white wooden structure, was cut on the East Coast and shipped around the Horn to Hawaii. That was back in 1821, when this Yankee-style building was used to house missionary families.

Like the nearby Chamberlain House and Depository and other structures here, the Frame House represents one of the missionaries' earliest centers in Hawaii. It was in 1820 that Congregationalists arrived in the islands; they immediately set out to build and proselytize. In 1831, they constructed the Chamberlain House and Depository from coral and used it as the mission store. The neighborhood's Printing Office, built of the same durable material ten years later, was used by the first press ever to print in the Hawaiian language. The Mission Houses complex tells much about the missionaries, who converted Hawaiian into a written language, then proceeded to rewrite the entire history of the islands. The museum is run by the Hawaiian Mission Children's Society. Guided tours daily. Closed Sunday and Monday. Admission.

KAWAIAHAO CHURCH ⬤idden
✉*957 Punchbowl Street* ✎*www.kawaiahao.org* Opposite the Mission Houses Museum, at South King and Punchbowl streets, is this renowned church. The imposing edifice required 14,000 coral blocks for its construction. Completed in 1842, it has been called the Westminster Abbey of Hawaii because coronations and funerals for Hawaiian kings and queens were once conducted here. Services are still performed in Hawaiian and English every Sunday at 9 a.m.; attending them is not only a way to view the church interior, but also provides a unique cultural perspective on contemporary Hawaiian life. Also note that the tomb of King Lunalilo rises in front of the church, and behind the church lies the cemetery where early missionaries and converted Hawaiians were buried.

MISSION MEMORIAL BUILDING ✉*Across South King Street* This brick structure with stately white pillars was constructed in 1916 to honor the same early church leaders held in esteem at Kawaiaho Church.

HONOLULU HALE ✉️*530 South King Street* 📞*808-768-4385* The nearby Renaissance-style building with the tile roof is Honolulu Hale, the City Hall. You might want to venture into the central courtyard, an open-air plaza surrounded by stone columns.

IOLANI PALACE _____ **h**idden

✉️*South King and Richards streets* 📞*808-522-0832* 📠*808-532-1051* 🖱️*www. iolanipalace.org, info@iolanipalace.org* If you walk along South King Street in a westerly direction toward the center of Honolulu, this stunning palace will appear on your right. The palace (*iolani* means "bird of heaven" in Hawaiian) is the only state residence of royalty on American soil.

The king who commissioned the Iolani Palace in 1882, David Kalakaua, was a world traveler with a taste for the good life. Known as the Merry Monarch, he planned for his coronation the greatest party Hawaii had ever seen. He liked to spend money with abandon and managed to amass in his lifetime a remarkable collection of material goods, not the least of which was his palace. This stunning Victorian-style mansion served as a royal residence until Queen Liliuokalani was overthrown in 1893.

Later the ill-starred monarch was imprisoned here; eventually, after Hawaii became a territory of the United States, the palace was used as the capitol building until 1969. Guided tours lead you past the koa staircases, the magnificent chandeliers and the Corinthian columns that lend a touch of European grandeur to this splendid building.

The land around the Palace was significant to the Hawaiian people even before the royalty set up house. A Hawaiian temple stood here until it was probably destroyed in 1819. King Kamehameha III relocated his court from Lahaina to this location in 1845. After his residence was torn down, the current palace incarnation was constructed.

Located on the palace grounds is **Iolani Barracks**, where the Royal Household Guards were stationed, and the **Coronation Pavilion**, upon which the King was crowned. The pavilion had been used for the inauguration of Hawaii's governors, and the Royal Hawaiian Band gives free concerts adjacent to the structure on most Fridays, weather permitting, between noon and 1 p.m. You can tour the palace grounds for free, but there's an admission charge for the building. Reservations are strongly advised; children under five are allowed only in the video theater and basement galleries. Tours are given Tuesday through Saturday. Closed Sunday and Monday.

KAMEHAMEHA STATUE Directly across the street from Iolani Palace rises a statue honoring Hawaii's first king. The spear-carrying

102

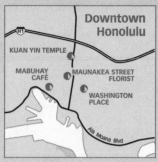

KUAN YIN TEMPLE

PAGE 107

Tranquil, incense-filled Buddhist sanctuary near verdant botanical gardens

MAUNAKEA STREET FLORIST

PAGE 114

Chinatown boutique brimming with fresh, fragrant leis of tuberoses and plumeria

MABUHAY CAFÉ

PAGE 112

Crispy pork *adobo*, soft white rice, flaky fried *lumpia* and other Filipino specialties in a hole-in-the-wall café

WASHINGTON PLACE

PAGE 103

Stately century-old mansion, now a public museum, that served as home to Hawaii's last royal family

warrior wears a feather cape and helmet. A huge gilt-and-bronze figure cast in Italy, it is covered with flower leis on special occasions.

ALIIOLANI HALE ☎808-539-4999 📠808-539-4996 🖰www.judiciaryhistory center.org, jhchawaii@yahoo.com Behind the Kamehameha Statue stands Aliiolani Hale, better known as the Judiciary Building, home to Hawaii's Supreme Court. Back in the days of the monarchy, it served as the House of Parliament. Self-guided tours of the Judiciary History Center are available Monday through Friday, and docent-led tours are available by appointment.

STATE CAPITOL BUILDING ✉415 South Beretania Street; Bounded by South Beretania, Richards and Punchbowl streets ☎808-586-0178 📠808-586-0019 Unlike the surrounding structures, this is an ultramodern building, completed in 1969. Encircled by flared pillars that resemble palm trees, the capitol represents a variety of themes. Near one entrance there's a **statue of Father Damien**, who tended to those with leprosy on Molokai Island; presiding over the other entrance is **Queen Liliuokalani**, Hawaii's last reigning monarch. The House and Senate chambers are designed in a cone shape to resemble volcanoes, and the open-air courtyard is a commentary on the state's balmy weather. Tours of the capitol building and the legislature are given Monday, Wednesday and Friday at 1:30 p.m.

HAWAII STATE ART MUSEUM ✉*One Capitol District Building; 250 South Hotel Street, second floor* ☎*808-586-0900* ✑*www.hawaii.gov/sfca* Since 1967 the State of Hawaii has set aside a percentage of revenues to fund the State Foundation on Culture and the Arts. The result is an art collection that has grown to more than 5000 pieces ranging from fabrics to paintings, glasswork to bronze sculpture. Art from the collection is exhibited in 285 buildings throughout the State, some of which is highlighted in an excellent historic walking tour booklet of downtown Honolulu. It's available free from the State Foundation for Culture and the Arts. To provide a museum setting for a portion of the collection, the State purchased the historic Richard Street YMCA, a noteworthy 1920s architectural monument across the street from Iolani Palace, and created the Hawaii State Art Museum (HiSAM), with three galleries on the second floor offering a total of 12,000 square feet of exhibit space. Closed Sunday and Monday.

WASHINGTON PLACE _____ **h**idden

✉*320 South Beretania Street* ☎*808-586-0248* Home to Hawaii's governors for 80 years, this building steeped in history is now a public museum. Captain John Dominis began construction in 1846, but never got to live here because he died at sea before the house was completed four years later. His famous daughter-in-law, however, made the house a palace. Queen Liliuokalani was living in Washington Place when she was overthrown, marking the end of the Hawaiian monarchy. When she was released from prison, she returned to Washington Place despite several other more comfortable living options. It has been speculated that her residence here was an act of politics and bravery: The home was cramped—at least by royal standards—but located near the new government's center of power. She did not, it would appear, wish to be forgotten. Washington Place has continued to serve its government over the years, providing living quarters for 12 governors and their families. Tours are available Monday through Friday; 48-hour advance reservations are required.

ST. ANDREWS CATHEDRAL ✉*229 Queen Emma Square* ☎*808-524-2822* ☎*808-537-4177* ✑*www.saintandrewscathedral.net, cathedral@saintandrewscathedral.net* Thought to be the only example of French-Gothic architecture in Hawaii, this cathedral was erected in 1862 of stone shipped from England. Its eight bells have the names of eight Hawaiian monarchs and the dates of their reigns engraved on them, and can perform 40,320 different melodic changes. One of the three Sunday masses is conducted partially in Hawaiian.

HONOLULU ACADEMY OF ARTS ✉*900 South Beretania Street* ☎*808-532-8700* ☎*808-532-8787* ✑*www.honoluluacademy.org, academypr@honoluluacademy.org* Another important cultural point and a jewel in Honolulu's art community is its arts academy. Founder Anna Rice Cooke originally donated over 4000 works in 1927. Today the internationally recognized museum boasts over 50,000 pieces and is worth spending an afternoon

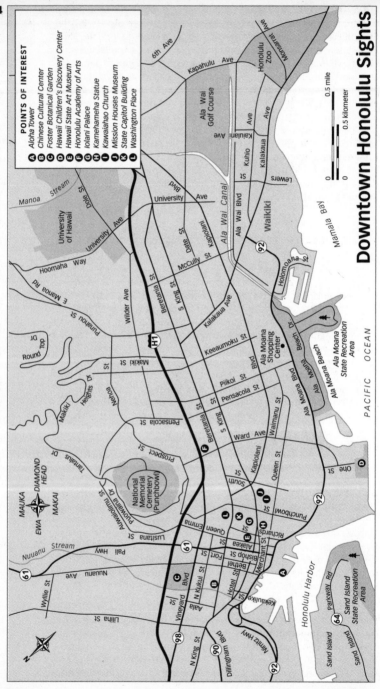

Downtown Honolulu Sights

POINTS OF INTEREST

- **A** Aloha Tower
- **B** Chinese Cultural Center
- **C** Foster Botanical Garden
- **D** Hawaii Children's Discovery Center
- **E** Hawaii State Art Museum
- **F** Honolulu Academy of Arts
- **G** Iolani Palace
- **H** Kamehameha Statue
- **I** Kawaiahao Church
- **J** Mission Houses Museum
- **K** State Capitol Building
- **L** Washington Place

perusing. Emphasizing Eastern and Western artworks, the museum may exhibit such items as author James Michener's collection of *ukiyo-e* prints from Japan or the Samuel H. Kress Foundation collection of Italian Renaissance paintings. In addition, traditional arts of Africa, the Pacific and the Americas are also displayed. Several elegantly landscaped courtyards add to the beauty. Guided tours are offered daily. Admission (first Wednesday of every month is free). Closed Monday.

HAWAII CHILDREN'S DISCOVERY CENTER ✉*111 Ohe Street* ☎*808-524-5437* 📠*808-524-5400* 🖥*www.discoverycenterhawaii.org, info@discovery centerhawaii.org* Let the kids burn off some steam at this 38,000-square-foot discovery center. Four major galleries sponsor interactive exhibits that are hands-on and educational (for example, "Fantastic You" will teach kids everything they need to know about the human body), but don't worry, they'll never catch on. You can picnic (or nap) at the park across the street. Be forewarned: Strollers are not allowed (although it is wheelchair accessible), so bring a carrier. Closed Monday. Admission.

Waterfront

To explore Honolulu's waterfront, head down Richards Street from the State Capitol Building toward Pier 7. This area of the city may not have the visual splendor of some of its neighbors, but it provides a historic and authentic glimpse into the maritime industry that keeps Honolulu bustling.

ALOHA TOWER ✉*Pier 9* When you reach the harbor, follow the roadway along the water to the right until you see the spire along the water's edge. In the early 20th century, when many visitors arrived in luxurious ocean liners, this slender structure was Hawaii's answer to the Statue of Liberty. It greeted guests when they arrived and bade them farewell upon departure. Now dwarfed by the skyscrapers of downtown Honolulu, proud Aloha Tower still commands an unusual view of the harbor and ocean. Any day between 9 a.m. and 5 p.m. you can ride an elevator to the tenth-floor observation deck for a crow's-nest view.

KEWALO BASIN HARBOR ✉*Ala Moana Boulevard and Ward Avenue* It's fun to wander the wharves along the waterfront, catching glimpses of the shops and pleasure boats that still tie up around Honolulu's historic port. You can take in the city's fishing fleet, as well as several tour boats, at this harbor, which is also known as Fisherman's Wharf, located midway between Waikiki and Downtown Honolulu.

HONOLULU FISH MARKET ✉*Near the Honolulu Harbor (Pier 38)* To see where all that delicious seafood you've been eating comes from, stop by this local fish market. Here auctioneers sell the day's catch. For the real experience, get there at 5:30 in the morning. Those not quite as industrious should note it's all over by noon.

FORT STREET MALL From the Honolulu Fish Market it's not far to this seven-block stretch of Downtown Honolulu. The mall is an attractive pedestrian thoroughfare with a few restaurants; it's also a good place to spend a little time shopping. Located miles from the Waikiki tourist beat, the stores here cater to local people, so you'll be able to discover objects unobtainable in kitschier quarters.

MERCHANT STREET Fort Street Mall leads you to the center of the Honolulu's old downtown section. The 19th- and early-20th-century buildings in this neighborhood re-create the days before Hawaii became the 50th state, when the islands were almost totally controlled by "The Big Five," an interlocking group of powerful corporations. Today the brick-rococo district remains much the same on the outside. But the interiors of the buildings have changed markedly. They now house boutiques and gourmet restaurants downstairs and multinational corporations on the upper floors.

Chinatown

Heading away from the waterfront all the way to the end of Merchant Street, take a right on Nuuanu Avenue, then a left on Hotel Street. As you walk along this thoroughfare, which seems to change its identity every block or two, you will pass from Honolulu's conservative financial district into one of its most intriguing ethnic neighborhoods, Chinatown.

The Chinese first arrived in Hawaii in 1852, imported as plantation workers. They quickly moved to urban areas after completing their plantation contracts, became merchants and proved very successful. Many settled right here in this weather-beaten district, which has long been a center of controversy and an integral part of Honolulu's history. When bubonic plague hit the Chinese community in 1900, the Caucasian-led government tried to contain the pestilence by burning down afflicted homes. The bumbling white fathers managed to raze most of Chinatown, destroying businesses as well as houses.

Chinatown has undergone a dramatic transformation over the past years in an effort to eliminate some of the seedier elements and red-light businesses. While it still has plenty of character, thanks to its quaint, time-worn stores and abundance of distinctive eateries, a thriving arts community has been established, breathing new life into the neighborhood.

Chinatown is where the locals go to buy leis, with most of the lei stands located on Maunakea Street and around the corner on North Beretania. Many of these shops are family-owned and -operated, and have been open for several generations. You can watch folks string leis or order garlands for special occasions or to take home.

Some of Chinatown's woodframe buildings still suggest the old days and traditions. Wander down side streets like Maunakea Street and you will encounter import stores, Chinese groceries and noodle factories. You might also pop into one of the medicinal herb shops, which feature unique potions and healing powders. There are chop suey joints, acupuncturists and outdoor markets galore, all lending a priceless flavor of the Orient.

MAUNAKEA MARKETPLACE ✉Hotel and Maunakea streets The ultimate emblem of Chinatown's revitalization is this often-crowded marketplace. This "Amerasian" shopping mall, with a statue of Confucius and one of Kuan Yin overlooking a brick courtyard, houses a Chinese teahouse and a Chinese art store. The most interesting feature is the produce market, a series of traditional hanging-ducks-and-live-fish stalls housed inside an air-conditioned building.

IZUMO TAISHAKYO MISSION Going north along Hotel Street across Nuuanu Stream, turn right on College Walk and follow it a short distance upstream. You'll pass this Japanese Shinto shrine. Take a minute to stop in to see the bell and gate.

FOSTER BOTANICAL GARDEN

✉50 North Vineyard Boulevard ☎808-522-7060, 808-522-7066 (reservations) ⌨www.co.honolulu.hi.us/parks/hbg/fbg.htm Proceed farther and you will arrive at this 14-acre plot planted with orchids, palms, coffee trees, poisonous plants and numerous other exotic specimens. There are about 4000 species in all, dotted around a garden that was first planted in 1853. You can meditate under a bo tree or wander through a "prehistoric glen," a riot of ancient ferns and unusual palms from all over the world. Or you can stroll through and marvel at the universe of color crowded into this urban garden. Visitors are advised to bring insect repellent. Guided tours are offered Monday through Saturday. Admission.

KUAN YIN TEMPLE

✉50 North Vineyard Boulevard When you're done enjoying Foster Botanical Garden, stop by the adjacent temple, where the smell of incense fills the air and Buddhist tranquility pervades. For a brief moment you'll feel like you're in ancient China rather than Honolulu.

CHINESE CULTURAL PLAZA On the way back to Chinatown, walk along the other side of Nuuanu Stream and stop at this Asian-style shopping mall bounded by Kukui, Maunakea and Beretania streets, and by the stream. You'll find porcelain, Chinese jewelry, housewares, gifts, medicinal herbs, Chinese cake shops and several restaurants. Don't miss the open-air market selling fresh vegetables, tropical fruits, fish, chicken feet, pigs' heads and other exotic items. The market entrance is in the back of the plaza.

HAWAII THEATRE ✉1130 Bethel Street; Between Hotel and Pauahi streets ☎808-528-0506 (box office), 808-791-1306 📠808-528-1675 ⌨www.hawaiitheatre.com After years of painstaking restoration, this revitalized theater on the outskirts of Chinatown is a study in neoclassical architecture. With gilded decor, Corinthian columns and striking mosaics, it has been elevated again to the grand status it enjoyed when the theater first opened in 1922. In 1929, it was the first movie theater in the islands to show movies with sound. Tours are available at this nationally registered historic place on Tuesdays. Shows, concerts, festivals, ethnic programs and films are presented here. Closed Monday. Admission.

LODGING

ASTON AT THE EXECUTIVE CENTRE HOTEL

$$$$　125 ROOMS　✉1088 Bishop Street　✆808-539-3000, 877-997-6667
📠808-523-1088　⌨www.astonhotels.com, res.exc@astonhotels.com

This highrise in the financial district, with its location and perks aimed at business folks (computer ports, in-room high-speed internet, daily newspaper) make it an ideal spot for a business trip. Other amenities include laundry facilities and complimentary breakfast.

NUUANU YMCA

$　70 ROOMS　✉1441 Pali Highway　✆808-536-3556　📠808-521-1181
⌨www.ymcahonolulu.org, tragossnig@ymcahonolulu.org

The Y has inexpensive one-person accommodations for men. Complete athletic facilities are available to make it more enticing. No reservations.

DINING

Downtown

As you get away from Waikiki you'll be dining with a more local crowd and tasting foods more representative of island cuisine, so I would certainly advise checking out some of Honolulu's eating places.

BA-LE SANDWICH SHOP

$　VIETNAMESE　✉1154 Fort Street Mall　✆808-521-4117
📠808-521-4117

The menu at this eatery specializes in the delicious concept of "gourmet Vietnamese sandwiches": loaves of French bread layered with various meats and marinated vegetables. Request it spicy; you can cool off your mouth after the meal with a choice from the long list of soothing puddings. No dinner on Saturday. Closed Sunday.

AUNTIE PASTO'S

$–$$　ITALIAN　✉1099 South Beretania Street　✆808-523-8855　📠808-524-6267
⌨www.auntiepastos.com

Auntie Pasto's is a popular Italian restaurant with oilcloth on the tables and a map of the mother country tacked to the wall. Pasta is served with any of a dozen different sauces—meat sauce, clams and broccoli, creamy pesto, carbonara and seafood. There are salads aplenty plus an assortment of entrées that includes veal marsala, chicken cacciatore and calamari piccata. No lunch on weekends.

PAE THAI

$–$$　THAI　✉1246 South King Street　✆808-596-8106

For a taste of Southeast Asian cuisine, try this café where you can savor *tom yum* (spicy lemongrass soup), chicken satay or a tasty garlic shrimp dish in this comfortable space decorated with trinkets from Thailand. Closed Sunday and Monday.

5 DOWNTOWN HONOLULU DINING

MAKAI FOOD LANAI

$ INTERNATIONAL ✉Aloha Tower Marketplace, Pier 8 ☎808-528-5700
📠808-524-8334

Up on the second level of the Aloha Tower Marketplace, toward the back overlooking the water, there's the Makai Food Lanai. This cluster of food stands ranges from **Casa Mia** (Italian) to **Aloha Tower BBQ** (local-style) to **Kabuto** (Japanese). There is comfortable seating at this food court.

CHAI'S ISLAND BISTRO

$$$$ PACIFIC RIM/AMERICAN ✉Aloha Tower Marketplace, 1 Aloha Tower Drive
☎808-585-0011 📠808-585-0012 ✐www.chaisislandbistro.com,
chai@chaisislandbistro.com

Satisfying your senses is easy here. Ample portions of distinctive dishes such as crispy snapper with sundried tomato citrus beurre blanc or grilled Mongolian lamb chops with brandy sate the taste buds, while the presentation pleases the eyes. The service is friendly and evening brings the sounds of Hawaii's contemporary musicians to touch your heart. No lunch Saturday, Sunday or Monday.

PEOPLE'S CAFÉ

$ LOCAL-STYLE ✉1310 Pali Highway ☎808-536-5789 📠808-536-5789

Near the city's financial center there's a funky restaurant that I particularly like. With a primarily Polynesian menu, this is a good spot to order poi, *lomi* salmon, *kalua* pig and other island favorites. *Ono, ono!* Closed Sunday.

BRASSERIE DU VIN

$$-$$$ FRENCH ✉1115 Bethel Street ☎808-545-1115
✐www.brasserieduvin.com

When Du Vin opened, Oahu residents cheered. Finally, authentic French fare in an unpretentious setting. There was much buzz about the wine bar, a stylish tavern that boasts a wine list with more than 250 selections. An outdoor patio leads to a second salon, giving patrons a choice of settings to enjoy favorites like duck confit, *croque monsieur* and shoestring *pommes frites* (which, naturally, come wrapped in newspaper). Located across the street from the Hawaii Theatre, it's an ideal stop for pre- or post-show drinks.

LA MARIANA SAILING CLUB

$$-$$$ AMERICAN/SEAFOOD ✉50 Sand Island Access Road
☎808-848-2800 📠808-841-2173

There is nothing else in Honolulu quite like this place. Located on the shores of the Keehi Lagoon and reached through the industrial port area off Sand Island Access Road, La Mariana plays host to tourists as well as an assortment of old salts who dance the hula, sing, party and provide more local color than you'll find just about anywhere else in town. What's more, the food, with a focus on fresh fish, seafood, prime rib and steaks, is good and the service friendly.

SUSHI KAHUNA

$ SUSHI   ✉ *212 Merchant Street* ☎ *808-545-7848*

A lunchtime-only spot for Japanese rolls, Sushi Kahama serves upscale-sushi-bar delicacies at downhome prices. Located in a downtown minimall, The Arcade, this four-table-and-counter café is a real find. Closed weekends.

Waterfront
FISHERMAN'S WHARF

$$–$$$ SEAFOOD   ✉ *1009 Ala Moana Boulevard* ☎ *808-538-3808* ✆ *808-521-5210*

Right next door to Honolulu's fishing fleet you'll find a tourist dining establishment that's been serving up platters for years. It has an authentic seafront feel because it is where the fishing boats actually come in. There are seafood dishes as well as pasta and steaks. No lunch on weekends.

JOHN DOMINIS

$$$–$$$$ SEAFOOD   ✉ *43 Ahui Street* ☎ *808-523-0955* ✆ *808-526-3758*
✑ *www.johndominis.com, jdominis@lava.net*

Fresh *onaga*, mahimahi, *opakapaka* and *ahi* highlight the vast seafood menu here. This sprawling establishment midway between Waikiki and Downtown Honolulu features huge pools filled with live fish. The wood-paneled dining room overlooks the water and the chefs know as much about preparing seafood as the original Polynesians. For landlubbers, steak and veal are also on the menu. The lounge features an extensive list of appetizers and wines by the glass. Sunday brunch; no dinner on Monday.

NICO'S PIER 38

$$ PLATE LUNCHES   ✉ *1133 North Nimitz Highway* ☎ *808-540-1377*
✆ *808-540-1376* ✑ *www.nicospier38.com*

Enjoy a meal of island favorites prepared with the skill and subtleties of chef Nicolas "Nico" Chaize's French culinary training. Plate lunches are elevated to another level with *hoisin* barbecue chicken and homemade hamburger steak with mushroom-onion gravy. Or try the grilled *ahi* baguette sandwich with arugula, tomato and wasabi aioli. In the morning, you can order sweet bread French toast or a hearty fried rice with ham, Portuguese sausage, bacon and *kamaboko* (fishcake). Breakfast and lunch only. Closed Sunday.

Chinatown
CHAR SIU HOUSE

$ CHINESE   ✉ *1134 Maunakea Street* ☎ *808-536-1588*

This tight and tidy spot in the Chinatown corridor is reputed to have the best *char siu* in the area. Yes, it's a meat market with cooked birds hanging in the window, but if you're looking for a filling and tasty lunch at an unbeatable price ($4–$6), this take-out joint is the way to go. They sell plates with generous scoops of rice and your choice of roast duck, roast chicken, roast pork and, of course, *char siu*, and they even throw in some greens to boot.

MYLAN RESTAURANT

$–$$ VIETNAMESE   ✉ *1160 Maunakea Street*   ✆ *808-528-3663*

Right in the heart of Chinatown, it may be small, but this café represents a triple threat to the competition—attractive decor, good prices and excellent food. The menu covers the spectrum of Vietnamese dishes, with a smattering of Italian and vegetarian fare, and the interior, lined with tropical paintings, is easy on the eyes.

CHAR HUNG SUT

$ CHINESE   ✉ *64 North Pauahi Street*   ✆ *808-538-3335*

This hole-in-the-wall take-out joint is short on ambience, but locals line up for the shredded-pork buns (*manapua*), pork hash, half-moon dumplings, sweet rice cakes and other tasty treats, buying dozens at a time. Get there early or you may be disappointed—favorites can, and do, run out before day's end. Closed Tuesday.

MAUNAKEA MARKETPLACE

$–$$ INTERNATIONAL   ✉ *Hotel and Maunakea streets*

There's a little bit of every other Asian cuisine in this compact food court that adjoins a fish and produce market. Here you'll find vendors dispensing steaming plates of Thai, Chinese, Japanese, Filipino, Korean and Vietnamese food. Small tables pushed together between the two rows of food stalls form an intimate but noisy eating area. Perfect for those counting pennies.

TAI PAN DIM SUM

$–$$ CHINESE   ✉ *Chinese Cultural Plaza, 100 North Beretania Street*
✆ *808-599-8899*

Drawing an overflow crowd of locals, Tai Pan is well-loved for its bite-sized delicacies such as *char siu* buns (baked and steamed), shrimp dumplings, bean curd rolls and pork ribs in black bean sauce. The fluorescent-lit room, tightly packed with tables, may lack pizzazz, but the authentic food is flavorful and reasonably priced.

LEGEND BUDDHIST VEGETARIAN RESTAURANT

$ CHINESE   ✉ *Chinese Cultural Plaza, 100 North Beretania Street*   ✆ *808-532-8218*

For anyone who thinks a meal without meat isn't a meal, a visit here might make a health food nut out of you. Yes, it's vegan (i.e., no animal products) and the decor is uninspired—but the dim sum is darn good. Run by the same people as Legend Seafood Restaurant, this eatery is located in the same building. No dinner. Closed Wednesday.

TO CHAU

$ VIETNAMESE   ✉1007 River Street   ☎808-533-4549

There's little atmosphere at this no-nonsense, formica-table place. What you will find, however, is excellent *pho*, the popular Vietnamese soup, and other simple dishes from that region at very low prices. But be prepared to wait a bit as it usually draws a crowd.

MABUHAY CAFÉ

$–$$ FILIPINO   ✉1049 River Street   ☎808-545-1956

For Filipino food, this café comes recommended by several readers. It's a plainly adorned place on the edge of Chinatown that serves a largely local clientele. The menu is extensive, covering all types of Filipino dishes like fried *lumpia* and pork *adobo*.

DUC'S BISTRO

$$–$$$ FRENCH-VIETNAMESE   ✉1188 Maunakea Street   ☎808-531-6325   🖰www.bucsbistro.com

Eating at Duc's Bistro is like entering a French salon. This quiet oasis may be on the edge of Chinatown, but it seems a world away. White tablecloths and vases full of flowers adorn the tables and gallery-quality paintings decorate the walls. A soothing atmosphere has gained this restaurant a loyal following among locals. Fresh fish, prawns, duck and chicken are prepared French fashion with a touch of Vietnam. Try the veal spring rolls with shiitake mushrooms and jicama, or, for an entrée, the lamb tenderloin with curry, *la lot* and roasted peanuts is delicious. No lunch on Saturday. Closed Sunday.

LITTLE VILLAGE NOODLE HOUSE

$–$$ CHINESE   ✉1113 Smith Street   ☎808-545-3008   🖷808-545-3738   🖰www.littlevillagehawaii.com

If you're looking for tasty pot stickers, stop at this delightful spot, which specializes in Chinese dumplings stuffed with a wide range of vegetarian and meat fillings. The pan-fried beef and walnut shrimp, garlic spinach and special fried rice are winners, too.

INDIGO

$$–$$$ ASIAN   ✉1121 Nuuanu Avenue   ☎808-521-2900   🖷808-537-4164   🖰www.indigo-hawaii.com, indigo@cchono.com

One of Chinatown's treats, this Eurasian dining room has bright art on white walls, white tablecloths and dark furniture. You can expect more than a dozen dim sum dishes. The soups and salads include tomato-garlic crab soup and goat cheese wontons. Among the entrées, they offer miso-marinated seared salmon and Mongolian lamb chops with mint-tangerine sauce. What an adventure! No lunch Saturday. Closed Sunday and Monday.

ZAFFRON RESTAURANT

$–$$ INDIAN   ✉69 North King Street   ☎808-533-6635   🖰www.zaffronhawaii.com, zaffronhawaii@zaffronhawaii.com

The decor belies the food at the Zaffron Restaurant. Fairly uninteresting red booths, stiff-backed chairs lining long picnic-like tables and a nightly buffet do not an exotic experience make. But the North Indian food itself will transport you and the prices will keep you there. Try the chick pea curry and the chai tea, and order as much *naan* bread as you can stuff in. No lunch Sunday; no dinner Sunday through Tuesday.

SAM CHOY'S BREAKFAST LUNCH & CRAB

$$–$$$ HAWAII REGIONAL   ✉*580 North Nimitz Highway*   📞*808-545-7979*
📠*808-545-7997*   🖥*www.samchoy.com*

A giant red neon sign announces that you've arrived at this noisy, bustling restaurant with marine decor accentuated by a dry-docked fishing boat. Chef Sam Choy, a local boy who has helped Hawaii Regional cuisine establish an international reputation, serves crab (Dungeness, Maryland Blue, Florida Gold, Alaskan king) fresh from the open kitchen. There's also lobster, shrimp, fish and, for those unclear on the concept, chicken and beef dishes.

SHOPPING

Downtown
LAI FONG DEPARTMENT STORE ✉*1118 Nuuanu Avenue* 📞*808-537-3497* This eclectic shop has been here for more than 70 years, and it is like an attic full of keepsakes stacked to the rafters. Among the Oriental antiques are carved pieces of ivory and jade, Chinese porcelain, teakwood and rosewood furniture, and *cheongsam*—silk dresses that are Shanghai's modern adaptation of the traditional *qipao*.

Waterfront
ALOHA TOWER MARKETPLACE ✉*Pier 8* 📞*808-528-5700* 🖥*www.alohatower.com* A California-style affair complete with white stucco walls and curved tile roof, this marketplace is located on the waterfront overlooking Honolulu Harbor. It's tucked between the Hawaii Maritime Museum and Aloha Tower, and is set near one of the busiest parts of the harbor. With its flagstone walkways and open-air courtyards, it's worth stopping by even if buying something is the last thing on your mind. Among the over 70 shops are about 25 devoted to apparel, a handful of galleries and perhaps three dozen specialty shops. Bring back a piece of Hawaii's musical tradition from **Hawaiian Ukulele** (808-536-3228; www.thehawaiianukulelecompany.com).

Chinatown
If you're seeking Asian items, then Chinatown is the place. Spotted throughout this neighborhood are small shops selling statuettes, pottery and other curios.

CHINESE CULTURAL PLAZA ✉*Corner of Beretania and Maunakea streets* 📞*808-521-4934* It's worthwhile to wander through this mall filled with Asian jewelers, bookstores and knickknack shops.

MAUNAKEA STREET FLORIST

✉*1189 Maunakea Street* ☎*808-537-2373* 🖱*www.flowerleis.net* Abundant on Maunakea Street are lei shops. Perhaps more than anything else, leis are symbolic of the beauty and generosity of Hawaii. Originally designed as a token of esteem for gods, family and oneself, they're still given on all types of occasions. You'll have no trouble tracking down a lei in Chinatown, but to narrow down your search, give Maunakea Street Florist a try. They're fairly inexpensive and are open late. You can also ship your purchases home.

TEA AT 1024 ✉*1024 Nuuanu Avenue* ☎*808-521-9596* Here they sell tea and assorted accessories for brewing the perfect cup. This shop also carries local artwork and contemporary clothing. Ladies and gentlemen are welcome to take high tea Tuesday through Saturday.

C-MUI CENTER

✉*1111 Bethel Street* ☎*808-536-4712* Crack seed, a variety of local snacks also known as *li hing mui*, is made from sweet-and-sour preserved fruit, a concept introduced by Chinese plantation workers. Crack seed stores are like candy stores for locals, and you'll find them sprinkled throughout the island. At C-Mui, big glass jars filled with crack seed favorites line the walls, offering dozens of lip-puckering, mouth-watering choices.

OPEN MARKET

✉*Along North King Street between River and Kekaulike streets* Don't miss this great place to shop for fresh foods. There are numerous stands selling fish, produce, poultry, meat, baked goods and island fruits, all at low-overhead prices. Arrive early, as the best picks are gone by noon.

PEGGE HOPPER GALLERY ✉*1164 Nuuanu Avenue* ☎*808-524-1160* 🖱*www.peggehopper.com, sales@peggehopper.com* At the edge of Chinatown along Nuuanu Avenue are several galleries and shops worthy of a visit. The Pegge Hopper Gallery displays acrylic paintings and the female portraits for which she is renowned. Open Tuesday through Friday or by appointment.

HILO HATTIE'S ✉*700 North Nimitz Highway* ☎*888-526-0299* 📠*888-526-5696* 🖱*www.hilohattie.com* Need a hula-girl duster, surfboard lamp, tiki mask or pineapple salad servers? You'll find this and much more at Hilo Hattie's, a tourist emporium of all things kitschy located just outside of Chinatown. They also sell more sedate items such as sarongs, slippers, silk aloha shirts, cookbooks and CDs. Though some of the food products (mac nuts, candies) are overpriced, they have the most extensive collection of island souvenirs you'll find under one roof.

NIGHTLIFE

HONOLULU THEATER FOR YOUTH ⊠*229 Queen Emma's Square* ☏*808-839-9885, 808-457-4254 (box office)* ✆*808-839-7018* ✍*www.htyweb.org, htymail@htyweb.org* A variety of youth- and family-oriented productions are performed by this young theater team at the Tenney Theatre at St. Andrew's Cathedral. The company also tours the neighbor islands. Reservations are recommended.

CHAMBER MUSIC HAWAII ☏*808-489-5038 (tickets)* ✍*www.chambermusichawaii.com* For something more refined and classical, consider an evening of fine vocal performance from this chamber group, which presents a series of concerts annually at several different locations around the city, including the Honolulu Academy of Arts. They also perform on the windward side of the island.

HONOLULU SYMPHONY ☏*808-524-0815, 808-792-2000 (box office)* ✆*808-528-2658* ✍*ww.honolulusymphony.com* The symphony's season runs from September to May, and provides a diverse schedule of programs. They perform at the Neal Blaisdell Center at Ward and King streets.

HAWAII OPERA THEATRE ⊠*987 Waimanu Street* ☏*808-596-7372, 808-596-7858 (box office)* ✍*www.hawaiiopera.org* Here you can see works such as Saint-Saens' *Samson and Delilah*, Puccini's *Madame Butterfly* and *Die Fledermaus* by Strauss. This regional company features stars from the international opera scene.

CHAI'S ISLAND BISTRO
⊠*Aloha Tower Marketplace, 1 Aloha Tower Drive* ☏*808-585-0011* ✍*www.chaisislandbistro.com, chai@chaisislandbistro.com* In a fairly intimate setting—you can get up close and personal, especially if you come early and have dinner—this bistro often hosts Hawaiian entertainers. Call and check who will be there—you're apt to find Jerry Santos, the Brothers Cazimero or Makaha Sons.

THIRTYNINEHOTEL ⊠*39 North Hotel Street* ☏*808-599-2552* ✍*www.thirtyninehotel.com* For a bit of swanky New York culture, join the young fashionistas at this pinnacle of hipness in Honolulu's Chinatown. Dance in the gallery, which is perpetually filled with quality, contemporary art, or sip a cocktail and soak in the well-populated, *trés chic* atmosphere. Closed Sunday and Monday.

LA MARIANA SAILING CLUB
⊠*50 Sand Island Access Road* ☏*808-848-2800* ✆*808-841-2173* Nightly live piano music adds to the party atmosphere at this oldtime tiki bar teeming with local color. A throwback to 1950s Hawaii.

THE LIVING ROOM ✉ *Fisherman's Wharf, 1009 Ala Moana Boulevard* ✆ *808-524-0150* ✎ *www.thelivingroomhawaii.com* Once the cool new kid on the block, this nightclub has come of age, but is not showing it one bit. The two-story club, formerly a ho-hum seafood restaurant, sits harborside, giving patrons looking out the window the distinct sensation of being at sea. Downstairs, the scene is more casual with pool tables, dartboards and a bar. A winding staircase leads to the upstairs lounge that features a bar on one end, a dancefloor on the other and large, comfy sofas (hence the name) in between. The jet-set crowd likes to gather here to dance to hip-hop, reggae, house and soul, spun by Honolulu's most prominent deejays.

INDIGO ✉ *1121 Nuuanu Avenue* ✆ *808-521-2900* ✎ *www.indigo-hawaii.com* An attractive Asian restaurant with a patio, this spot has hip-hop dancing, acoustic jazz and contemporary music Tuesday through Saturday. On several nights the sound is live; other nights it's deejay driven. Closed Sunday and Monday. Occasional cover.

ARTS AT MARK'S GARAGE ✉ *1159 Nuuanu Avenue* ✆ *808-521-2903* ✎ *www.artsatmarks.com* Stop at this gallery and performance space to catch some improvisational comedy. Other nights, Mark's also hosts art exhibits, jazz and dance performances and poetry slams.

HAWAII THEATRE ✉ *1130 Bethel Street* ✆ *808-791-1306, 808-528-0506 (tickets)* ✎ *www.hawaiitheatre.com* Shows here run the gamut from the best in Broadway performances to dance troupes, classical music and much more. The **Hawaii International Film Festival** (www.hiff.org) is held here late in the year (among other venues).

REGAL DOLE CANNERY 18 THEATRES ✉ *735-B Iwilei Road* ✆ *808-528-3653* If you're in the mood for a movie fix, head to this theater complex, a short drive from Chinatown. Hawaii's largest cineplex with 18 screens, it also features the state's best cinematic selection, including foreign films you'll find nowhere else on the island.

BEACHES & PARKS

KAKAAKO
WATERFRONT PARK
✉ *End of Cooke Street off Ala Moana Boulevard*

🏃 Located near downtown Honolulu and popular with local picnickers, this rock-fringed park has a promenade with an uninterrupted view spanning from Diamond Head to the harbor. There are picnic tables, pavilions, showers, restrooms and large, grassy plots. There's no swimming here, but at the east end of the park is an excellent surf spot called "Kewalos" that is dear to waveriders—so dear, in fact, that a coalition of surfers fought to stave off a luxury development that threatened to limit public access to the park. A short paddle away, there is also a surf spot called "Point Panic," the only wave on the island reserved exclusively for bodysurfers.

SAND ISLAND STATE RECREATION AREA

✉ *From Waikiki, take Ala Moana Boulevard and Nimitz Highway several miles west to Sand Island Access Road* ☎ *808-587-0300*

🛶 This 140-acre park wraps around the south and east shores of Sand Island, with sections fronting both Honolulu Harbor and the open sea. Despite the name, there's only a small sandy beach here, and jet traffic from nearby Honolulu International might disturb your snoozing. But there is a great view of Honolulu. While the swimming and snorkeling are poor here, you'll find a summertime surf break and fishing is usually rewarding. Watch out for the coral and sharp rocks on the bottom; the sharks and pollution can also put a damper on your rides. *Papio* and *moano* are the prime catches. Facilities include restrooms and a picnic area.

▲ Tent camping available in the grassy area facing the ocean, Friday through Sunday nights only. State permit required.

GREATER HONOLULU

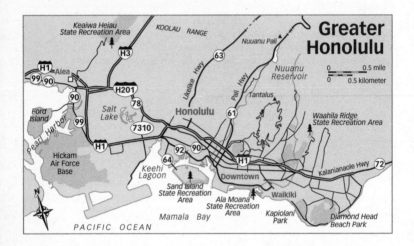

Framed by the Waianae Range in the west and the Koolau Range to the east, Honolulu is a nonstop drama presented within a natural amphitheater. Honolulu Harbor sets the stage to the south; at the center lie Waikiki and Downtown Honolulu. Wrapped around these tourist and business centers is a rainbow-shaped congeries of sights and places that, for lack of a better name, constitutes "Greater Honolulu."

Greater Honolulu is where most of the people of Honolulu live. It extends from navy-gray Pearl Harbor to the turquoise waters of the prestigious Kahala district and holds in its ambit some of the city's prettiest territory. Here are working-class enclaves with neat, even rows of houses and wonderful ethnic restaurants. Here, too, is the realm of the well-to-do with their neighborhoods by the waterfront and homes perched on the hillsides overlooking the city.

Each part of greater Honolulu is defined not only by its geographic characteristics but also by the type of people who settled there. Manoa Valley, for example, became home to the descendants of the early missionaries, who built New England saltbox–style homes quite different than those in other areas. Portuguese immigrants, many of whose families had come to work on the sugar plantations, put down roots on the slopes of Punchbowl and named their streets after Lisbon, the Azores, Madeira and other places that reminded them of home.

The points of interest are dotted all across the city and require a bit of planning to see. You'll need to ride buses or taxis or rent a car, but it is well worth the extra effort. You'll be away from the crowds of tourists and get a chance to meet the locals and get a singular perspective on island life and culture.

SIGHTS

Kalihi–Nuuanu Avenue Area

The first district in Greater Honolulu is actually within walking distance of Downtown Honolulu, but it's a relatively long walk, so transportation is generally advised. Nuuanu Avenue begins downtown and travels uphill in a northeasterly direction past several noteworthy points.

SOTO MISSION OF HAWAII ✉ *1708 Nuuanu Avenue* ✆ *808-537-9409*
Home of a meditative Zen sect, Soto Mission is one of the first spots you'll see along Nuuanu Avenue. Modeled after a temple in India where the Buddha gave his first sermon, this building is marked by dramatic towers, and beautiful Japanese bonsai plants decorate the landscape.

HONOLULU MYOHOJI TEMPLE ✉ *2003 Nuuanu Avenue* ✆ *808-524-7790*
Here and at the nearby Soto Mission the city seems like a distant memory. This building, placidly situated along a small stream, is capped by a peace tower.

HONOLULU MEMORIAL PARK ✉ *22 Craigside Place* ✆ *808-537-4303*
✐ *www.honolulumemorialpark.com* Uphill from Honolulu Myohoji Temple and Soto Mission lies this memorial park. There is an ancestral monument here, bordered on three sides by a pond of flashing carp and a striking three-tiered pagoda. This entire area is a center of simple yet beautiful Asian places of worship.

HAWAII TENRI CULTURAL CENTER ✉ *2236 Nuuanu Avenue* ✆ *808-538-7671* This is a woodframe temple that was moved here all the way from Japan. One intriguing fact about this fragile structure is that large sections were built without nails.

ROYAL MAUSOLEUM
✉ *2261 Nuuanu Avenue* The Hawaiian people have an important center here–the Royal Mausoleum, which is situated across the street from the Hawaii Tenri Cultural Center. This was the final resting place for two of Hawaii's royal families, the Kamehameha and Kalakaua clans. Together they ruled 19th-century Hawaii. Today the area is a state monument landscaped with palms, ginger, plumeria and other beautiful tropical plants and flowers. Closed weekends.

KALIHI One of the oldest neighborhoods, Kalihi, still thrives as a working-class enclave west of downtown. As Honolulu grew, wealthy and middle-class people moved farther eastward and northward to the outer reaches of the city. The poorer Hawaiian residents of Kalihi were joined by immigrants and people leaving the plantations for an urban lifestyle. In Kalihi, they were close to factory jobs and small farms still

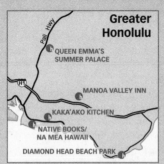

scattered through the area. They opened clubs and restaurants and established schools and churches, many of which still exist today.

Punchbowl and Tantalus

It is a few miles from Downtown Honolulu to Punchbowl, the circular center of an extinct volcano. You'll find it northeast of town, at the end of Ward Avenue and just off Prospect Drive, which circles the crater. A youngster in geologic terms, the volcano is a mere 150,000 years old. From the lip of the crater, there is a marvelous vista sweeping down to Diamond Head, across Honolulu and all the way out to the Waianae Range.

NATIONAL MEMORIAL CEMETERY OF THE PACIFIC ✉2177 *Puowaina Drive* ☎808-532-3720 The most important feature in Punchbowl is the National Memorial Cemetery, located in the crater known as *Puowaina*, Hawaiian for "hill of sacrifice." Over 42,000 war dead have been interred, including victims of both World Wars, as well as the Korean, Spanish-American, Vietnam and Iraq wars. President Barack Obama has stopped here to pay homage to his grandfather, a WWII veteran.

There is also an impressive monument to the "Courts of the Missing," which lists the names of soldiers missing in action. Ironically, of all the people buried here, the most famous was not a soldier but a journalist—Ernie Pyle, whose World War II stories about the average GI were eagerly followed by an entire nation. Near his grave you will also find the burial site of Hawaii's first astronaut, Ellison Onizuka, who died in the *Challenger* space shuttle disaster. Guided walking tours (fee) are arranged through the American Legion (808-946-6383).

TANTALUS

You can explore the heights by following Tantalus Drive as it winds up the side of this 2013-foot mountain. Together with Round Top Drive, Tantalus Drive forms a loop that circles through the residential areas hidden within this rainforest. There are spectacular views all along the route, as well as hiking trails that lead from the road into verdant hilltop regions. Here you'll encounter guava, banana and eucalyptus trees as well as wildflowers such as ginger, and an occasional wild pig.

CONTEMPORARY MUSEUM ✉2411 Makiki Heights Drive ✆808-526-0232 ✆808-536-5973 ✐www.tcmhi.org, info@tcmhi.org For art lovers, a stop at this museum is a must. In addition to changing exhibitions of contemporary art, it features the works of several well-known artists in its sculpture garden and galleries, including David Hockney, Robert Arneson, Charles Arnoldi and Tom Wesselman. Boasting five galleries, an inspired gift shop and a gourmet café, the museum is nevertheless upstaged by its magnificently landscaped grounds. Closed Monday. Admission.

PUU UALAKAA PARK One of the best views in all of the Punchbowl–Tantalus area is found at this lovely retreat located along the drive. The vista here extends from Diamond Head west to Pearl Harbor, encompassing in its course a giant swath of Honolulu and the Pacific. If you were a fan of *Blue Hawaii*, you might recall the view from here. It's where Elvis decides he wants to become a tour guide.

Cross-Island Express

Along the outskirts of Honolulu, there are several more points of interest. The best way to tour them is while traveling along the two highways that cut across the Koolaus, connecting Honolulu directly with the island's Windward Coast: the Likelike Highway (Route 63) and the Pali Highway (Route 61). The Likelike Highway can be reached from Route H-1, the superhighway that serves Honolulu. Before heading up into the mountains to tour other sites, you will encounter the Bishop Museum near the intersection of Routes 63 and H-1.

BISHOP MUSEUM

✉1525 Bernice Street ✆808-847-3511 ✆808-841-8968 ✐www.bishop museum.org, membership@bishopmuseum.org Founded in 1889 by Charles Reed Bishop in honor of his late wife, Princess Bernice Pauahi

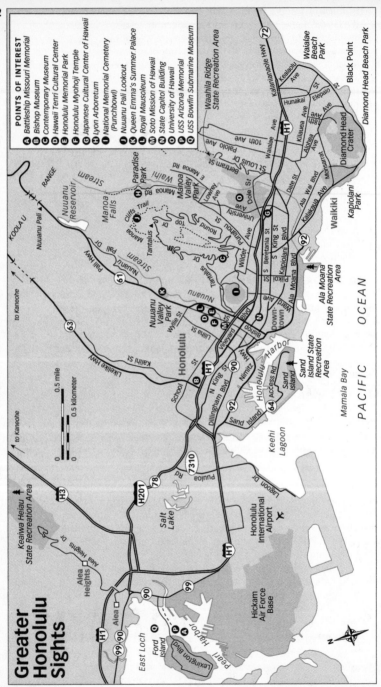

Greater Honolulu Sights

POINTS OF INTEREST

A Battleship Missouri Memorial
B Bishop Museum
C Contemporary Museum
D Hawaii Tenri Cultural Center
E Honolulu Memorial Park
F Japanese Cultural Center of Hawaii
G Honolulu Myohoji Temple
H Lyon Arboretum
I National Memorial Cemetery (Punchbowl)
J Nuuanu Pali Lookout
K Queen Emma's Summer Palace
L Royal Mausoleum
M State Capitol Building
N Soto Mission of Hawaii
O University of Hawaii
P USS Arizona Memorial
Q USS Bowfin Submarine Museum

Bishop, the last descendant of the royal Kamehameha family, the Bishop Museum now includes a plethora of artifacts, documents and photographs about Hawaii, as well as other Pacific island cultures. Built on the original site of the Kamehameha Schools for Boys, a school established to educate Hawaiian children, the museum was created to augment their education and instill a greater pride in their Hawaiian heritage. The one remaining building from the school, which was relocated in the '60s, is Bishop Hall. The museum is a must-see for anyone interested in Hawaiiana.

Here you'll also find an outrigger canoe, thrones, primitive artworks and fascinating natural history exhibits. There are drums made with shark skin, and helmets decorated with dog teeth and pearl shells. The 19th-century whaling trade is represented with menacing harpoons and yellowing photographs of the oil-laden ships. Of all the exhibits, the most spectacular are cloaks worn by Hawaiian kings and fashioned from tens of thousands of tiny feathers. There are displays capturing the Japanese, Chinese and Filipino heritage in Hawaii and a hall devoted to other cultures of the Pacific. The museum also houses a planetarium, various children's activities, and a gift shop. The Bishop is truly one of the finest museums of its kind in the world. Admission.

QUEEN EMMA'S SUMMER PALACE

✉ *2913 Pali Highway* ✆ *808-595-6291* 📠 *808-595-4395* ✐ *www.daughtersof hawaii.org* The other, more scenic road across the mountains is the Pali Highway, Route 61. As it ascends, it passes Queen Emma's Summer Palace. Constructed in 1848, the palace was originally used as a mountain home by King Kamehameha IV and his wife, Queen Emma. Today the gracious white-pillared house is a museum. Here you can view the Queen's personal artifacts, as well as various other period pieces. The Palace's gardens are especially beautiful; you can almost see the Queen entertaining her guests by the lily pond. The gift shop has a nice selection of local crafts and books. Admission.

NUUANU PALI DRIVE When visiting Queen Emma's Summer Palace, you can also walk the tree-shaded grounds of this scenic road and follow until it rejoins the highway. This residential boulevard, with its natural canopy and park-like atmosphere, is one of Honolulu's many idyllic hideaways.

NUUANU PALI LOOKOUT
Along Pali Highway there is a turnoff to a lookout—a point that must not be missed, and is without a doubt Oahu's finest view. Gaze down the sheer, rugged face of the Koolau cliffs as they drop 3000 feet to a softly rolling coastal shelf. Your view will ex-

tend from Makapuu Point to the distant reaches of Kaneohe Bay, and from the lip of the cliff far out to sea. It was from these heights, according to legend, that a vanquished army was forced to plunge when Kamehameha I captured Oahu in 1795. On the last Saturday of April, there is a sunrise ceremony commemorating this decisive battle. If dawn is too early, visit later when there's a free day-long cultural fair.

Pearl Harbor

Many people consider a trip here a pilgrimage. It was here on a sleepy Sunday morning, December 7, 1941, that the Japanese launched a sneak attack on the United States naval fleet anchored in the port, immediately plunging the nation into World War II. As Japanese planes bombed the harbor, over 2400 Americans lost their lives. Eighteen ships sank that day in the country's greatest military disaster. Pearl Harbor, several miles northwest of Downtown Honolulu, can be reached by car or bus.

USS ARIZONA MEMORIAL ✉ *Pearl Harbor* ✆ *808-422-2771* 🕾 *808-483-8608* ⌨ *www.nps. gov/usar* The battleship USS *Arizona* was hit so savagely by aerial bombs and torpedoes that it plunged to the bottom, entombing over 1100 sailors within its hulk; today they remain in that watery grave. A special USS *Arizona* Memorial was built to honor them; it's constructed directly above the ship, right in the middle of Pearl Harbor. The memorial includes a shrine with the name of each sailor who died aboard the ship carved in marble. Gazing at this too, too long list of names, and peering over the side at the shadowy hull of the ship, it's hard not to be overcome by the tragic history of the place. Daily from 7:30 a.m. to 5 p.m., there's a 75-minute program that includes free boat tours out to this fascinating memorial. Remember, no bathing suits, bare feet or bags are permitted.

USS BOWFIN SUBMARINE MUSEUM ✉ *Pearl Harbor* ✆ *808-423-1341* 🕾 *808-422-5201* ⌨ *www.bowfin.org, info@bowfin.org* Anchored nearby the *Arizona* visitors center, this World War II–era submarine is a window into life beneath the waves. It provides an excellent opportunity to tour the claustrophobic quarters in which 80 men spent months at a time. The accompanying museum, filled with submarine-related artifacts, will help provide an even fuller perspective. Admission.

BATTLESHIP MISSOURI MEMORIAL ✉ *Pearl Harbor* ✆ *808-455-1600, 877-644-4896* ⌨ *www.ussmissouri.org, mightymo@ussmissouri.org* For another perspective on World War II, visit this battleship memorial. Launched in 1944, the *Missouri*, or Mighty Mo as it is usually called, was the last U.S. battleship ever built. It was aboard this 887-foot vessel on September 2, 1945, that General Douglas MacArthur accepted the surrender of the Japanese forces, thus ending World War II. The decommissioned battleship is now docked in Pearl Harbor, off Ford Island, within sight of the USS *Arizona* Memorial. Tours depart from the ticket office of the *Bowfin* submarine. Guided tours are available, or you can tour the Mighty Mo on your own, getting a first-hand glimpse of its massive armaments, the surrender deck and the commanding bridge. Plan to spend an hour on the self-guided tour. Admission.

MOANALUA GARDENS ✉*Entrance and parking lot are along the Puuloa Road off-ramp from westbound Moanalua Freeway* ☎*808-833-1944* Following a heavy dose of historic WWII remembrance, Moanalua Gardens is an ideal place for quiet contemplation. Take a stroll or picnic on the 26-acre expanse of manicured lawns, part of a once-private estate now open to the public. The park is often deserted, perhaps due to the lack of facilities, so you'll be assured plenty of solitude for wandering among the native plants, koi pond and meandering stream. Kamehameha V's summer home is here as well. The trees, especially the centuries-old monkeypods, are the most outstanding feature of the park.

KEAIWA HEIAU STATE RECREATION AREA

✉*End of Aiea Heights Drive, Aiea 808-537-0800* A peaceful respite from the bustling city, this sacred site is named for an ancient temple that was once used for medicinal healing. Here, *kahuna*, or Hawaiian priests, would treat patients using plants and herbs from the surrounding forest, applying a holistic approach known as *laau lapaau*. See "Beaches & Parks" for more information.

Ala Moana Area

Bordering the *ewa* direction of Waikiki, just Diamond Head–side of Downtown Honolulu, is Ala Moana (which means "pathway to the sea"). Its claim to fame is a very large family-oriented park that extends from the Ala Wai Yacht Harbor along the ocean to Kewalo Basin.

ALA MOANA BEACH PARK Honolulu residents flock here on the weekends to hold family reunions or company picnics, or to play volleyball, softball or tennis with their friends; even President Obama has brought his family here for swimming and picnics. The sandy beach that lines the park is a safe place for swimmers, especially near **Magic Island** (Ala Moana Regional Park), the peninsula on the east side of the park. Long-distance swimmers practice swimming the length of the park, while joggers run alongside the shore to get into shape. Watching the sun set from this spot is the sport of choice for many locals and tourists alike.

ALA MOANA CENTER ✐*www.alamoana.com* Across the street from Ala Moana Beach Park, this shopping center is the shop-'til-you-drop capital of the islands (and almost anywhere else in the U.S.). In addition to over 209 shops, Ala Moana Center is the main transfer point for most island buses, so if you ride TheBus, you'll likely end up here at some point.

Moiliili–Kapahulu–Kaimuki Area

Just *mauka* (toward the mountains) of Ala Moana are several working-class communities—Moiliili, Kapahulu and Kaimuki. They skirt the University of Hawaii on one side and Waikiki on the other. What's best about these neighborhoods is the handful of restaurants that are far enough away from the madding crowd of Waikiki to make eating out a pleasure. Restaurants in every budget category can be found in these enclaves, and best of all, you'll more than likely be dining with a local crowd.

JAPANESE CULTURAL CENTER OF HAWAII

✉ *2454 South Beretania Street* ☎ *808-945-7633* 📠 *808-944-1123* 🖥 *www.jcch.com, info@jcch.com* In Moiliili, this cultural center sponsors a permanent exhibit focusing on the history of Japanese culture in Hawaii. In addition to the gallery, there's a gift shop, traditional martial arts dojo and teahouse. The Resource Center contains an extensive collection of books, pamphlets, periodicals and oral histories. The center also hosts cultural events and festivals marking traditional Japanese holidays; call ahead for details. Closed Sunday and Monday. Admission.

Manoa Valley Area

Residents of a different sort are found in the city's beautiful Manoa Valley, a couple of miles northeast of Waikiki. In the early 19th century, this upscale valley neighborhood that is home to the University of Hawaii served as a popular retreat of Hawaiian royalty. It was later settled by descendants of missionaries, who built homes reminiscent of their New England origins. The estate of the Cooke family, who founded Castle & Cooke, one of the Big Five companies that controlled the state, can also be found in Manoa.

The neighborhood was also settled by Chinese, who favored Manoa for its excellent *feng shui*. Because the mountains on both sides act as protection and funnel energy through the valley, the Chinese people believed living there would bring good luck. Manoa owes its natural heritage partly to the founder of the Lyons Arboretum, who at the turn of the 20th century planted trees from around the world in what was to become a verdant valley.

UNIVERSITY OF HAWAII ✉ *2444 Dole Street* ☎ *808-956-8111* 🖥 *www.hawaii.edu* The state university has its main campus in Manoa; almost 21,000 students and 1300 faculty members attend classes and teach on these beautifully landscaped grounds.

UNIVERSITY OF HAWAII ART GALLERY ✉ *Art Building, University of Hawaii at Manoa* ☎ *808-956-6888* 📠 *808-956-9659* 🖥 *www.hawaii.edu/artgallery, gallery@hawaii.edu* Don't miss the opportunity to visit the university's art gallery. Employing modular and movable walls, it constantly reinvents itself to the configurations of visiting exhibits. Exhibits here have included intricately patterned Japanese fishermen's coats, ethnic clothing from southwest China, and contemporary Korean art. You never know what the gallery will offer up. Closed Saturday and from mid-May to mid-August.

JOHN YOUNG MUSEUM OF ART ✉ *Krauss Hall, 2500 Dole Street* ☎ *808-956-3634* 🖥 *www.outreach.hawaii.edu/jymuseum* On a hot day, the John Young Museum of Art on campus may be just the place to take refuge. The museum centers around Asian art, including ancient Chinese tomb figures, modern Japanese pottery, Korean Buddha figurines and works from many other Asian nations. There's also tribal art and a variety of works from other parts of the world. After wandering around the exhibition area, take time to walk the grounds as well; there's a quiet courtyard with sculptures, a water garden and a reflecting pool. Closed Saturday.

EAST-WEST CENTER

✉ *John Burns Hall, 1601 East-West Road* ☎ *808-944-7111* 📠 *808-944-7376* 🖫 *www.eastwestcenter.org, ewcinfo@eastwestcenter.org* A non-profit research facility, this center is also part of the university. Designed by noted architect I. M. Pei, the center strives to promote the mutual understanding and cooperation among Pacific Rim cultures. The center also contains a number of priceless Asian artworks, a Japanese garden, waterfall and teahouse, well worth viewing. Closed Saturday and Sunday.

WAIOLI TEA ROOM ✉ *2950 Manoa Road* ☎ *808-988-5800* 🖫 *www.thewaioli tearoom.net* From campus you can head deeper into Manoa Valley along Oahu Avenue and Manoa Road. You'll pass this cozy dining room tucked into a garden setting where you can enjoy breakfast, lunch or high tea, a bakery and a gift shop. Here also is the **Little Grass Shack** that was once occupied by novelist Robert Louis Stevenson (or so the story goes), and a small chapel replete with stained-glass windows.

LYON ARBORETUM

✉ *3860 Manoa Road* ☎ *808-988-0456* 📠 *808-988-0462* 🖫 *www.hawaii.edu/ lyonarboretum* Farther down Manoa Road is a magnificent 194-acre garden with over 8000 plant species. The many trails offer leisurely walks throughout the gardens—my favorite is the "Ti Walk," which takes you up to the Bromeliad Garden and Inspiration Point. Cockatoos, mynas, thrushes, the endemic *amakihi* and numerous other bird species abound. You will also find, perhaps, the world's largest collection of palm trees. This is a wonderful place to while away a quiet afternoon. Closed Sunday.

Kahala Area

DIAMOND HEAD BEACH PARK This twisting ribbon of white sand is nestled directly below the famous crater. Whenever the wind and waves are good, you'll see windsurfers and surfers galore sweeping in toward the shoreline. The coral reef here makes for good skindiving, too. It's a pretty beach, backdropped by the Kuilei cliffs and watched over by the **Diamond Head Lighthouse**.

KAHALA DISTRICT From Diamond Head, continue east along Diamond Head Road and Kahala Avenue. These will lead through the Kahala District, home to the island's elite. Bordered by the ocean and the exclusive Waialae Country Club is a golden string of spectacular oceanfront homes with carefully manicured lawns. This neighborhood remains quiet and peaceful, blessed by the breezes that blow in from its shores and unsullied by the kind of development that has commercialized other urban beach areas. Although the beach is shaded by coconut palms, local residents don't have to worry about falling coconuts. They're all picked by local Tongan tree climbers, hired to prevent the dropping fruit from bonking heads.

SHANGRI LA

For details and tour options contact the Honolulu Academy of Arts 📞808-532-3853 🖥*www.shangrilahawaii.org* Tobacco heiress Doris Duke, a socialite celebrity of the mid-20th century, built a fantasy home on a five-acre site on the lava rock headland called **Black Point**, just to the east of Diamond Head. Duke, who died in 1993, created a museum of the house, which she'd romantically named Shangri La, after the legendary Himalayan valley where peace and good health prevailed. Intrigued by Islamic art, Duke designed the home with Islamic architectural features, furnishings and artworks. The museum is open to a limited number of visitors daily, with guided, small group tours departing from the Honolulu Academy of Arts. Advance bookings are recommended for the informative and entertaining docent-led tour.

LODGING

Pearl Harbor Area
BEST WESTERN PLAZA HOTEL

$$–$$$ 274 ROOMS ✉3253 North Nimitz Highway 📞808-836-3636, 800-800-4683 📠808-834-7406 🖥www.bestwesternhonolulu.com, info@bestwesternhonolulu.com

This is a convenient location that's just a half-mile away from the airport, a stone's throw from downtown and a great home base for visiting Pearl Harbor. The rooms are basic and comfortable; all have refrigerators. Amenities include a pool, a restaurant and free wi-fi. There's free shuttle service 24 hours a day to and from the airport.

PACIFIC MARINA INN

$$ 119 ROOMS ✉2628 Waiwai Loop 📞808-836-1131, 800-548-8040 📠808-833-0851 🖥www.castleresorts.com/pmi

Pacific Marina Inn bills itself as a "little oasis near the Honolulu airport." That may be hyperbolic, but it *is* convenient and comfortable: All the rooms have wi-fi, the suites have refrigerators, and there's free shuttle service to the airport, a swimming pool, a restaurant and laundry facilities, as well as karaoke in the bar. In addition, the hotel is adjacent to the Keehi Lagoon Park, where there are picnic areas and tennis courts.

Ala Moana Area
PAGODA HOTEL

$$$ 359 ROOMS ✉1525 Rycroft Street 📞808-941-6611, 800-367-6060 📠808-955-5067 🖥www.pagodahotel.com, pagres@hthcorp.com

Sufficiently removed from the crowds but still only a ten-minute drive from the beach is this bright, tropical-style hotel. Spacious studio and one-bedroom units put the accent on rattan furniture. The carpeted rooms feature views of the hotel garden or distant mountains. Units in the adjoining Pagoda Terrace offer kitchens. Ask for a room in the new wing, which is substantially nicer than the old one.

AQUA MARINA HOTEL

$$$ 136 ROOMS   ✉ *1700 Ala Moana Boulevard*   ☎ *808-942-7722, 866-406-2782*   📠 *808-942-1873*   🖱 *www.aquaresorts.com/marina*

In the same neighborhood as the Pagoda, you'll find the 40-floor Aqua Marina Hotel. The rooms have high-speed internet access, air conditioning, in-room refrigerators, coffee makers and cable television. Some of the units include kitchenettes; others have partial ocean views, although a cityscape is more common. The Aqua Marina is run more like a condominium than a hotel, with maid service just twice a week. It has a swimming pool and sauna, coin-operated laundry and on-site parking for a fee. The accommodations here are basic, but the locale is excellent.

YMCA CENTRAL BRANCH

$ 114 ROOMS   ✉ *401 Atkinson Drive*   ☎ *808-941-3344*   📠 *808-941-8821*   🖱 *www.ymcahonolulu.org, centralymca@ymcahonolulu.org*

This inexpensive place for both men and women is handily situated across the street from Ala Moana Center and a block from the beach. And you're welcome to use the gym, pool, saunas and television room. There's a Vietnamese restaurant on-site. You can also expect the usual Y ambience—long sterile hallways leading to an endless series of identical, cramped, uncarpeted rooms. The 20 rooms for women are a few dollars more than the dormitories for men, but they have private bathrooms. The low prices here help make up for the lack of amenities.

ALA MOANA HOTEL

$$$$ 1058 ROOMS   ✉ *410 Atkinson Drive*   ☎ *808-955-4811, 800-367-6025*   📠 *808-944-6839*   🖱 *www.alamoanahotel.com, reservations@alamoanahotel.com*

Here you'll find a nice balance of luxury and Hawaiian culture. The guest rooms are on the small side, but they have all the basic amenities and many have at least a partial view of the Koolau Mountains or the ocean. Hawaiians from other islands often stay here: You can walk to Ala Moana Shopping Center and Ala Moana Regional Park. The Hawaii Convention Center is just across the street, and Polynesian music and fire dance is performed nightly.

Manoa Valley Area
FERNHURST YWCA

$ 40 ROOMS   ✉ *1566 Wilder Avenue*   ☎ *808-941-2231*   📠 *808-945-9478*   🖱 *www.ywcaoahu.org, fernhurst@ywcaoahu.org*

In Manoa Valley, the Fernhurst YWCA is an appealing three-story low-rise that provides a residence for women and children (boys up to five years old). Rooms are single or double occupancy with shared baths. Among the facilities are high-speed internet, microwaves, laundry, dining room and lounge. Rates include breakfast and dinner.

HOSTELLING INTERNATIONAL—HONOLULU

$ 35 BEDS   ✉ *2323-A Sea View Avenue*   ☎ *808-946-0591*   📠 *808-946-5904*   🖱 *www.hostelsaloha.com, hihostel@lava.net*

This dormitory-style crash pad has separate living quarters for men and women, although there are two private rooms available. Shared kitchen facilities, television lounge, garden patio, laundry and internet access are available. Visitors can book island tours through the hostel.

MANOA VALLEY INN

$$ 8 ROOMS ✉2001 Vancouver Drive ☎808-947-6019 ☏808-946-6168
🖫www.manoavalleyinn.com, manoavalleyinn@aloha.net

Hawaii's foremost bed-and-breakfast inn rests in a magnificent old mansion near the University of Hawaii campus. Set in the lush Manoa Valley, this B&B is a 1912 cream-colored Victorian featuring seven guest rooms and an adjacent cottage. Decorated with patterned wallpaper and old-style artworks, the rooms are furnished in plump antique armchairs. Guests enjoy a spacious veranda and lawn. For luxury and privacy, this is a historic jewel. Complimentary breakfast.

Kahala Area
KAHALA HOTEL & RESORT

$$$$ 312 ROOMS ✉5000 Kahala Avenue ☎808-739-8888, 800-367-2525
☏808-739-8800 🖫www.kahalaresort.com, reservations@kahalaresort.com

For a real splurge, you might want to check into this resort. Located right on a secluded beach, this exclusive hostelry offers myriad activities for adults and kids. There's a lagoon where you can get up-close and personal (read: swim) with the resident dolphins. Or you can attend some of the complimentary fitness and cultural (lei-making, ukulele-playing) classes. From 10:30 a.m. to 9 p.m., guests at the Kahala Hotel & Resort have access to a free shopping shuttle that hits all the biggies: Ala Moana Center, Kahala Mall and the Royal Hawaiian Shopping Center.

DINING

Kalihi–Nuuanu Avenue Area

MEG'S DRIVE-IN

$ PLATE LUNCHES ✉743 Waiakamilo Road ☎808-845-3943

In Kalihi, Meg's is a small eatery serving breakfast, local-style plate lunches and daily specials. You can take your meal to go or dine on the adjoining lanai. No dinner Saturday. Closed Sunday.

HELENA'S
HAWAIIAN FOODS

$ HAWAIIAN ✉1240 North School Street ☎808-845-8044

Quietly hidden away in a tiny storefront in the Kalihi district, Helena's has been dishing up *kalua* pig, *lomi* salmon and *pipi-kaula* for more than 50 years. The food is served in tiny dishes, so you can sample a selection. The luau chicken cooked with taro leaves and coconut milk is a knockout. The place only has 13 ta-

bles, which means there's often a wait—but it's worth it. Closed
Saturday through Monday.

LILIHA BAKERY

$-$$ LOCAL-STYLE/AMERICAN   ✉*515 North Kuakini Street*   ☎*808-531-1651*

Ask any Honolulu resident about the best pastry in town, and chances
are they'll point you here. This half-century-old institution is home to
the "coco puff," a chocolate-filled cream puff topped with chantilly
frosting—they sell more than 3600 a day. Complementing the busy
bakery is an old-fashioned diner that has one long counter and 15 or so
barstools. It's open 24 hours and popular with the after-hours crowd
who like to soak up their drink with a hearty plate of sausage and eggs.

LILIHA
SEAFOOD RESTAURANT

$$$ PLATE LUNCHES/LOCAL-STYLE   ✉*1408 Liliha Street*   ☎*808-536-2663*

This neighborhood café out past Downtown Honolulu, comes
highly recommended by local folks. This could very well be the
only Hawaiian dining spot that offers sweet-and-sour sea bass,
squid with sour mustard cabbage and fried squid with *ong choy*.
In addition to two dozen seafood dishes, they have a host of
chicken, pork, vegetable and noodle selections.

Punchbowl and Tantalus Area
CONTEMPORARY CAFÉ

$$ AMERICAN   ✉*2411 Makiki Heights Drive*   ☎*808-523-3362*   📠*808-536-5973*
💻*www.tcmhi.org*

For a light but satisfying lunch, stop by the Contemporary Museum's
Contemporary Café. The ever-changing menu features well-done salads and sandwiches, like the soba noodle salad with garlic-*shoyu* dress-
ing or the Hawaiian chicken wrap with avocado and creamy pineapple
chutney. Sit inside surrounded by modern artwork or outside in a pleasant garden setting. No dinner. Closed Monday.

Ala Moana Area

Situated midway between Waikiki and Downtown Honolulu is this
area packed with shopping centers that feature a wide range of eateries
worth visiting.

BIG CITY DINER

$-$$ AMERICAN/LOCAL-STYLE   ✉*1060 Auahi Street*   ☎*808-591-8891*

Located below the theaters at the sprawling Ward Entertainment Centre, this restaurant adds island flair to a winning American concept.
Voted the "best restaurant for under $20," the eatery serves burgers,
salads, sandwiches and typical diner fare. It also offers a variety of local-
style favorites like chilled tofu, kimchi, *panko*-crusted calamari tempura and boiled edamame. The baby-back ribs with guava barbecue
sauce and Uncle Danny's Fried Rice consistently get rave reviews, and
rightfully so.

RYAN'S GRILL

$$–$$$ AMERICAN/PAN-ASIAN   ✉ *Ward Centre, 1200 Ala Moana Boulevard*
📞 *808-591-9132* 📠 *808-591-0034* 🖰 *www.r-u-i.com/rya*

Ryan's is one of Honolulu's hottest after-work hangouts for singles who want to become un-single, and the place is packed from 5 p.m. until after 1 a.m. Comfortable leather chairs and marble-topped tables create a cozy, modern atmosphere. Grilled and steamed fish and fowl, pizzas, salads and fettuccine are among the many culinary options for those who go to eat instead of drink.

Plate Lunches

There's nothing more Hawaiian than the plate lunch. It's soul food at its finest, but not for the faint of heart, nor for those counting calories or concerned about the fat content of their food. A local culinary tradition, the plate lunch combines Japanese, Chinese, Korean, Hawaiian, American and Filipino fare into a meal that is not only delicious but more food for the price than you're likely to find anywhere.

The plate lunch tradition began in the sugar plantation days, when women would deliver plates of food to family plantation workers. These plates would usually consist of two scoops of white rice, a scoop of potato or macaroni salad and a variety of meat and fish, including teriyaki pork, beef, chicken or fish; pork or chicken *luau*; or *kalua* pig. Some entrepreneurial villagers started up businesses selling lunches to field workers without families.

Little-changed today, the plate lunch still consists of two scoops of white rice and possibly a third scoop of macaroni or potato salad, as well as the main selections, which could be just about anything. A local favorite is *loco moco*, a hamburger steak topped with fried egg and gravy. There are also *kalbi* (Korean beef ribs), teriyaki beef, chicken and pork *katsu*, and stir-fried shrimp.

Plate lunches are served in simple restaurants, usually a drive-in or coffee shop. They also can be found at any of the lunch trucks parked at places around Honolulu, near the University of Hawaii or on the North Shore. Although there are probably as many opinions on the best plate lunches as there are people in Oahu, here are a few favorites.

LIKE LIKE DRIVE INN ✉ *745 Keeaumoku Street* 📞 *808-941-2515* Like Like Drive Inn is one of the oldest and most well-established plate lunch eateries in Honolulu and very popular with the locals. This comfy coffee shop has the feel of the '50s and serves up some good home-style comfort food.

GRACE'S INN ✉ *1296 South Beretania Street* 📞 *808-593-2202* Grace's Inn, with several locations around Oahu, is famed for its chicken *katsu* and homemade kim chi. It also serves beef stew, beef curry and a variety of other dishes. Their Beretania eatery is the best known of the "chain."

L & L DRIVE-INN ✉ *1711 Liliha Street* 📞 *808-533-3210* You'll never be far from an L & L Drive-Inn. With more than 20 restaurants around Oahu, the chain has been voted by *Honolulu Advertiser* readers as serving the best plate lunches. Stir-fried shrimp and hamburger steak are among the offerings, and the breakfasts come with rice and a Hawaiian favorite, Spam. Visit the original diner.

KAKA'AKO KITCHEN

$$ PLATE LUNCHES ⊠Ward Centre, 1200 Ala Moana Boulevard
☎808-596-7488 ✎808-596-9114

Local dishes get dressed up with fresh ingredients and a gourmet touch at Kaka'ako Kitchen. Popular choices include the blackened *ahi* wrap with wasabi aioli, crispy sweet chili chicken, *kalbi* short ribs with kimchi and an island-style linguine with sun-dried tomatoes and chili-*hoisin* cream sauce. There's usually a line during peak meal times, when service can be slow. Sit inside or out on the covered lanai. The inventive food would cost much more in a full-service restaurant, but the disposable plates and order-at-the-counter service keep prices affordable.

MAKAI MARKET

$ INTERNATIONAL ⊠Ala Moana Center, 1450 Ala Moana Boulevard

Weary shoppers recharge at this giant food court on the lower level of Ala Moana Center. Take your pick from two dozen vendors at this United Nations of fast food. Generous plates of rotisserie chicken are available at **Lahaina Chicken Company** (808-946-4588), steaming bowls of noodles are found at **Donburiya Dondon** (808-944-3618), and **Little Café Siam** (808-943-8424) serves fragrant Thai and Vietnamese curries. Or take the escalator up to the upper level, where a medley of stand-alone restaurants offer a more relaxed atmosphere. Try **Assaggio** (808-942-3446) and **Romano's Macaroni Grill** (808-356-8300) for Italian or **Genki Sushi** (808-942-9102) and **Kyoto Ohsho** (808-949-0040) for sushi.

THE PINEAPPLE ROOM BY ALAN WONG

$$$ HAWAII REGIONAL ⊠Macy's 3rd floor, Ala Moana Center, 1450 Ala Moana Boulevard ☎808-732-8645 ✎www.alanwongs.com

Don't be fooled by its department-store locale: This eatery has all the flavor of Alan Wong's cuisine without the hype (or the price tag) of his flagship restaurant on South King Street. The contemporary dining room is a can't-miss lunch stop for the ultrajuicy *kalua* pig BLT, the calamari *somen* salad or the kimchi reuben. Reservations recommended. No dinner Sunday.

DON QUIJOTE

$ INTERNATIONAL ⊠801 Kaheka Street ☎808-973-4800

A few blocks from Ala Moana Center is this gaudy, Japanese-leaning superstore that sells affordable food items, household goods and Hawaii kitsch. If you can navigate your way through the chaotic aisles to the seafood department, you'll discover some tasty *poke* options. Outside, there's a food court that's popular with nearby residents and office workers. Offerings include noodles, dim sum, local-style plate lunches and Korean barbecue. For a heaping plate lunch, head to neighborhood favorite **AAA Barbecue** (808-941-9998). **Leo's Taverna Express** (808-949-2225) serves quick, quality gyros and falafel.

PAGODA FLOATING RESTAURANT

$$$$ INTERNATIONAL ✉ 1525 Rycroft Street 📞 808-948-8356 📠 808-946-4635
🖫 www.pagodahotel.com

For prime rib, crab legs, shrimp and vegetable tempura, try this "floating" restaurant. A restaurant-in-the-round, it sits above a pond populated with gaily colored tropical koi. Several cascades and a fountain feed the pond. The surrounding grounds have been carefully landscaped. This buffet restaurant offers a continental breakfast spread with a few Asian touches, while the dinner service features changing entrées such as oxtail stew, *misoyaki*, butterfish and *kalua* pork. No lunch.

Moiliili–Kapahulu–Kaimuki Area

ALAN WONG'S RESTAURANT

$$$$ HAWAII REGIONAL ✉ 1857 South King Street 📞 808-949-2526
📠 808-951-9520 🖫 www.alanwongs.com

To go where the local gentry dine, head to Alan Wong's for locally caught fish, home-grown produce and a wealth of poultry and meat dishes like macadamia nut and coconut–crusted lamb chops. One of the *in* places to dine on Hawaii Regional cuisine, so reservations are suggested. Dinner only.

JIMBO'S RESTAURANT

$ JAPANESE ✉ 1936 South King Street 📞 808-947-2211

The decor at Jimbo's Restaurant is simple but the noodles are superb. Jimbo's serves Japanese udon—thick, white and perfectly cooked—in a broth so delicious your taste buds will rejoice. This is Japanese soul food at its finest and no doubt the best udon this side of Tokyo. No wonder there's always a line outside.

CHEF MAVRO'S

$$$$ FRENCH ✉ 1969 South King Street 📞 808-944-4714 🖫 www.chefmavro.com,
chef@chefmavro.com

This top-of-the-line restaurant is a star in the Honolulu culinary scene. Chef George Mavrothalassitis, formerly of the Four Seasons Resort in Wailea, presides over his own corner in Honolulu. The unassuming building on South King Street does not hint at what awaits inside—an elegant yet understated dining room adorned with local artwork. The French-inspired cuisine arrives at the table in an equally sublime presentation. The dishes are five-star and the service impeccable. One claim to fame of Chef Mavro is the perfect pairing of the wine with every item on the menu. A place for that special night. Dinner only. Closed Monday.

GENKI SUSHI

$$ SUSHI ✉ 885 Kapahulu Avenue 📞 808-735-7700 📠 808-735-7708
🖫 www.genkisushiusa.com

With a conveyor belt that propels the meandering sushi bar, Genki Sushi is one of Honolulu's most enjoyable and best-priced sushi restaurants. Be prepared for a 15- to 20-minute wait for a table, then dig in.

ONO HAWAIIAN FOODS

$$　LOCAL-STYLE/PLATE LUNCHES　✉*726 Kapahulu Avenue*
✆ *808-737-2275*

A must for all true Hawaii lovers, this hole-in-da-wall eatery is located on a busy street. But if you're lucky enough to get one of the few tables, you can feast on *laulau, kalua* pig, *pipikaula,* poi and *haupia.* The walls are papered with signed photographs of local notables and the place is packed with locals, notable and otherwise. Closed Sunday.

IRIFUNE

$$　JAPANESE　✉*563 Kapahulu Avenue*　✆ *808-737-1141*

This warm and friendly Japanese eatery is also frequented by a local crowd. In fact, around dinnertime, you will likely find yourself in line. The decor gives off a fun, casual air: fishing nets, Kabuki masks and other assorted wallhangings. On the menu are tasty curry, sushi, teriyaki and tempura dishes, plus several other Asian delectables like the over-the-top delicious garlic *ahi.* Closed Sunday and Monday.

UNCLE BO'S

$$-$$$　AMERICAN/PAN-ASIAN　✉*559 Kapahulu Avenue*　✆ *808-735-8311*
✐ *www.unclebosrestaurant.com*

Open from 5 p.m. to 2 a.m. daily, Uncle Bo's attracts a young, social crowd with its extensive *pupu* offerings and lively bar. Its proximity to Waikiki makes it a convenient choice for visitors who want to sample Asian fusion without pretension. Ordering lots of starters to share—like *hamachi* carpaccio, sweet chili calamari and spinach-artichoke-crab dip with won ton chips—is a good alternative to the pricier individual entrées. If you are going big, the fresh fish comes in a variety of tantalizing preparations.

RAINBOW DRIVE-IN

$　PLATE LUNCHES　✉*3308 Kanaina Avenue*　✆ *808-737-0177*
✐ *www.rainbowdrivein.com*

For local-style plate lunches, cruise in to Rainbow's. Popular with *kamaaina* and tourists alike, the menu includes hamburger steak, beef stew, shoyu chicken, breaded mahimahi, chili and fried chicken served with two scoops of rice and various salads. Breakfast plates include two eggs, rice, toast and your choice of meat, including the ubiquitous Spam.

TOWN

$$-$$$　ITALIAN/AMERICAN　✉*3435 Waialae Avenue*　✆ *808-735-5900*
✐ *www.townkaimuki.com, info@townkaimuki.com*

Owner, chef and Oahu native Ed Kenney is a champion of the slow food movement, and his restaurant adheres to its principles, serving Mediterranean-inspired dishes made with love and locally grown, organic produce. The menu changes daily depending on the freshest ingredients available, and Kenney makes them burst with flavor. The busy restaurant has simple, contemporary decor and a dog-friendly outdoor patio.

AZTECA MEXICAN RESTAURANT
$$ MEXICAN ✉3617 Waialae Avenue ☎808-735-2492
Waialae Avenue, a neighborhood strip a mile or so outside Waikiki, has developed into a gourmet ghetto. Azteca's is a vinyl-booth-and-plastic-panel eatery that serves a delicious array of Mexican food.

3660 ON THE RISE

$$$–$$$$ HAWAII REGIONAL ✉3660 Waialae Avenue ☎808-737-1177
📠808-735-6105 🖎www.3660.com, 3660@cleanwire.net
This award-winning restaurant is a local favorite, blending island ingredients with a definite touch of European cuisine. Try their signature *ahi katsu*: deep-fried *ahi* wrapped in nori with a wasabi-ginger sauce. Finish off the meal with Harlequin crème brûlée, which is difficult to describe without salivating but basically involves vanilla-bean custard and chocolate mousse glazed with caramel. Dinner only. Closed Monday.

HALE VIETNAM
$$ VIETNAMESE ✉1140 12th Avenue ☎808-735-7581
For spicy and delicious Asian dishes, it is hard to find a more appealing place than this one. A family restaurant that draws a local crowd, it has traditional Vietnamese soup and a host of excellent entrées.

Kahala Area
OLIVE TREE CAFE
$$ GREEK-MIDDLE EASTERN ✉4614 Kilauea Avenue ☎808-737-0303
After shopping at the upscale Kahala Mall, slip over to the Olive Tree for some delightful Greek and Middle Eastern food served in a no-nonsense atmosphere. Classics like falafel, *souvlaki*, *babaghanouj* and hummus are excellent, and the salads, lamb, fish and chicken dishes are also good. The tasty cuisine makes up for the spartan dining room. You can also bring your own beer and wine for a nominal corkage fee. Dinner only.

HOKU'S

$$$$ HAWAII REGIONAL ✉Kahala Hotel & Resort, 5000 Kahala Avenue
☎808-739-8760 🖎www.kahalaresort.com/dining/hoku.cfm
Year after year, this is voted one of Honolulu's best restaurants. Chef Wayne Hirabayashi is known for his inventive style that highlights the flavor of fresh local ingredients, and the evolving menu sets a standard for contemporary island cuisine. Patrons walk away saying it's the best meal they ever had—mouth-watering selections like slow-braised pork belly and pancetta-crusted *onaga*—but keep in mind that the price tag is as lofty as the compliment. That said, if you're looking to have one special

meal, this is the place. The presentation of each dish is simply
beautiful, matching the panoramic ocean view that completes
the dining experience. Dinner only. Sunday brunch.

SHOPPING

Pearl Harbor Area

KAM SUPER SWAP MEET

✉ *98-850 Moanalua Road* ✆ *808-483-5535* ✑ *www.kamswapmeet.com*
Expect a variety of secondhand items here. It's a great place to
barter for bargains, meet local folks and find items you'll never
see in stores. It's open on Wednesday, Saturday and Sunday
from 5 a.m. to 1 p.m. and Friday from 6 a.m. to 1 p.m.

PEARLRIDGE CENTER ✉ *231 Pearlridge Center, Aiea* ✆ *808-488-0981*
✆ *808-488-9456* ✑ *www.pearlridgeonline.com* A monorail shuttles shoppers
between the two main buildings that house this massive shopping
complex. It has all the standard mall offerings—boutiques, kiosks, food
court, movie theaters, restaurants—and is anchored by **Macy's** (808-
486-6701) and **Sears** (808-487-4212). **Borders Books and Music** (808-
487-1818) takes up a big chunk of real estate, as does **Toys 'R' Us** (808-
487-5811) across the street. Word to the wise: These parking lots are
typically full each weekend, so be prepared to exercise patience.

ALOHA STADIUM SWAP MEET ✉ *99-500 Salt Lake Boulevard, Aiea*
✆ *808-486-6704* ✑ *www.alohastadiumswapmeet.net* If you love bargains, you'll
enjoy browsing through the Aloha Stadium Swap Meet, the biggest
shopping experience of its kind on Oahu. This flea market, just north of
Pearl Harbor, costs just one dollar to get in; you'll cruise among vendors, many of them regulars selling cheap T-shirts, handmade crafts
and artworks, and others setting up for the day to sell household goods.
Open Wednesday, Saturday and Sunday from 6 a.m. to 3 p.m.

Cross-Island Express

SHOP PACIFICA

✉ *1525 Bernice Street, near the intersection of Routes 63 and H-1* ✆ *808-848-*
4158 ✆ *808-847-8249* ✑ *www.bishopmuseum.org* Out at the Bishop
Museum, be sure to stop by this shop, which offers a fine selection of Hawaiiana. There are books on island history and geography, an assortment of instruments that include nose flutes and
gourds, plus cards, souvenirs and wooden bowls.

Ala Moana Area

WARD CENTRE ✉ *1200 Ala Moana Boulevard* This is one of Honolulu's
sleeker shopping malls located on Ala Moana Boulevard. Streamlined
and stylized, it's an enclave filled with designer shops, spiffy restau-

rants, boutiques and children's shops. Adorned with blond-wood facades, brick walkways and brass-rail restaurants the center is anchored at the far end by **Borders Books & Music** (808-591-8995), a superstore that is chockablock with everything for your reading and listening pleasure. Just down the walkway, you'll find **Hawaiian Moon** (808-596-2294), a locally owned family business that specializes in island-style clothing that is more contemporary than the aloha wear sold at places like Hilo Hatties. Many of the garments are made from original prints that reflect Hawaii's culture and landscape. In the same complex, **Town & Country Surf Shop** (808-592-5299), offers an excellent selection of surf wear and beach apparel, as well as surf, skate and body boards, and all the accessories and gear needed to enjoy those sports. **Black Pearl Gallery** (808-597-1477), features lustrous Tahitian black pearls that highlight its jewelry collection.

Ala Moana Center may be the biggest, but the smaller Ward Warehouse, between Waikiki and Downtown Honolulu, is a shopping center worth visiting.

NATIVE BOOKS/
NA MEA HAWAII

✉ *Ward Warehouse, 1050 Ala Moana Boulevard* 📞 *808-596-8885* This community resource/bookstore is *the* venue for finding Hawaiian books, CDs and other cultural items of the Pacific Islands. If you have questions about Hawaii's history, myths or politics, they have answers, or know where to get them.

NOHEA GALLERY

✉ *1050 Ala Moana Boulevard* 📞 *808-596-0074* This store displays quilts, jewelry, pottery, glassware, lamps and wooden bureaus—all made in Hawaii by local artists.

ALA MOANA CENTER ✉ *1450 Ala Moana Boulevard* 📞 *808-955-9517* 📠 *808-949-0985* 🖱 *www.alamoanacenter.com* On the outskirts of Waikiki is the state's largest shopping center. This multitiered complex has practically everything. Ala Moana features three department stores: **Sears** (808-947-0252), **Macy's** (808-941-2345) and a Japanese emporium called **Shirokiya** (808-973-9111). **Longs Drug Store** (808-941-4433) is a good place to buy inexpensive Hawaiian curios. You'll also find an assortment of stores selling liquor, tennis and golf supplies, stationery, leather goods, cameras, shoes, tobacco, etc. You name it, they have it. The designer shops, appropriately, are located on the upper levels.

Moiliili–Kapahulu–Kaimuki Area

SATURDAY FARMER'S MARKET AT KAPIOLANI COMMUNITY COLLEGE ✉ *Kapiolani Community College, 4303 Diamond Head Road* 📞 *808-848-2074* Although the farmer's market is open but one day a week (7:30 to 11:00 a.m.), it's worth a mention as a place to get something tasty from one of the food vendors. You can purchase locally grown and made items, including fresh fish, produce and flowers, plants, free-range beef, leis, bread, jams and honey, salad dressings, cookies, exotic fruits and more. It's well-known as a great place for brunch from one of the vendors offering fresh breakfast fare, so get there early and bring a shopping bag (or three). It's held in the shady KCC parking lot off Diamond Head Road.

Kahala Area

KAHALA MALL ✉ *4211 Waialae Avenue* ☎ *808-732-7736* 🌐 *www.kahalamall center.com* One of Honolulu's more upscale shopping centers is Kahala Mall, where you'll find designer shops and national chains galore. This complex also hosts almost 100 moderately priced stores.

NIGHTLIFE

Outside Honolulu there are usually a couple of spots to hear Hawaiian music. Pick up a copy of *Spotlight's Oahu Gold*, *The Honolulu Weekly* or *This Week Oahu* magazine to see what's going on.

Ala Moana Area

RUMOURS ✉ *410 Atkinson Drive* ☎ *808-955-4811* 🌐 *www.alamoanahotel.com* Theme nights are the spice of life here. Friday nights the deejay plays current Top-40 hits, while Saturday is a Flashback Night and you can dance to tunes from the '70s and '80s. Located in the Ala Moana Hotel, this club is decorated with artwork and neon fixtures. Open Friday and Saturday nights. Cover.

WARD ENTERTAINMENT CENTRE ✉ *Kamakee and Auahi streets* This bustling destination is a draw for both tourists and *kamaaina*. On the ground floor, **Dave & Buster's** restaurant/entertainment center has an extensive video arcade, billiards and shuffleboard. Escalators to the second level lead to a 16-screen **movie theater**. Or just grab a cup of coffee at Starbucks and enjoy a little people-watching.

KINCAID'S ✉ *Ward Warehouse, 1050 Ala Moana Boulevard* ☎ *808-591-2005* A harbor view and Hawaiian contemporary music played on Thursday, Friday and Saturday by acoustic guitarists and bands make this a good choice for a relaxing evening. The lounge is part of a popular Honolulu restaurant in Ward Warehouse.

WALLACE THEATRES AT RESTAURANT ROW ✉ *500 Ala Moana Boulevard* ☎ *808-526-4171* The Wallace Theatres at Restaurant Row have the greatest movie bargain in town: 50-cent shows starting before 3:30. Miss the mid-afternoon cutoff? Not to worry—it's a mere $1 at all other times. Free validated parking and $1.50 hot dogs make this a must for wallet-conscious cinephiles.

Manoa Valley Area

ANNA BANNANA'S ✉ *2440 South Beretania Street* ☎ *808-946-5190* 📠 *808-946-6959* Over by the University of Hawaii's Manoa campus, Anna Bannana's has been a popular hangout for years. This wildly decorated spot has all types of live entertainment nightly, from open-mic Monday and turntable Tuesday to live bands on the weekends. Occasional cover.

MANOA VALLEY THEATRE ✉️2833 *East Manoa Road* 📞*808-988-6131* 📠*808-988-3179* 🖱️*www.manoavalleytheatre.com* A half dozen Broadway and off-Broadway productions with local actors are staged here. Recent offerings include *Tuesdays with Morrie* and *The 25th Annual Putnam County Spelling Bee.*

Moiliili–Kapahulu–Kaimuki Area

DIAMOND HEAD THEATRE ✉️*520 Makapuu Avenue* 📞*808-733-0274 (box office)* 🖱️*www.diamondheadtheatre.com* Musicals are the mainstay at Kaimuki's community theater that's located across the street from Kapiolani Community College.

BEACHES & PARKS

Pearl Harbor Area
KEAIWA HEIAU STATE RECREATION AREA

✉️*To get there from Honolulu, take Route 90 west to Aiea, then follow Aiea Heights Drive to the park.* 📞*808-537-0300*

🏃 Amazing as it sounds, this is a wooded retreat within easy driving distance of Honolulu. Situated in the Koolau foothills with sweeping views of Pearl Harbor and Greater Honolulu, it contains the remains of a *heiau*, a temple once used by Hawaiian healers. Day visitors can walk the Aiea Loop Trail, a peaceful circuit through groves of Norfolk pines and fragrant eucalyptus trees. Facilities include picnic area, showers and restrooms.

▲ Four campsites are available from Friday through Wednesday for tent camping only. State permit required.

Ala Moana Area
ALA MOANA REGIONAL PARK

✉️*On Ala Moana Boulevard at the west end of Waikiki, across from Ala Moana Center*

🏊 🎣 🚣 🏄 This 119-acre park is a favorite with Hawaii residents. On weekends every type of outdoor enthusiast imaginable turns out to swim, snorkel, fish (common catches are *papio*, bonefish, goatfish and *moano*), jog, sail model boats and so on. It's also a good place to surf; there are three separate breaks here: "Concessions," "Tennis Courts" and "Baby Haleiwa" all have summer waves. There's a curving length of beach, a grassy park area, a helluva lot of local color and facilities that include a picnic area, restrooms, showers, concession stands, tennis courts, a recreation building, a bowling green and lifeguards.

Kahala Area

DIAMOND HEAD BEACH PARK

✉️*Just beyond Waikiki along Diamond Head Road at the foot of Diamond Head; watch for parked cars.*

🏊 🎣 🚣 🏄 Heaven to windsurfers, this twisting ribbon of white sand sits directly below the crater. It's close enough to Waikiki for convenient access but far enough to shake most of the crowds. The Kuilei cliffs, covered with scrub growth, loom behind the beach. Snorkeling is good—a coral reef extends off-shore through this area. There's also a year-round surf break called "Lighthouse." And for the anglers, your chances are good to reel in *ulua*, *papio* or *mamao*. A shower is the sole facility.

KUILEI CLIFFS BEACH PARK AND KAALAWAI BEACH
✉ *Located east of Diamond Head Beach Park*

🏊 🤿 🏄 🎣 🚿 Extending east from Diamond Head Beach Park, these sandy corridors are also flanked by sharp sea cliffs. Together they extend from Diamond Head Lighthouse to Black Point. The aquatic attractions are the same as at Diamond Head Beach Park and both beaches can be reached from it (or from cliff trails leading down from Diamond Head Road). A protecting reef makes for good swimming at Kaalawai Beach (which can also be reached via a public accessway off Kulumanu Place).

WAIALEA BEACH PARK
✉ *4900 block of Kahala Avenue in Kahala*

🏊 🤿 🚿 Smack in the middle of Honolulu's prestigious Kahala district, where a million dollars buys a modest house, sits this tidy beach. Its white sand neatly groomed, its spacious lawn shaded by palms, Waialae is a true find, and its beauty makes for a popular wedding spot. It has good swimming and fishing. There are bathhouse facilities, beachside picnic tables and a footbridge arching across the stream that divides the property. To the west of the park lies Kahala Beach, a long, thin swath of sand that extends all the way to Black Point. Snorkeling is best near the Kahala Hotel & Resort.

SOUTHEAST OAHU

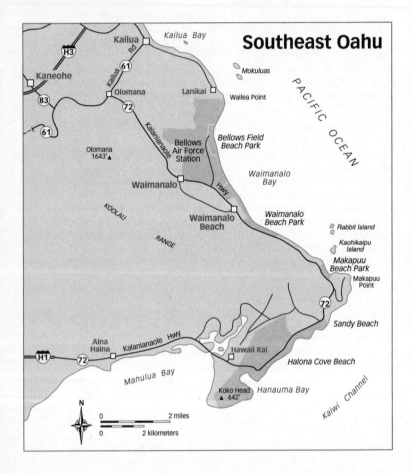

Southeast Oahu

Out past Honolulu, beyond the glitter of Waikiki and the gilded neighborhoods of Kahala, the pace slows down, the vistas open up and Oahu begins to look more like a tropical island. The road—Route 72, the Kalanianaole Highway—leads out of Honolulu and hugs the rugged coastline as it climbs up and down and back and forth along the edge of a series of volcanic ridges. The jagged, jade-colored peaks of the Koolau Mountains on one side and the sparkling blue sea on the other provide some of the most striking scenery the state has to offer.

Fortunately, there are lots of places to stop and admire it along the way. Some of Hawaii's best snorkeling is at Hanauma Bay, a marine nature preserve. Koko Head and Koko Crater have hiking trails, and a swim is an option at any of a number of pocket beaches that dot the shore. For those who long for more "traditional" amusements, there is also Sea Life Park, a marine theme park, about midway along the Southeast Coast.

Although it's technically part of Honolulu, the rural landscape here stands in sharp contrast to the congestion and hustle-bustle of town. This is despite the creeping expansion of residential communities like family-oriented Aina Haina, which was developed on the old dairy lands of Aina Haina Valley, and upscale Hawaii Kai, which sprawls over former farm lands closer to the coast. Both are popular bedroom communities for town workers who want a little space and don't mind the commute.

Still, you don't hit true country until the road drops down closer to sea level and begins to skirt the fields that are clustered around Waimanalo, one of Oahu's major farming regions. Sugar has gradually been replaced here with small family-owned fruit and flower farms that grow much of the fresh produce sold in smaller Honolulu markets and exported to the neighboring islands.

Life shifts into a slower, more comfortable gear in these parts, and when combined with the beautiful scenery, gives Waimanalo a personality and charm all its own. This bucolic area offers up a very different side of multifaceted Oahu, and one that warrants a closer look.

SIGHTS

KOKO HEAD Kalanianaole Highway streams through Hawaii Kai and other residential areas, then ascends the slopes of an extinct volcano, 642-foot Koko Head. Here Madame Pele is reputed to have dug a hole for the last time in search of fiery volcanic matter.

KOKO CRATER

The second hump on the horizon is this crater, which rises to over 1200 feet. This fire-pit, according to Hawaiian legend, is the vagina of Pele's sister. It seems that Pele, goddess of volcanoes, was being pursued by the handsome demigod, Kamapuaa. Her sister, trying to distract the hot suitor from Pele, spread her legs across the landscape.

HANAUMA BAY NATURE PRESERVE ✉*7455 Kalanianaole Highway; 10 miles east of Waikiki* ✆*808-396-4229* ⌖*www.hanaumabayhawaii.org* From the top of Koko Head, a well-marked road and sidewalk lead down to one of the prettiest beaches in all Hawaii. The word *hanauma* means "curved bay," and you will clearly see that Hanauma Bay was once a circular volcano, one wall of which was breached by the sea. This breathtaking place is a marine preserve filled with multicolored coral and teeming with underwater life. Little wonder that Hollywood chose this spot as the prime location for Elvis Presley's movie, *Blue Hawaii*. Elvis' grass shack was right here, and the strand was also a setting in the classic film *From Here to Eternity*.

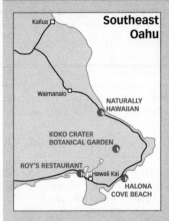

The swimming and snorkeling are unmatched anywhere and the mazework of coral formations along the bottom adds to the snorkeling adventure. You can also hike along rock ledges fringing the bay and explore some mind-boggling tidepools like **Toilet Bowl**, a tidepool that "flushes" as the waves wash through it. Crowded though it is, this is one strand that should not be bypassed (though park officials are now regulating access to prevent overuse). Hanauma Bay is an extremely popular picnic spot among local folks, so it is also advisable to visit on a weekday rather than face bucking the crowds on Saturday and Sunday. Because of its popularity, the preserve cuts off entrance to the park when the parking lot is full (another good reason to arrive early). All guests entering this nature preserve are required to watch a short educational video that explains how to keep this beautiful place clean and healthy for generations to come. Closed Tuesday. Admission.

From Hanauma Bay, the highway corkscrews along the coast. Among the remarkable scenes you'll enjoy en route are views of Lanai and Molokai, two of Oahu's sister islands. On a clear, clear day you can also see Maui, an island that requires no introduction.

HALONA BLOWHOLE ⊠*North of Hanauma Bay off Kalanianaole Highway* At an overlook you will encounter this lava tube through which geysers of seawater blast. During high tide and when the sea is turbulent, these gushers reach dramatic heights. *Halona* means "peering place," and that is exactly what everyone seems to do here. You can't miss the spot, since the roadside parking lot is inevitably crowded with tourists. Between December and April this vista is also a prime whale-watching spot.

SANDY BEACH Just beyond Halona Blowhole spreads this stretch of sand, one of Hawaii's most renowned bodysurfing spots. It's a long, wide beach piled with fluffy sand and complete with picnic areas and showers. Inexperienced bodysurfers are better off enjoying the excellent sunbathing here, since the dramatic shorebreak that makes the beach so popular among bodysurfers is dangerous for beginners.

KOKO CRATER
BOTANICAL GARDEN

 hidden

⊠*Kokonani Street, off Kalanianaole Highway* ☎*808-522-7060* ✐*www.honolulu.gov/parks/hbg* Just beyond Sandy Beach, a sign points you to a side road that leads up to this 60-acre collection of cacti, plumeria and other water-thrifty plants. A brochure at the start of the two-mile loop trail guides you through the drought-resistant landscape, which is divided into four major collections of different geographic areas: Africa, Madagascar, the Americas and Hawaii. Pay careful attention in the Hawaii section to the grove of *wiliwili* trees. These native trees, known for their fiery-orange flowers that bloom in the fall, have all been but wiped out by a nefarious, alien gall wasp that eats their leaves. Hawaiians once used the wood to build outriggers, fish floats and surfboards. Scientists are experimenting with biological controls to help stop the wasps' destruction.

MAKAPUU POINT Route 72 rounds Oahu's southeastern corner and sets a course along the eastern shoreline. It also climbs to this scenic point from which you can take your first view of the Windward Coast. You will be standing on Makapuu Point. Above you rise sharp lava cliffs, while below are rolling sand dunes and open ocean. The paved trail to the lighthouse at Makapuu Point offers amazing views of the Windward Coast. The slope-faced islet just offshore is Rabbit Island. Humpback whales can be seen in winter months in the water here, which separates Oahu and Molokai. The distant headland is Makapuu Peninsula, toward which you are bound.

SEA LIFE PARK HAWAII ⊠*41-202 Kalanianaole Highway, Waimanalo* ☎*808-259-2500* ✆*808-259-7373* ✐*www.sealifeparkhawaii.com* From Makapuu Point's perfect perch, you can also spy this marine attraction comparable to those in California and Florida. Among the many features at this park is the "Hawaiian Reef Tank," a 300,000-gallon oceanarium inhabited by about 4000 sea creatures. To see it you wind through a spiral viewing area that descends three fathoms along the tank's glass perimeter. At times a scuba diver will be hand-feeding the fish. Swimming about this

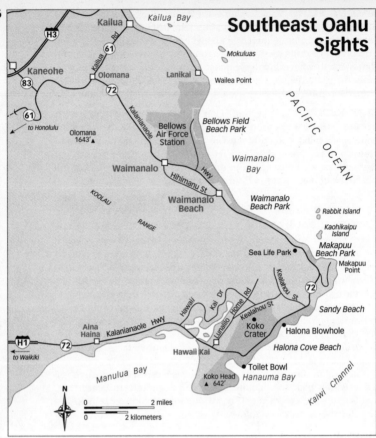

Southeast Oahu Sights

Kailua

Kailua Bay

Mokuluas

Kaneohe

Olomana

Lanikai

Wailea Point

to Honolulu

Olomana
1643'

Bellows
Air Force
Station

Bellows Field
Beach Park

PACIFIC OCEAN

Waimanalo

Hihimanu St

Waimanalo
Bay

KOOLAU

Waimanalo
Beach

Waimanalo
Beach Park

Rabbit Island

RANGE

Kaohikaipu
Island

Makapuu
Beach Park

Sea Life Park

Makapuu
Point

Kealahou St

Kai Dr

Hawaii

Kealahou St

Sandy Beach

Aina
Haina

Kalanianaole Hwy

Hawaii Kai

Koko
Crater

Halona Blowhole

Halona Cove Beach

to Waikiki

Manulua Bay

Koko Head
642'

Toilet Bowl
Hanauma Bay

Kaiwi Channel

N

0   2 miles

0   2 kilometers

underwater world are sharks, stingrays, turtles and a variety of lesser-known species. As well as several interactive programs, the park also features a turtle lagoon, penguin habitat and the only known *wholphin* (half whale, half dolphin) living in captivity. Admission.

MAKAPUU BEACH PARK ✉*41-095 Kalanianaole Highway* Across the road from Sea Life Park spreads this other fabled but daunting body-surfing spot set in a particularly pretty location. Nearby black lava cliffs are topped by a white lighthouse and **Rabbit Island** is anchored just off-shore. Rabbit Island resembles a bunny's head, but was actually named for a former rabbit-raising farm there. Makapuu Beach itself is a short, wide rectangle of white sand. It's an ideal place to picnic, but when the surf is up, beware of the waves. This is where *expert* bodysurfers show their stuff.

KOOLAU RANGE The road from Makapuu Beach continues along the shoreline between soft sand beaches and rugged mountain peaks. During the next 30 miles your attention will be drawn back continually to those rocky crags. They are part of the Koolau Range, a wall of precipitous mountains that vault up from Oahu's placid interior. Their spires, minarets and fluted towers are softened here and there by lush, green valleys, but never enough to detract from the sheer beauty and magnitude of the heights. Light and shade play games along their moss-covered surfaces, while rainbows hang suspended between the peaks. If wind and weather permit, you will see hang gliders dusting the cliffs as they sail from the mountains down to the distant beach.

WAIMANALO The road from Makapuu Beach continues through this tiny seaside village that spans all of three square miles. This former ranching town is now a farming community, and you'll pass numerous nurseries set up for fruit and flower cultivation. Extended families with deep Waimanalo roots live in harmony with the land that supports them, growing organic produce in their yards and sharing with each other. Life moves slowly here, maintaining the steady rhythm of old Hawaii that development has yet to alter. The green, open space is easy on the eyes, a welcoming gateway to the Windward Coast.

OLOMANA PEAK Outside Waimanalo you will see this peak favored by rock climbers. It is a three-peaked mountain that seems to belong in the Swiss Alps.

LODGING

BEACH HOUSE HAWAII ✉*Beach lots throughout Waimanalo* ☎*808-259-7792, 866-625-6946* 📠*808-259-0203 wwww.beachhousehawaii.com, info@beachhouse hawaii.com* This is a lodging service that offers rental homes and suites ranging from studios to six-bedroom units, each with private bath, kitchenette, lanai, queen-sized beds, fresh flowers and ceiling fans. Boogieboards, snorkeling gear, beach chairs, a hot tub and a barbecue round out the amenities. Fresh papaya grow on the trees, and for a lazy afternoon in the sun, sink into the hammock with a good book. For those who can't get away from it all, there's even internet access.

DINING

Spotted along Oahu's southeastern shore are a couple of moderately priced restaurants (and an expensive but worthy one) that may prove handy if you're beachcombing or camping. All are located on or near Route 72 (Kalanianaole Highway).

AINA HAINA SHOPPING CENTER
$–$$ INTERNATIONAL   ✉*Kalanianaole Highway at West Hind Street*
The food court here might be a good stop on your way to Hanauma Bay. If you're looking for snacks, head to **Chang's Doe Fang Company** (808-373-3402), where you'll find unusual flavors of Icees, *manapua* and *musubi*, and a big selection of candy and crack seed. A few stores away, **Cake Couture** (808-373-9750) sells delectable cupcakes topped with buttercream frosting that look too good to eat.

ROY'S RESTAURANT

$$$–$$$$ HAWAII REGIONAL   ✉*6600 Kalanianaole Highway, Hawaii Kai*
📞*808-396-7697* 📠*808-396-8706* 🖱*www.roysrestaurant.com,*
honolulu@roysrestaurant.com

Tucked away in unassuming fashion in a business park is one of my favorite dining spots. You'll have to travel all the way to Hawaii Kai, several miles east of Waikiki, to find the original Roy's. It is, to say the least, ultracontemporary, from the magazine clips framed on the walls to the cylindrical fish tank near the door. One of the most innovative of Hawaii's Pacific Rim cuisine dining rooms, it specializes in fresh local ingredients. It's also wildly popular, so reserve in advance. Dinner only.

ASSAGGIO HAWAII KAI

$$$ ITALIAN   ✉*Koko Marina Shopping Center, 7192 Kalanianaole Highway, Hawaii Kai*
📞*808-396-0756* 📠*808-396-0757*

This is an excellent neighborhood-style Italian restaurant with an extensive menu. You'll find dishes like butter-steamed Manila clams, chicken linguine and osso buco, as well as a fresh catch-of-the-day and seafood. There are four other locations in Mililani, Ala Moana, Manoa and Kailua, though I like this one for its yacht-club ambience and marina-side seating. No lunch on weekends.

TEDDY'S BIGGER BURGERS

$ AMERICAN   ✉*7192 Kalanianaole Highway, Hawaii Kai* 📞*808-394-9100*
🖱*www.teddysbiggerburgers.com, rstula@teddysbiggerburgers.com*

Also at Koko Marina Shopping Center is this zippy '50s-style diner painted in primary colors. This local chain, voted Best Burger by *Honolulu Advertiser* readers, uses quality ingredients and homemade sauces on the charbroiled made-to-order menu items.

THAI VALLEY CUISINE

$–$$ THAI   ✉*Kalama Village Center, 501 Kealahou Street, Hawaii Kai* 📞*808-395-9746*

This great find is tucked away in a tiny shopping center in Kalama Village, a suburban residential neighborhood built in the center of Koko Head Crater. The restaurant serves a variety of Thai appetizers, curries, noodles and such entrées as basil eggplant, fresh mushrooms sautéed in garlic, stuffed chicken wings and deep-fried snapper. No lunch.

KENEKE'S PLATE LUNCH

$ PLATE LUNCHES   ✉*41-857 Kalanianaole Highway, Waimanalo*
📞*808-259-9811* 🖱*www.kenekes.net*

For breakfast, plate lunches and sandwiches at greasy-spoon prices, drop in here. No gourmet's delight, this tiny eatery is well placed for people enjoying Waimanalo's beaches. No dinner.

DAVE'S ICE CREAM

$ DESSERT   ✉*41-1537 Kalanianaole Highway, Waimanalo* 📞*808-259-0356*

Dave's scoops up gourmet ice cream in flavors like adzuki bean, cotton candy and *poha*, made from gooseberries grown on the Big Island. It also serves guava and passion fruit sherbet, among many other selections.

SHOPPING

AINA HAINA SHOPPING CENTER ✉*Kalanianaole Highway at West Hind Street* With its relatively meager offerings, this is the retail mecca in this region, which has an overall dearth of shopping. Foodland Farms, an upscale version of the former ubiquitous supermarket Foodland, with a deli, a wine shop and locally grown and organic produce, anchors the center.

NATURALLY HAWAIIAN

✉*41-1025 Kalanianaole Highway, Waimanalo* ✆*808-259-5354* ✎*808-259-5350* ✐*www.naturallyhawaiian.com* There aren't many places on Oahu more Hawaiian than Waimanalo, so this place fits the landscape nicely. Featuring fine art and homemade gifts, the shop sells puka-shell necklaces, koa wood pieces, prints and paintings, and Hawaiian commemorative stamps.

NIGHTLIFE

KONA BREWING COMPANY ✉*7192 Kalanianaole Highway* ✆*808-394-5662* ✐*www.konabrewingco.com* Located on the docks of Koko Marina, this casual restaurant-pub boasts 24 taps, out of which flow Kona Brewing Company's signature microbrews—island-inspired beers like Longboard Lager and Fire Rock Pale Ale. It is Hawaii's second KBC; the other is its original location in Kona. There's live traditional and contemporary music every Friday, Saturday and Sunday, and plenty of outdoor seating with a magnificent view of the Koolau mountains that loom over Hawaii Kai. A choice place to enjoy a frosty pint at the end of the day.

BEACHES & PARKS

HANAUMA BAY
NATURE PRESERVE

✉*Take Kalanianaole Highway (Route 72) to Koko Head, then turn onto the side road near the top of the promontory. This leads to a parking lot; leave your vehicle and walk the several hundred yards down a somewhat steep path to the beach.* ✆*808-396-4229* ✐*www.hanaumabayhawaii.org*

🏊 🤿 One of Oahu's prettiest and most popular beaches, this bay is located about nine miles east of Waikiki. A curving swath of white sand, it extends for almost a half-mile. The bottom of the bay is a maze of coral reef, and the entire area has been designated a marine preserve; fishing is strictly prohibited. As a result, the skindiving is unmatched and the fish are tame enough to eat from your hand. The spectacular coral labyrinth makes this one of Oahu's top snorkeling spots. While most people stay within the confines of the nearshore reef, some of the best snorkeling is on the other side. Strong swimmers and experienced snorkelers can walk along the rock ledge at the south end of the bay and jump in just outside the fringing reef—it's a rewarding experience, one that you won't have to share with a hundred of your closest friends. (Just beware of "Witch's Brew," a turbulent area on the bay's right side, and the "Molokai Express," a wicked current sweeping across the mouth of the bay.) If you're feeling a little water weary, you can hike along the rock ledges that fringe the bay and explore the amazing tidepools. Get here early—April through September the beach closes at 7 p.m., 6 p.m. the rest of the year (it opens at 6 a.m.), and the parking lot fills up quickly. In addition, you are required to watch a short film on the bay's ecosystem and proper snorkeling etiquette. Facilities include a picnic area, restrooms, showers, a snack bar, snorkeling equipment rentals, a gift shop and lifeguards. Closed Tuesday. Parking fee, $1; nonresident day-use fee, $5 per person.

HALONA COVE BEACH

✉ *Stop at the Halona Blowhole parking lot on Kalanianaole Highway (Route 72), about ten miles east of Waikiki. Follow the path from the right side of the lot down to the beach.*

This is the closest you'll find to a hidden beach near Honolulu. It's a patch of white sand wedged between Halona Point and the Halona Blowhole lookout. Located directly below Kalanianaole Highway (Route 72), this is not exactly a wilderness area. But you can still escape the crowds massed on the nearby beaches. And you and your special someone can emulate the famous love scene in the move *From Here to Eternity*, which was filmed here. Swimming and snorkeling are good when the sea is gentle but extremely dangerous if it's rough. Prime catches are *ulua, papio* and *mamao*. There are no facilities.

SANDY BEACH

✉ *On Kalanianaole Highway (Route 72) about 10 miles east of Waikiki.*

A long, wide beach, this is a favorite among Oahu's youth. The shorebreak makes it one of the finest, and most dangerous, bodysurfing beaches in the islands. In fact, more neck and back injuries happen here than all of Oahu's other beaches combined. That says a lot about the surf-riding skills of President Obama, who was photographed bodysurfing the sizeable shorebreak in perfect form while he was on vacation. East swells bring good waves for shortboarding at the two outer surf breaks, "Half-point" and "Full-point," but beware of rip currents. Lifeguards are on duty. It's a pleasant place to sunbathe, but if you go swimming, plan to negotiate a pounding shoreline. Anglers try for *ulua, papio* and *mamao*. There are picnic areas, restrooms and showers. Should you want to avoid the crowds, head over to **Wawamalu Beach Park** next door to the east.

MAKAPUU POINT STATE WAYSIDE

✉Off Kalanianaole Highway between Sandy Beach and Makapuu Lookout; trailhead is a half-mile past the golf course on the right.

🏃 This 38-acre state park encompasses Makapuu Beach, lookout and the lighthouse that overlooks the east Oahu coast. The mile-long asphalted trail leading to the lighthouse has become a popular family excursion; you can take the trail's uphill segments at a leisurely pace. The heat can be draining by midday, so a morning or afternoon hike is recommended, particularly on weekends when crowds abound. Panoramic views are the reward, with brisk tradewinds likely. The two islands offshore nearby are bird sanctuaries. The large one is known as Rabbit Island. The Hawaiians call it Manana Island, which means to stretch out or protrude.

MAKAPUU BEACH PARK

✉41-095 Kalanianaole Highway

🏊 🏐 Set in a very pretty spot with lava cliffs in the background and Rabbit Island just offshore is this short, wide rectangle of white sand. It is Hawaii's most famous bodysurfing beach. With no protecting reef and a precipitous shoreline, Makapuu is inundated by awesome swells that send wave riders crashing onto shore. As at Sandy Beach, necks and backs are broken with frightening regularity here, so if the waves are large and you're inexperienced—play the spectator. If you take the plunge, prepare for a battering! Snorkeling is usually poor and surfing is not permitted here. Common catches are *ulua*, *papio* and *mamao*. The only facilities are restrooms and a lifeguard.

WAIMANALO BEACH PARK AND
WAIMANALO BAY BEACH PARK

✉Waimanalo Beach Park is at 41-741 Kalanianaole Highway (Route 72) about 15 miles east of Waikiki. Waimanalo Bay Beach Park is on Aloiloi Street a mile farther north.

🏊 🏐 This spacious 75-acre park is located at the southeast end of Waimanalo's three-and-a-half-mile-long beach. It's studded with ironwood trees and equipped with numerous recreation facilities, including a playground, a basketball court and a baseball field. Waimanalo Beach Park and Waimanalo Bay Beach Park, a mile farther north, are both excellent spots for picnicking, swimming, sunbathing and bodysurfing at a shallow sandbar known as "Sherwoods." The latter is farther removed from the highway in a grove of ironwood trees. Waimanalo is a good place to fish for *papio*, bonefish, milkfish and goatfish. Be careful you don't get stung by Portuguese man-of-war jellyfish or *limu* seaweed—both of these are prevalent along the beachfront here. There are picnic areas, restrooms and showers at both parks.

▲ A county permit required at both of the parks for tent and trailer camping.

BELLOWS FIELD BEACH PARK

✉Turn off Kalanianaole Highway (Route 72) toward Bellows Air Force Station. The park is located near Waimanalo, about 17 miles east of Waikiki.

🏊 🎣 🏕 🏐 One of Oahu's prettiest parks, Bellows is a broad whitesand beach bordered by ironwood trees and a marvelous view of the Koolau Mountains. The clear water sparkles under the sun, and though beachgoers can engage in every variety of water sport here, the shallow sandbar creates waves that are best for bodyboarding and bodysurfing. Snorkelers and swimmers should be aware that Portuguese man-of-war jellyfish are common in these waters and often wash up onto the shore. If you cast a line, you might hook *papio*, bonefish or goatfish. Note: Because Bellows is located on a military base, there is a section of the beach that is off limits to civilians, a rule that is readily enforced. Also, it is open to visitors only from Friday noon until 8 a.m. Monday. Facilities include a picnic area, showers and a restroom.

▲ County permit required.

WINDWARD COAST

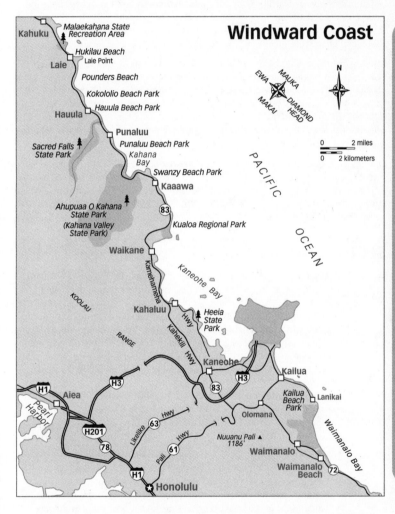

Windward Coast

Kahuku
Malaekahana State Recreation Area
Hukilau Beach
Laie Point
Laie
Pounders Beach
Kokololio Beach Park
Hauula Beach Park
Hauula
Punaluu
Sacred Falls State Park
Punaluu Beach Park
Kahana Bay
Swanzy Beach Park
Kaaawa
Ahupuaa O Kahana State Park
(Kahana Valley State Park)
Kualoa Regional Park
Waikane
Kaneohe Bay
Kahaluu
Heeia State Park
KOOLAU
Kamehameha Hwy
Kahekili Hwy
RANGE
Kaneohe
Kailua
H1
Aiea
H3
Kailua Beach Park
Lanikai
Pearl Harbor
H201
Olomana
Likelike Hwy 63
78
Pali Hwy 61
Nuuanu Pali ▲ 1186'
Waimanalo
H1
Waimanalo Bay
Waimanalo Beach
72
★ Honolulu

EWA MAUKA
MAKAI DIAMOND HEAD

N

PACIFIC OCEAN

0   2 miles
0   2 kilometers

Named for the trade winds that blow with soothing predictability from the north-east, this sand-rimmed shoreline lies on the far side of the pali from Honolulu. Between these fluted emerald cliffs and the turquoise ocean are the bedroom communities of Lanikai, Kailua and Kaneohe and the agricultural regions of the Waiahole and Waikane valleys. As suburbs give way to small farms, this florid region provides a relaxing transition between the busy boulevards of Honolulu and the wild surf of the North Shore.

Kailua, which was previously a quiet suburb, has become a windsurfing mecca, attracting beginning and intermediate sailors from around the world to its shores. A protective reef, a lack of breakers and on-shore trade winds create near perfect conditions for the sport, and the residents of Kailua haven't overlooked the opportunities. Scores of families operate bed and breakfasts in residential neighborhoods, and windsurfers have become a part of the community. It's the kind of low-key place where even the likes of Robin Williams, who reportedly vacations there, can find an escape.

Moving north, the highway hugs the coast, revealing a steady succession of beaches, and passes through sleepy rural communities, where life seems little changed by the procession of tourists in rental cars and buses that pass by daily. In Laie, the Mormons set about creating a religious community that draws students from throughout the South Pacific to a branch of Brigham Young University and tourists to the Polynesian Cultural Center, which the students operate as the most popular tourist attraction on Oahu.

Leaving Laie, one returns to the sleepy ambience of rural Oahu, although even this bucolic region has not escaped the influence of tourism. A case in point is nearby Kahuku, a former sugar cane town whose mill has been converted into a small shopping center catering to visitor traffic. But the little town is better known for its sweet corn and aquaculture, evidence that agriculture is still alive in the country.

SIGHTS

KAILUA   From the southeastern corner of the island, the Kalanianaole Highway flows into Kailua, where it intersects with Route 61, or Kailua Road. This charming residential town is only 15 minutes from downtown Honolulu, but it feels like a world away. Bordered by an unspoiled white-sand beach on one side and the verdant Koolau Mountains on the other, Kailua boasts endless options for outdoor recreation. The community is big on canoe paddling, kite surfing, hiking and cycling, and it's the training ground for many of the island's triathletes. A string of strip malls along the main drag, Oneawa Street, offers a variety of smoothie and coffee shops, cute boutiques, small eateries and basic conveniences.

ULUPO HEIAU

✉*Take Route 61 to Kailua Road. Turn right and go about a quarter of a mile; the monument is behind the YMCA.*   The original purpose of this massive monument has been lost over time; it may have been a site once dedicated to the gods of agriculture or war. According to Hawaiian legend, this temple (which stands 30 feet high and measures 150 feet in length) was built by *Menehune*, who passed the building stones across a six-mile-long bucket brigade in a one-night construction project. The *Menehune*, in case you haven't been introduced, were tiny Hobbit-like creatures who inhab-

Windward Coast

Kahuku

MALAEKAHANA STATE
RECREATION AREA CABINS

KUALOA
REGIONAL PARK

Kailua

HOOMALUHIA
BOTANICAL GARDEN

BOOTS
AND KIMO'S
HOMESTYLE
KITCHEN

Honolulu

MALAEKAHANA STATE RECREATION AREA CABINS

PAGE 163

Six rustic beach houses offering back-to-nature accommodations in a tropical forest

KUALOA REGIONAL PARK

PAGE 168

Beachfront park backdropped by fluted cliffs and lush forests with a shoreline ideal for serene snorkeling

HOOMALUHIA BOTANICAL GARDEN

PAGE 157

Scenic nature conservancy with hundreds of acres of fruit trees, rainbow blossoms and panoramic ocean views

BOOTS AND KIMO'S HOMESTYLE KITCHEN

PAGE 165

Generous portions of macadamia nut pancakes, charbroiled Pulehu short ribs and savory turkey plates in a lively café

---

ited Hawaii even before the Polynesians arrived. They were reputed to be superhumanly strong and would work all night to build dams, temples and other structures. Several mysterious humanmade objects in the islands that archaeologists have trouble placing chronologically are claimed by mythmakers to be *Menehune* creations.

LANIKAI BEACH   A slight detour down Route 61 toward the Pacific will bring you to one of Oahu's premier neighborhoods—**Lanikai**—and one of its most beautiful beaches—Lanikai Beach. Actually, Lanikai has one of the *world's* best beaches. The sand is powder-fine; palm trees sway in the wind, providing enough shade to make for ideal sunbathing; and the water, protected by an offshore reef, is the color of Indian turquoise. When accessing Lanikai, use the public walkways so as not to disturb the local residents who live near this beach.

MOKULUAS   Offshore are two small islands, **Moku Iki** and **Moku Nui**, bird sanctuaries known as the Mokuluas. Moku Iki is off-limits, but you can kayak (or swim) out to dry, barren Moku Nui from Lanikai Beach; you'll find a fine-sand beach, where hundreds of birds will prob-

Windward Coast Sights

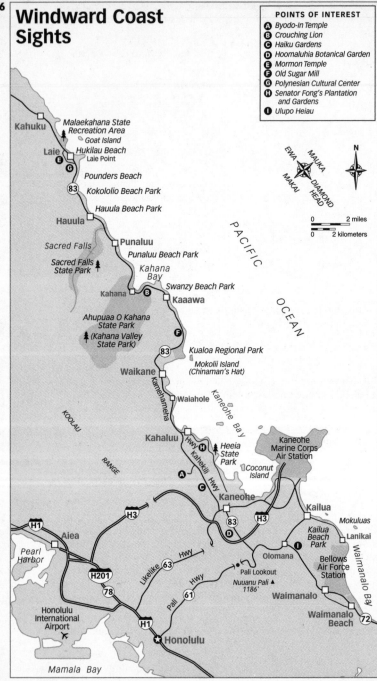

POINTS OF INTEREST

- **Ⓐ** Byodo-In Temple
- **Ⓑ** Crouching Lion
- **Ⓒ** Haiku Gardens
- **Ⓓ** Hoomaluhia Botanical Garden
- **Ⓔ** Mormon Temple
- **Ⓕ** Old Sugar Mill
- **Ⓖ** Polynesian Cultural Center
- **Ⓗ** Senator Fong's Plantation and Gardens
- **Ⓘ** Ulupo Heiau

EWA, MAUKA, MAKAI, DIAMOND HEAD

N

0   2 miles
0   2 kilometers

Kahuku

Malaekahana State Recreation Area
Goat Island
Laie
Hukilau Beach
Laie Point
Ⓔ Ⓖ
Pounders Beach
83
Kokololio Beach Park

Hauula Beach Park

Hauula

Sacred Falls

Punaluu

Punaluu Beach Park

Sacred Falls State Park

Kahana Bay

Kahana
Ⓑ
Swanzy Beach Park
Kaaawa

Ahupuaa O Kahana State Park
(Kahana Valley State Park)

Ⓕ
83
Kualoa Regional Park

Waikane
Mokolii Island (Chinaman's Hat)

Kamehameha

Waiahole

Kaneohe Bay

KOOLAU

RANGE

Kahaluu
Ⓗ
Heeia State Park
Kaneohe Marine Corps Air Station

Kahekili Hwy

Ⓐ
Coconut Island
Ⓒ
Kaneohe
83
H3

Kailua
Mokuluas

Ⓘ
Kailua Beach Park
Lanikai

H3

H1
Aiea

H3
Ⓓ

Pearl Harbor

Likelike Hwy
63
Hwy

Olomana
Bellows Air Force Station

H201
78

Pali Hwy
61
Pali Lookout
Nuuanu Pali 1186'

Waimanalo

Waimanalo Bay

Honolulu International Airport
H1
Honolulu ★

Waimanalo Beach
72

PACIFIC OCEAN

Mamala Bay

ably be your only company. The strand where you disembark from your kayak has a unique feature—the waves come from both sides of the island and create an enormous clashing sound. Around the back of the island is a little cove where people often swim, though the currents can be dangerous and the surf quite high, so be cautious.

HOOMALUHIA BOTANICAL GARDEN

✉ *45-680 Luluku Road, Kaneohe* ☎ *808-233-7323* 📠 *808-233-7326* Heading back to the main highway from Lanikai, you will find that Route 72 immediately merges into Route 61, which then continues for two miles to Route 83, the Kamehameha Highway. Above this thoroughfare, spreading across more than 400 acres at the foot of the *pali* is this botanical garden, a relaxing nature conservancy. With sheer cliffs rising on one side and a panoramic ocean view opening in the distance, it is a special place indeed. There is a 32-acre lake (no swimming) as well as a visitors center and hiking trails. Camping is available on weekends (permit required—get one at the garden office, open daily). The fruits, flowers and trees include hundreds of species native to Hawaii as well as tropical regions around the world.

HAIKU GARDENS

✉ *46-336 Haiku Road, Kaneohe* ☎ *808-247-0605* 📠 *808-247-5886* 🖥 *www.haikugardens.com* The Kahekili Highway (Route 83) carries you to these graceful gardens, located just outside Kailua. Formerly a private estate, the gardens rest in a lovely spot with a lofty rockface backdrop. Within this preserve are acres of exotic plant life, including an enchanting lily pond as well as numerous species of flowers. Hawaii specializes in beautiful gardens; the frequent rains and lush terrain make for luxuriant growing conditions. This happens to be one of the prettiest gardens of all.

VALLEY OF THE TEMPLES ✉ *47-200 Kahekili Highway, Kaneohe* ☎ *808-239-8811* Along the Kahekili Highway (Route 83) you'll encounter this verdant chasm folded between the mountains and the sea. Part of the valley has been consecrated as a cemetery honoring the Japanese. Highlighting the region is the **Byodo-In Temple**. Rimmed by 2000-foot cliffs, this Buddhist shrine is a replica of a 900-year-old temple in Kyoto, Japan. It was constructed in 1968 in memory of the first Japanese immigrants to settle in Hawaii. The simple architecture is enhanced by a bronze bell weighing seven tons that visitors are permitted to ring. A statue of Buddha dominates the site. Walk along the placid reflecting pool with its swans, ducks and multihued carp and you will be drawn a million miles away from the bustle of Honolulu. Admission.

KANEOHE BAY ✉ *Located along Kamehameha Highway (Route 836), a few hundred yards before it merges with Route 83* This sparkling bay is the state's largest sheltered body of water. About eight miles long and a little less than three miles wide, it possesses the only barrier reef in the islands. Viewed from on high, the various shades of blue are quite dramatic—from light blues, aqua, to royal blue. They reflect the diverse bottom conditions of Kaneohe: the coral reefs, shallows and greater depths. There's also a sandbar that is completely submerged during high tides. Because of its unique conditions, Kaneohe Bay is one of the most studied bays in the world. It is also one of the most picturesque spots on Oahu.

CORAL QUEEN ✉️*Heeia Kea Harbor, Kamehameha Highway* 📞*808-292-8470* 📠*808-236-0722* For a closer look, without getting wet, you can take an hour-long glass-bottom boat ride aboard the *Coral Queen*. Not only will you see patch reefs, fringe reefs and scads of tropical fish, a sea turtle might just glide by the finger or rice corals that have been transplanted in the bay. To get there, simply follow North Kalaheo Avenue through Kailua, then pick up Kaneohe Bay Drive, and turn right on Route 836, which curves for miles before linking with Route 83. Closed Sunday.

HAWAIIAN FISHPONDS

Along the bay shores are ancient Hawaiian fishponds, rock-bound enclosures constructed by the early Polynesians to raise fresh seafood. Though they once lined the shores of Oahu, today only a quarter (about 100) of the ponds remain in usable condition. Several rest along this Windward Coast. One of the largest is located near Heeia State Park. It's an impressive engineering feat that measures 500 feet in length and once contained an 88-acre fish farm. The stone walls in places are 12 feet thick. Ancient Hawaiians would have fared well on the television series *Survivor*; they had fishtrapping down pat. Using enclosed brackish water off the coast, fish were bred and maintained in fishponds through ingenious use of *makaha*, sluice gates that controlled the in- and outflow of water. Designed to allow young fish in and keep the ready-to-eat fish from escaping, the gates also helped control the growth of algae, the lowest but most vital rung on the pond food ladder. This ancient technique is still practiced in the bay, where the **Kualoa Ranch** (808-237-7321; www.kualoa.com) maintains an operational pond, a cattle ranch and sells its produce.

HEEIA STATE PARK

✉️*46-465 Kamehameha Highway at Kealohi Point* 📞*808-247-3156* Continuing along Route 836 you'll come to this state park, a small greensward located on Kealohi Point, anchored by a lighthouse. Kealohi Point was a significant spot for ancient Hawaiians: It was thought to be a jumping-off point of the soul into the spirit world. This park is a perfect spot for a picnic with lovely views of the bay and the ancient fishpond. Offshore you'll see **Coconut Island**, made famous in the opening of TV's *Gilligan's Island*. Adjacent to the park is **Heeia Kai Boat Harbor**.

SENATOR FONG'S PLANTATION AND GARDENS

✉ *47-285 Pulama Road, Kaneohe* ☎ *808-239-6775* 📠 *808-239-6469* ⬧ *www. fonggarden.com, info@ fonggarden.com* High above Kaneohe, gazing down upon the bay, is Senator Fong's. Here you can take an hour-and-a-half long leisure walk throughout 700 acres of gardens and orchards. This luxurious preserve was donated by one of Hawaii's most famous U.S. senators, so be prepared to venture from Eisenhower Valley to Kennedy Valley (sugar cane) to the Johnson Plateau (fruit orchards) to Nixon Valley (gardens) to the Ford Plateau (pine trees). Guides will take you on a one-mile walking tour (that can expand to two miles if you're up for it). Admission.

WAIAHOLE VALLEY AND WAIKANE VALLEY   Route 83 soon becomes known as the Kamehameha Highway as it courses past lazy fishing boats then enters these valleys, some of the last places on the island where Hawaiian farmers grow crops in the traditional way. Fruit stands line the highway. The roads off the highway lead to small Hawaiian enclaves, where you'll see taro patches and papaya trees in the people's backyards.

KUALOA REGIONAL PARK ✉*49-479 Kamehameha Highway* As you round the bend you'll come to one of the loveliest regional parks on the island. Kualoa in Hawaiian means "long back," and this area is rich in ancient and sacred history (see "Beaches & Parks" below).

CHINAMAN'S HAT   That cone-shaped island offshore is Chinaman's Hat. It was named for its resemblance to a coolie cap, though the Hawaiians had another name for it long before the Chinese arrived in the islands. They called it Mokolii Island, or "little dragon," and claimed it represented the tail of a beast that resided under the water. Watch for frigate birds and delicate white-tailed tropical birds flying overhead.

KUALOA RANCH & ACTIVITY CLUB ✉*45-560 Kamehameha Highway, Kaaawa* ☎*808-237-7321* ⬧*www.kualoa.com* Right past the entrance to the regional park on the *mauka* side of the highway is Kualoa Ranch & Activity Club, one of the settings for *Jurassic Park* and *Godzilla*. Unfortunately, you're only likely to see horses grazing in the pasture with white herons on their back. Today the ranch offers visitors a variety of sporting activities, including kayaking, horseback riding and tours. The ranch is also the site of **Molii Fishpond**, one of the ancient fishponds used by Hawaiians, and there's a visitors center.

OLD SUGAR MILL   Just down the road from Kualoa Ranch is Oahu's first sugar mill, which lies in ruin along the side of the road. Built during the 1860s, it fell into disuse soon after completion and has since served only as a local curiosity.

KAAAWA   Along Kamehameha Highway you'll pass the sleepy community of Kaaawa and **Swanzy Beach Park** (see "Beaches & Parks" section below). Behind the scattering of homes along the road, **Kaaawa**

Valley reaches far inland, flanked by daunting, knife-edged cliffs on either side. The area is steeped in legend, a place where chiefs trained for battle, fishponds were built by *Menehune* and night marchers (ghosts of warriors) made their way to the sea. A powerful energy presides over the valley, still largely untouched by development, and it remains one of the most beautiful places on the island.

CROUCHING LION A few miles after Swanzy Beach, be on the lookout for the Hawaii Visitors Bureau marker noting Crouching Lion (there's also a restaurant by the same name just below the mountain). To the ancient Hawaiians, who had never experienced the king of the jungle, the stone face was, in fact, that of Kauhi, a demigod from the island of Tahiti who was turned into stone during a struggle between Pele and her sister Hiiaka.

KAHANA BAY

✉ *52-222 Kamehameha Highway, across from Kahana Valley State Park* Once the sight of a burgeoning Hawaiian fishing village, this coral-studded bay is now a tranquil spot for a picnic or swim in the sea. Be sure to look out for **Huilua Fishpond** located at the mouth of the Kahana Stream. Constructed more than 800 years ago, the seven-acre pond is among the oldest of the 100 or so ponds that once provided food for the Hawaiian population. Fish from the ocean entered the pond through a sluice gate that could be closed to keep them from escaping. On the north side of the bay, look for a fishing shrine called **Kapaeleele Koa**, where rituals were held and fishermen would leave offerings in hopes of a good catch.

KAHANA VALLEY STATE PARK

✉ *55-222 Kamehameha Highway (Route 83) about 14 miles north of Kaneohe* ☎ *808-587-0300* 🖳 *808-587-0311* Across the highway from the Huilua Fishpond is this state park (it's official name is Ahupuaa O Kahana State Park, but few call it by that moniker). If you like to hike there's a trail up the valley through lush foliage that weaves past old farmsteads. The valley was once filled with taro patches, another primary source of food for the Hawaiians who lived here. The *auwai*, irrigation canals that diverted water from the stream to feed the taro, are still visible, and there is also evidence of sacred *heiau*, or temples. Also once abundant in the valley were *hau* trees, a low-lying hibiscus with heart-shaped leaves that produces brightly colored red and yellow flowers in the summer. This tree was important to Hawaiians, who built outriggers for their canoes from the wood, wove rope from the bark, and used the sap and flowers for medicine. Check out the visitors and orientation centers here. Please be respectful of those who live here.

PUNALUU After Kahana Valley Park, the highway, still crowding the coastline, traverses the roadside community of Punaluu, legendary home of the demigod Kamapuaa, one of Pele's lovers. There's a long, narrow strand of sand and ocean at **Punaluu Beach Park**, which offers pleasant swimming opportunities because of an offshore reef. (However, use caution when the weather is stormy.)

HAUULA The roadway continues up to this small town with its old **Hauula Door of Faith Church**, a small chapel of clapboard design surrounded by palms. Not far from it is another aging woodframe sanctuary, **Hauula Congregational Christian Church**, built of wood and coral back in 1862.

LAIE Once thought to have been an ancient place of refuge for Hawaiians, this town is now a stronghold for Mormons. The Hawaii campus of **Brigham Young University** is located here, as well as the **Mormon Temple**. The Mormons settled in Hawaii back in 1864; today they make up about two percent of the population in Hawaii. The courtyards and grounds of the temple are open to the public, but only Mormons are permitted to enter the temple sanctuary.

POLYNESIAN CULTURAL CENTER ✉ *55-370 Kamehameha Highway, Laie* ✆ *808-293-3333, 800-367-7060* ✆ *888-722-7339* ⌂ *www.polynesia.com* The Mormons own this cultural center, Oahu's most popular tourist attraction. Set right on Kamehameha Highway in Laie, it represents one of the foremost theme parks in the entire Pacific, a 42-acre attempt to recreate ancient Polynesia. As you wander about the grounds you'll encounter ersatz villages portraying life in the Marquesas, Tahiti, Fiji, Tonga, New Zealand and old Hawaii. Step over to the Tahitian hamlet and you will experience the rocking *tamure* dance. Or wander onto the islands of Samoa, where the local inhabitants demonstrate how to climb coconut trees. In Tonga a native will be beating tapa cloth from mulberry bark, while the Fijians are pounding rhythms with poles of bamboo. These mock villages are linked by waterways and can be visited in canoes. The boats will carry you past craftsmen preparing poi by mashing taro roots, and others husking coconuts.

The most popular shows are the "Rainbows of Paradise," in which the boats head up a lagoon amid a flurry of singing and dancing, and "Horizons." The latter is an evening show similar to Waikiki's Polynesian revues, though generally considered more elaborate. Most of the entertainers and other employees at this Hawaiian-style Disneyland are Mormon students attending the local university. Closed Sunday. Admission.

LAIE POINT ✉ *Head toward the ocean on Anemoku Street, off Kamehameha Highway, then turn right on Naupaka Street* Be sure to take in this point, the town's natural wonder. The headland provides extraordinary ocean views sweeping for miles along the shoreline. Since the breezes and surf are wilder here than elsewhere on the Windward Coast, you'll often encounter waves lashing at the two offshore islets with amazing force. The island with the hole in it is **Kukihoolua** or, as the locals call it, Puka Rock.

MALAEKAHANA STATE RECREATION AREA ✉*Kamehameha Highway (Route 83) in Laie about 23 miles north of Kaneohe* Along the oceanside, a few miles outside of Laie, hidden behind the vines hugging the road is Malaekahana (see "Beaches & Parks" for added description). This gem of a park offers a long strand of white sand lined with ironwood trees.

GOAT ISLAND Offshore of Malaekahana State Recreation Area is Goat Island, or Mokuauia, a bird sanctuary you can actually wade over to when the tide is right (be sure to wear reef slippers or some such foot covering and be careful of the currents).

LODGING

HAWAII'S HIDDEN HIDEAWAY B&B

$$–$$$ 3 ROOMS   ✉*1369 Mokolea Drive, Kailua* ☎*808-262-6560, 877-443-3299* 📠*808-262-6561* ✎*www.ahawaiibnb.com, hhhideaway@yahoo.com*

Out in the suburban town of Kailua, where trim houses front a beautiful white-sand beach, you'll discover Hawaii's Hidden Hideaway B&B, which I recommend for more than just its name. It really is a lovely bed and breakfast, with lots of privacy. There are a suite and two studios available; the suite has an outdoor spa with an ocean view. All three have private entrances, parking and decks, and kitchenettes stocked with breakfast goodies. You're quite close to the beaches of Lanikai and Kailua, and a 30-minute or so drive to Waikiki. Three-night minimum stay—not that that will be difficult.

SHARON'S KAILUA SERENITY

$ 3 UNITS   ✉*127 Kakahiaka Street, Kailua* ☎*808-262-5621, 800-914-2271* ✎*www.sharonsserenity.com*

Located in a quiet canal-side neighborhood four blocks from Kailua Beach, Sharon's is a popular bed and breakfast with two rooms and a suite. Guests have use of the swimming pool and access to a comfortable, spacious living room. Host Sharon Price serves an expanded continental breakfast and offers up plenty of advice to those who want it. This B&B can be booked directly; there is a three-night minimum stay. Children over eight years of age are welcome.

PAT'S KAILUA BEACH PROPERTIES

$$–$$$ 31 ROOMS   ✉*204 South Kalaheo Avenue, Kailua* ☎*808-262-4128, 808-261-1653* 📠*808-261-0893* ✎*www.patskailua.com, info@patskailua.com*

Overlooking Kailua Beach Park and about 100 yards from the beach sits this cluster of woodframe cottages. Each is equipped with a full kitchen, cable television and a telephone. Some of the furniture is nicked, but these units (from studios to five-bedroom homes) are clean and cozy. They sit in a yard shaded with monkeypod, coconut and breadfruit trees and provide an excellent value.

SCHRADER'S WINDWARD COUNTRY INN

$$–$$$ 50 ROOMS   ✉47-039 Lihikai Drive, Kaneohe   ☎808-239-5711, 800-735-5071   📠808-239-6658   🖥www.schradersinn.com, info@schradersinn.com

You can't get much closer to the water than Schrader's. It's an unusual resting place consisting of several woodframe buildings right on the edge of Kaneohe Bay. There are picnic tables, barbecue grills and a pool on the two-acre property, as well as a tour boat that can take you snorkeling, kayaking or sightseeing on the bay. The guest rooms are cottage-style with kitchenettes; many have lanais and bay views. Prices include continental breakfast.

ALI'I BLUFFS BED & BREAKFAST

$ 2 ROOMS   ✉46-251 Ikiiki Street, Kaneohe   ☎808-235-1124, 800-235-1151   🖥www.hawaiiscene.com/aliibluffs, donm@lava.net

This contemporary Hawaiian B&B offers two rooms with private baths. The Victorian room features antiques and vintage paintings; the Circus room has large circus posters, many of them originals, from around the world. Furnished in antiques and Persian rugs, this charming home offers a full breakfast served poolside every morning.

LAIE INN

$–$$ 49 ROOMS   ✉55-109 Laniloa Street, Laie   ☎808-293-9282, 800-526-4562   📠808-293-8115   🖥www.laieinnhawaii.com, laieinn@hawaii.rr.com

A low-slung motel with two floors of rooms surrounding a swimming pool, the Laie Inn is a standard soda-machine-in-the-courtyard facility located next to the Polynesian Cultural Center.

MALAEKAHANA STATE RECREATION AREA CABINS

hidden

$ 7 UNITS   ✉Kamehameha Highway (Route 83) in Laie about 23 miles north of Kaneohe   ☎808-293-1736   📠808-293-2066   🖥www.malaekahana.net

For a back-to-nature experience, this tropical forest has six beach houses with two or three bedrooms, private baths and kitchens (starting at $80 per night) and a four-room cabin with a game room and a commercial kitchen ($250 per night). There are five yurts that sleep two to four people ($50 to $100 per night) and 10 "li'l grass shacks" ($40 per night for two people). Keep in mind that the cabins here are more like indoor camping than motel accommodations: They're equipped with beds, kitchen facilities and bathrooms. Bring your own bedding and cooking gear and be prepared for very rustic accommodations.

DINING

BUZZ'S ORIGINAL STEAK HOUSE

$$$ STEAK   ✉413 Kawailoa Road, Kailua   ☎808-261-4661   🖥www.buzzssteakhouse.com

Kailua has a collection of eating establishments spread throughout the town. Among them is Buzz's, right across the street from the beach. The place is popular not only with windsurfers, but with Honolulu residents who drive out on the weekends to enjoy the surf and a meal at this upscale beach shack, which has been in business since 1962. Burgers, steaks and seafood are the specialties here, and all entrées include a trip to the salad bar at dinnertime.

CINNAMON'S RESTAURANT

$$ CONTINENTAL ✉ *Kailua Square Shopping Center, 315 Uluniu Street, Kailua* ✆ *808-261-8724* 🕿 *808-262-9910* 🖅 *www.cinnamonsrestaurant.com, cinnamonrest@aol.com*

Known for years as a prime breakfast and lunch place, Cinnamon's draws a local crowd, which sits beneath the dining room gazebo or out on the patio. The menu is best described as Continental cuisine with local flavors. Try the chicken cashew sandwich or the carrot pancakes—all made from scratch! No lunch Sunday, no dinner.

ASSAGGIO RISTORANTE ITALIANO

$$$ ITALIAN ✉ *354 Uluniu Street, Kailua* ✆ *808-261-2772* 🖅 *www.assaggiokailua.clearwire.net*

Assaggio Ristorante Italiano in the downtown Kailua Business Center has a spacious, breezy dining room that still manages to feel cozy. It's ideal for a relaxed meal of pasta, stuffed eggplant, veal scallopine and other well-prepared Italian dishes, and is popular with the lunchtime business crowd. No lunch on weekends.

BACI BISTRO

$$–$$$ ITALIAN ✉ *30 Aulike Street, Kailua* ✆ *808-262-7555* 🕿 *808-261-2857* 🖅 *www.restauranteur.com/bacibistro*

Kailua residents will tell you the pastas here are all homemade and beautifully prepared. You have the option of sitting in the small dining room with greenhouse windows or in the romantic covered lanai. There are veal and fish entrées, risotto dishes and an array of antipasti. No lunch on Saturday and Sunday.

SAKU

$$–$$$ JAPANESE/SUSHI ✉ *20 Kainehe Street, Kailua* ✆ *808-262-5661*

This *izakaya* (featuring tapas-like small plates) restaurant provides Kailuans with Japanese cuisine that some would argue rivals the best in Honolulu. Their signature *tebakara*, garlic-soy-coated chicken wings, are a must-try. The modern, deep red dining room is warm and inviting, and the welcoming Japanese owners pride themselves on food that is healthy rather than greasy—a major selling point for health-conscious Kailua residents. Sharing a variety of selections from the *izakaya* menu keeps the meal affordable, or you can splurge on *nigiri* and designer sushi rolls. Closed Sunday.

TIMES COFFEE SHOP

$ AMERICAN/LOCAL-STYLE ✉ *153 Hamakua Drive, Kailua* ✆ *808-262-0300*

Slide into a booth at this coffee shop, where breakfast brings together local favorites (Portuguese sausage omelettes, Spam and eggs) and American classics (pancakes, waffles). Fried rice, hamburger steaks, grilled mahimahi and sandwiches make an appearance on the lunch menu. No dinner.

BOOTS AND KIMO'S HOMESTYLE KITCHEN

$ AMERICAN/LOCAL-STYLE   ✉*131 Hekili Street #102, Kailua*
📞*808-263-7929*

Generous portions of American and local dishes are what keep customers coming back to Boots and Kimo's. The mac-nut pancakes and charbroiled Pulehu short ribs are favorites, as well as omelettes like the Maui Wowie (a vegetarian option with jalapeños) and the Pakalolo (ham and veggies). At lunch, there's teri chicken and turkey plates, too. You'll wait in line on the busy weekends. Breakfast and lunch only. Closed Monday (unless it is a holiday).

SAENG'S THAI CUISINE

$–$$ THAI   ✉*315 Hahani Road, Kailua* 📞*808-263-9727*

Saeng's is a freshly decorated Southeast Asian restaurant with a hardwood bar and potted plants all around. Located in a strip mall, it nevertheless conveys a sense of elegance. The menu focuses on vegetarian, seafood and curry dishes. No lunch on weekends.

FORMAGGIO GRILL

$$$ ITALIAN   ✉*305 Hahani Street, Kailua* 📞*808-263-2633*
✍*www.formaggio808.com*

Sister to the award-winning wine bar in Honolulu, this jovial restaurant has a warm and happy atmosphere with tables of smiling patrons engaged in lively conversation that gets louder beneath the vaulted ceiling as the wine continues to flow. The bistro menu selections range from simple, like pizza and panini, to extravagant—beef bourguignon *grande mère* and foie gras crostini. There are numerous options for steak-lovers and vegetarians alike and, of course, a dizzying wine list that makes it hard to resist raising a glass. Dinner is accompanied by live music Wednesday through Saturday, and the lights stay on until midnight on Wednesday and Thursday, and 1 a.m. on Friday and Saturday.

KOA PANCAKE HOUSE

$$ AMERICAN   ✉*46-126 Kahuhipa Street, Kaneohe* 📞*808-235-5772*

This tastefully appointed restaurant features a breakfast bill of fare that includes pancakes and crêpes suzette and a lunch menu with salads, sandwiches, teriyaki chicken and seafood. No dinner.

HALEIWA JOE'S SEAFOOD GRILL

$$–$$$ STEAK/SEAFOOD   ✉*46-336 Haiku Road, Kaneohe* 📞*808-247-6671*
📠*808-247-5886* ✍*www.haleiwajoes.com*

What sets Haleiwa Joe's apart is its idyllic setting. A terraced dining area overlooks sharp cliffs and peaceful flower beds, making this a choice stop for dinner. The menu consists of steak, seafood and prime rib with a Pan-Asian influence. Dinner only; brunch available on Sunday.

SUMO RAMEN AND CURRY HOUSE

$ LOCAL-STYLE   ✉*Kaneohe Shopping Center, 46-047 Kamehameha Highway, Kaneohe* ☎*808-234-6868*

Serving up tasty local food, ranging from Spam curry to seafood ramen bowls and beef stew, this place is a sure bet. Prices range from $3.50 to $6.50, making it one of the cheapest eateries in the area.

CROUCHING LION INN

$$$–$$$$ AMERICAN   ✉*51-666 Kamehameha Highway, Kaaawa* ☎*808-237-8981* ⌨*www.crouchinglionhawaii.com*

The setting is the draw at this vintage 1927 English Tudor–style house at the foot of verdant mountains. The food isn't remarkable, but they do have the most extensive menu in the area. Try the specialties: honey garlic shrimp, macadamia chicken and flame-broiled scallops. The beautiful ocean view makes it a worthy stop, even without food. One drawback: It's popular with tour buses, so try to arrive at an off-hour.

SHOPPING

Shopping on the Windward Coast is not a major activity. Kailua and Kaneohe both have large shopping centers but the stores are not noteworthy. There are, however, a few places to stop by and browse.

ISLAND SNOW ✉*Kailua Beach Center, 130 Kailua Road, Kailua* ☎*808-263-6339* Locals recommend Island Snow for shave ice, an island favorite. Rainbow (a combination of banana, strawberry and vanilla) is probably the most popular cone, but you can customize your treat further with adzuki beans, ice cream or a "snowcap" sweet topping. T-shirts, sunglasses and other beachy merchandise are also available.

KAILUA SHOPPING CENTER ✉*Kailua Road and Hahani Street, Kailua* Kailua Shopping Center offers a wide range of services at 20 stores.

KAILUA FARMERS' MARKET ✉*Kailua Town Center Parking* ⌨*www.hfbf. org/FarmersMarket.html* On Thursdays, you can visit the Kailua Farmers' Market, held from 5 to 7:30 p.m. at Kailua Town Center Parking.

ISLAND TREASURES ART GALLERY

✉*629 Kailua Road, Suite 103, Kailua* ☎*808-261-8131* Peruse an exceptional collection of pottery, wooden boxes, jewelry, paintings, handcrafted wooden furniture, shell candles and etched glass with island designs, all created by artists living in Hawaii.

OLIVE BOUTIQUE ✉*43 Kihapai Street, Kailua* ☎*808-263-9919* ⌨*www.iheart olive.com* Oahu native Ali McMahon's boutique speaks to smart island fashion, featuring contemporary women's clothing lines—Indah, Free People, Ella Moss and more—that combine style and comfort (read:

lots of popular cottons). There's an uplifting vibe to the place, perhaps leftover karma from the flower shop that used to be there. Olive also sells jewelry, candles, greeting cards and other gift items.

KANEOHE SHOPPING CENTER ✉*45-934 Kamehameha Highway, Kaneohe* Kaneohe Shopping Center, located across Kamehameha Highway from Windward Mall, is anchored by a Safeway and Longs Drugs and is designed to offer one-stop shopping for practical purchases.

LANCE FAIRLY GALLERY ✉*53-839 Kamehameha Highway, Punaluu* ☎*808-293-9009, 888-293-1188* ✐*www.lancefairly.com* Expect original paintings by local artists, limited-edition prints and enameled tropical fish at this Punaluu shop.

NIGHTLIFE

BOARD RIDERS BAR AND GRILL ✉*201 Hamakua Drive #A, Kailua* ☎*808-261-4600* ✐*www.boardriderskailua.com* Nights on the Windward Coast are quiet and peaceful, and most people like it that way, aside from the large number of military personnel who frequent the night spots. For those who prefer a bit of action, head to Kailua, where there's always something going on at Board Riders. This sports bar has a pool table and dartboards; on many nights there are dance tunes ranging from reggae to rock. Occasional cover on Friday and Saturday.

TIARE'S SPORTS BAR & GRILL ✉*120 Hekili Street, Kailua* ☎*808-230-8911* ✐*www.tiares.com* Tiare's boasts seven television screens, darts and pool. A sports bar that attracts a slightly rowdy clientele when the hour grows late, it's the only Windward club open until 4 a.m. It tends to be loud, and gets louder Thursday through Saturday nights when local live music is featured after 10 p.m. and folks start drinking hard and dancing. There is free karaoke on Tuesdays, with some interesting jam sessions. Burgers and *pupus* available on weekend nights only.

BEACHES & PARKS

KAILUA BEACH
✉*Off Kalaheo Avenue*

Stretching for two miles with white sand all the way and tiny islands offshore, this is one of the prettiest beaches around. It's in the suburban town of Kailua, so you'll trade seclusion for excellent beach facilities. The center of activity is **Kailua Beach Park**, off Kawailoa Road near the south end of the beach. This 30-acre facility has a grassy expanse shaded by ironwood and coconut trees and is perfect for picnicking. There are restrooms and a pavilion. **Kalama Beach County Park** (250 North Kalaheo Avenue), a small park with restrooms in the middle of Kailua Beach, is less crowded. Swimming, surfing and bodysurfing are good all along the strand and windsurfing is excellent, but exercise caution.

LANIKAI BEACH

✉The strand parallels Mokulua Drive. Lanikai can be reached by driving south along the beachfront roads in Kailua.

 Everyone's dream house is on the beach at Lanikai. This sandy stretch, varying from 20 to 100 feet in width, extends for over a mile. The entire beach in this residential community is lined with those houses everybody wants. The water is the color of cobalt and the protecting reef offshore makes the entire beach safe for swimming. Lanikai has also become a windsurfing favorite. No facilities; the nearest facilities are at Kailua Beach.

HEEIA STATE PARK

✉46-465 Kamehameha Highway; Just outside of Kaneohe

This small pocket park located off of Kamehameha Highway at Kealohi Point is an ideal spot to picnic when traveling around the island. The views of Kaneohe Bay and the ancient Hawaiian fishpond are noteworthy. Numerous indigenous plants thrive here and there are educational programs offered by Friends of Heeia State Park. In addition, there's a pavilion, picnic tables and restrooms.

KUALOA REGIONAL PARK

✉49-479 Kamehameha Highway (Route 83) about ten miles north of Kaneohe

You could search the entire Pacific for a setting as lovely as this one. Just 500 yards offshore lies the islet of Mokolii, better known as Chinaman's Hat. Behind the beach the *pali* creates a startling background of fluted cliffs and tropical forest. The beach is a long and narrow strip of sand paralleled by a wide swath of grass parkland. Little wonder this is one of the Windward Coast's most popular picnic areas. It is usually a favorite for swimming, snorkeling and fishing, but high bacteria levels during rainy seasons sometimes result in beach closures. Facilities include picnic areas, restrooms and showers.

▲ Tent camping permitted. County permit required.

SWANZY BEACH PARK, PUNALUU BEACH PARK AND HAUULA BEACH PARK

✉These parks are all located along Kamehameha Highway (Route 83). Swanzy lies about 12 miles north of Kaneohe, Punaluu is about four miles north of Swanzy, and Hauula is about three miles beyond that.

These three county facilities lie along Kamehameha Highway (Route 83) within seven miles of each other. Swimming is generally good at each. Along this coast the most abundant fish is *papio*, followed by bonefish, milkfish and goatfish. Camping is allowed at all except Punaluu, but none compare aesthetically with other beaches to the north and south. Swanzy is located on the highway but lacks a sandy beach. However, it has the best diving. Its surf break, "Crouching Lion," is for experts only; Punaluu, possessing a pretty palm-fringed beach, has great swimming year-round; and Hauula, a spacious park with a beach and a winter surf break for beginners, is visited periodically by tour buses. So put these beach parks near the bottom of your list, and bring them up only if the other beaches are too crowded. All three beaches have picnic areas and restrooms.

▲ Tent and trailer camping allowed at Hauula Beach Park, as well as at Swanzy Beach Park on weekends. A county permit is required. 808-523-4525 or 808-768-3440.

KAHANA VALLEY STATE PARK

✉ *52-222 Kamehameha Highway (Route 83) about 14 miles north of Kaneohe*
📞 *808-587-0300* 🖨 *808-587-0311* 🖱 *www.hawaiistateparks.org*

🏃 🛶 🚣 Officially called Ahupuaa O Kahana State Park, this 5228-acre paradise, set on a white-sand beach, offers something for every adventurer. You can pick fruit in a lush forest, picnic in a coconut grove and see an ancient fishpond. You can also fish for *papio*, bonefish, milkfish and goatfish. Swimming is generally good. Surfing is a possibility but is mediocre at best. Facilities include an orientation center, picnic areas and restrooms.

▲ There's tent camping on the beach; $5 per night. No camping on Thursday. State permit required.

KOKOLOLIO BEACH PARK

✉ *55-017 Kamehameha Highway (Route 83) in Laie about 20 miles north of Kaneohe*

🚣 🎣 🚣 Here's one of the prettiest beaches on the Windward Coast. With trees and a lawn that extends toward the white-sand beach, it's a highly recommended spot for day-tripping. It's a popular place for speardiving when the ocean is calm, and the shorebreak offers fun bodysurfing and bodyboarding action. In the winter, north swells bring sizeable waves to a surf spot called "Statues," best when the winds are variable or out of the south. Common catches include *papio*, bonefish, goatfish and milkfish. There are picnic areas and restrooms.

▲ Camping allowed with county permit, call 808-768-3440.

POUNDERS BEACH

✉ *Kamehameha Highway north of Kakela Beach*

🚣 🚣 Named for the crushing shorebreak that makes it a popular bodysurfing beach, this quarter-mile-long strand features a corridor of white sand and a sandy bottom. Swimming is good near the old landing at the western end of the beach. Be careful of currents when swimming anywhere along the beach. Anglers try for *ono*, *moi* and *papio*. There are showers, but no other facilities here.

HUKILAU BEACH

✉ *55-692 Kamehameha Highway (Route 83) in Laie about 22 miles north of Kaneohe*

🚣 🛶 🎣 🚣 This privately owned facility fronts a beautiful white-sand beach that winds for more than a mile. Part of the beach is lined with homes, but much of it is undeveloped. Several small islands lie offshore, and the park contains a lovely stand of ironwood trees. All in all this enchanting beach is one of the finest on this side of the island.

Swimming is good; bodysurfing is also recommended. Snorkeling is usually fair and there are small surfable waves with left and right slides. The principal catch is *papio*; milkfish, bonefish and goatfish are also caught. There are no facilities here.

MALAEKAHANA STATE RECREATION AREA AND GOAT ISLAND _____

✉*Kamehameha Highway (Route 83) in Laie about 23 miles north of Kaneohe*

🏊 🎣 ⛺ 🚿 This is a rare combination. The Malaekahana facility is one of the island's prettiest parks. It's a tropical wonderland filled with palm, *hala* and ironwood trees, and graced with a curving, white-sand beach. Goat Island or Mokuauia, lies just offshore. When the tide is right, you can wade out to it. Other times, grab a boogie board or surf board and paddle out with a picnic lunch. It's a small, low-lying island covered with scrub growth and scattered ironwood trees. On the windward side is a coral beach; to leeward lies a crescent-shaped white-sand beach. It's a good place to swim because it is shallow and well-protected. There are also good places for snorkeling and, in winter, you can paddle out to a break with a left slide. Feel like fishing? You may well reel in *papio*, the most abundant fish along here; goatfish, milkfish and bonefish are also caught. Goat Island is now a state bird refuge, so you might see wedge-tailed shearwaters nesting. Whatever activity you choose, make sure you don't disturb the birds. Goat Island will return the favor—there'll be nothing here to disturb you either. Facilities include showers, bathrooms and barbecue pits.

▲ There are two sections to the park. The Laie section includes Goat Island and is administered by the state. The Kahuku section (Puuhonua o Malaekahana, or Place of Refuge) is operated by the Friends of Malaekahana, the first native Hawaiian group to operate a park in the islands.

Laie Section: Tent camping allowed. State permit required.

Kahuku Section: There are rustic cabins available here. These beachfront units include 27 campsites and seven beach cabins that make for an indoor-camping experience (see "Windward Coast Lodging" for more information). Tent sites are $8.50 per person, per night. Information: 808-293-1736, fax 808-293-2066; www.malaekahana.net.

NORTH SHORE

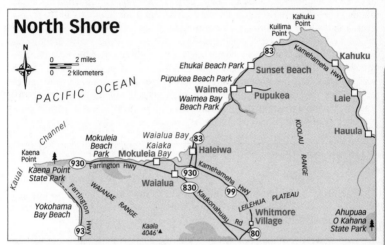

North Shore

PACIFIC OCEAN

Kauai Channel

Kahuku Point
Kuilima Point
83
Kamehameha Hwy
Kahuku
Ehukai Beach Park
Pupukea Beach Park
Sunset Beach
Waimea
Waimea Bay Beach Park
Pupukea
Laie
Mokuleia Beach Park
Waialua Bay
Kaiaka Bay
Mokuleia Bay
83
Haleiwa
Hauula
Kaena Point
930
Farrington Hwy
Kamehameha Hwy
99
Kaena Point State Park
930
Waialua
830
Kaukonahuav Rd
LEILEHUA PLATEAU
KOOLAU RANGE
Whitmore Village
Ahupuaa O Kahana State Park
Yokohama Bay Beach
WAIANAE RANGE
Farrington Hwy
Kaala 4046'
93
80

Wide, wide beaches heaped with white, white sand roll for miles along the North Shore, which curves from Kahuku Point in the east to Kaena Point in the west. Although they can compete with the most beautiful beaches anywhere, it's not the sand nor their size that is the main attraction here. Rather it is the winter waves, and these waves have made Oahu's North Shore legendary and very busy during surf season. Surfers come from around the world to try their skill at one of the world's most renowned spots for the sport.

If you have ever owned a surfboard, or even a Beach Boys album, you know Waimea Bay and Sunset Beach. The names are synonymous with surfing. They number among the most challenging and dangerous surf spots anywhere. During the winter, 15- to 20-foot waves are as common as bleached hair and beach buggies. The infamous "Banzai Pipeline," where surfers risk limb and longevity as thunderous waves pass over a shallow reef, is here as well.

The surf is not the only thing that's superb. The setting is stunning. Oahu's two mountain ranges form the backdrop, while 4025-foot Mt. Kaala, the island's highest peak, towers above all. Small ranches and farms checkerboard the tableland between the mountains and the sea. The old-time farmers, the surfers and the counterculture types who live in the area all come to Haleiwa for shopping, dining and socializing. Haleiwa, a restored plantation town with old clapboard buildings and wooden sidewalks, preserves the spirit of a rural way of life that is rapidly disappearing.

The plantations that established Oahu's economic base have all closed. In fact, the last sugar mill on the island, located in the North Shore town of Waialua, shut down in 1996, marking the end of a major chapter in Oahu's history. Although the Waialua Sugar Company now no longer processes cane, this low-key village west of Haleiwa still has the feel of a sugar town. The mill, which stands at its center, and the old Bank of Hawaii building, serve as reminders of a past that just yesterday was the present.

As the hub of sugar production has shifted to other areas of the world, the farmers of Oahu have filled the vacuum. Coffee experienced a bum crop when it was first planted here in the early 1800s. Locals gave it a more successful try in 1825, however, and it's now experiencing a production boom. The soil and climate of this island lend themselves to excellent crops of the beans, which thrive in moist soil rich in the organic matter of volcanic rock and leaf mold. The land near Waialua, the sleepy little sugar plantation town, is ideal for coffee production: The absorbent soil is loose enough to drain excess water, and the temperature and elevation further the perfect conditions. The sorghum and *wiliwili* trees of the North Shore currently protect the crop; ultimately, the recently planted Norfolk pines will become the primary guardian against wind damage to the coffee trees.

SIGHTS

KAHUKU   Kamehameha Highway winds its way to the North Shore, beginning with this former plantation town that is home to approximately 1200 residents. Stop at one of the roadside stands for a taste of fresh, local sweet corn and island-renowned Kahuku shrimp.

KAHUKU SUGAR MILL   Kahuku is also the home of the Kahuku Sugar Mill, a turn-of-the-20th-century plant. In an effort to refurbish the old mill, the entire complex was turned into a shopping mall. The shops never quite made it and now the mall hosts local services (including a bank and post office).

JAMES CAMPBELL NATIONAL WILLDLIFE REFUGE

✉ 66-590 Kamehameha Highway, Haleiwa ✆ 808-637-6330 🖥 www.fws.gov/jamescampbell Facilitating the recovery of four endangered bird species—the black-necked Hawaiian stilt, Hawaiian moorhen, Hawaiian coot and Hawaiian duck—this wildlife refuge consists of two units: The Punamaoo Pond is a spring-fed marsh; the Kii Unit is made up of former sugar cane waste–settling basins. Free guided tours of the 164-acre wetlands are offered Thursday and Saturday, from late October to late February. Reservations required.

KAHUKU POINT   If you continue along Kamehameha Highway from the wildlife refuge, you will skirt **Kaihalulu Beach**, which continues out to Kahuku Point, the northernmost point on Oahu. The current here is strong and the rocky bottom makes swimming difficult, but it is a wonderful spot to spend the afternoon beachcombing.

KUILIMA COVE   The road from Kahuku Point makes a bend past Kuilima Cove, the windswept white-sand strand fronting the Turtle Bay Resort. Access to the cove is on the east side of the hotel next to the restaurant Ola. Although the snorkeling here is far from good, the protected cove is one of the few safe places to swim in the winter, when raging swells pummel the rest of the coast. Just past the cove, there is also a

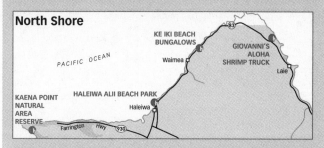

North Shore

PACIFIC OCEAN

KE IKI BEACH BUNGALOWS

GIOVANNI'S ALOHA SHRIMP TRUCK

Waimea

Laie

KAENA POINT NATURAL AREA RESERVE

HALEIWA ALII BEACH PARK

Haleiwa

Farrington Hwy 930

KAENA POINT NATURAL AREA RESERVE

PAGE 177

Remote, legendary mountaintop site believed to be where spirits ascended to the afterlife

HALEIWA ALII BEACH PARK

PAGE 185

Prime surfing destination with 20-foot swells on a powdery gold beach lined with palm trees

KE IKI BEACH BUNGALOWS

PAGE 178

Palm-shrouded woodframe cottages with bamboo and ratan furnishings just steps from the ocean

GIOVANNI'S ALOHA SHRIMP TRUCK

PAGE 179

Lemon-and-butter or hot-and-spicy shrimp served with two scoops of sticky rice—Oahu's best plate lunches

walking and jogging trail that runs along the shoreline through a peaceful grove of swaying ironwood trees. The resort reserves about a dozen free parking spaces for beachgoers who are not hotel guests. Request a beach pass at the parking booth.

ROADSIDE VENDORS

Roadside vendors at locations along the Kamehameha Highway sell sweet corn, watermelon, papaya, mango and tropical flowers from local farms and gardens, fresh-caught fish and shrimp from the area's aquaculture ponds. You'll get a warm welcome and a chance to "talk story" with the locals as well as the opportunity to enjoy some of Hawaii's natural delicacies.

SUNSET BEACH ✉59-104 Kamehameha Highway Stretching for two miles and averaging 200 feet in width, this is one of Hawaii's largest strands. It is home to a wave by the same name, located near Lifeguard Tower 27.

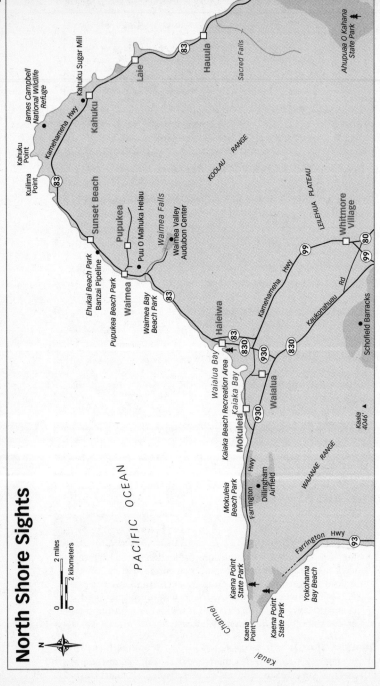

North Shore Sights

N

PACIFIC OCEAN

0   2 miles
0   2 kilometers

Kaena
Channel

Kauai

Kaena Point

Kaena Point
State Park

Kaena Point State Park

Yokohama Bay Beach

Mokuleia Beach Park

Dillingham Airfield

Farrington Hwy

Farrington Hwy

93

WAIANAE RANGE

Kaala
4046'

Mokuleia

930

Waialua

Kaiaka Bay

Kaiaka Beach Recreation Area

Waialua Bay

Haleiwa

83

830

930

830

Kaukonahua Rd

Schofield Barracks

LEILEHUA PLATEAU

99

99

80

Whitmore Village

Kamehameha Hwy

99

KOOLAU RANGE

Waialua Bay
Beach Park

Waimea

Pupukea Beach Park

Ehukai Beach Park
Banzai Pipeline

Sunset Beach

Pupukea

Puu O Mahuka Heiau

Waimea Falls

Waimea Valley
Audubon Center

83

Kahuku Point

Kuilima Point

Kahuku Point

83

Kamehameha Hwy

James Campbell
National Wildlife
Refuge

Kahuku Sugar Mill

Kahuku

Laie

83

Hauula

Sacred Falls

Ahupuaa O Kahana
State Park

The Sunset Beach community encompasses Ehukai Beach to the south and the exclusive gated community at Velzyland to the north. All along this shoreline, you can watch world-class athletes shoot the curl when the surf is up; when conditions are flat, usually in summer, Sunset becomes a great place to swim.

EHUKAI BEACH PARK ✉ *Off Kamehameha Highway about seven miles northeast of Haleiwa* This is one of the best places to surf on Oahu. Just 100 yards to the west (Ke Nui Road) sits the **Banzai Pipeline**, where a shallow coral shelf creates tubular waves so powerful and perfect they actually resemble pipes. First surfed in 1957, it lays claim to cracked skulls, lacerated legs and some of the sport's greatest feats.

PUU O MAHUKA HEIAU

✉ *From Kamehameha Highway, turn left near the Sunset Beach Fire Station onto Pupukea Road, then follow the Hawaii Visitors & Convention Bureau signs.* On a plateau between Sunset Beach and Waimea Bay you'll find Oahu's oldest temple. A split-level structure built of stone, it once was used for human sacrifices. Today there is nothing more menacing than a spectacular view and perhaps a gentle breeze from the ocean.

ST. PETER & PAUL A beautiful religious site built on a former rock-crushing plant, this quaint church, with its steeple constructed from the remaining rocks of the plant, seems to stand watch over Waimea Bay.

WAIMEA VALLEY _____ ⓗidden

✉ *Kamehameha Highway, five miles northeast of Haleiwa* ☎ *808-638-9199* ☏ *808-638-9197* Here you can wander through a tropical preserve and cultural park stretching across 1800 acres. Once a Hawaiian village, it is crisscrossed with hiking trails and archaeological ruins. Weather permitting, you can picnic and swim at **Waimea Falls**, or browse the arboretum featuring tropical and subtropical trees from around the world, or the beautiful botanical gardens with 6000 species of rare plants. Then there are the birds that populate the complex; since this nature park serves as a bird sanctuary, it attracts a varied assortment. Activities for visitors include guided nature walks and cultural talk-story sessions with resident *kapuna*.

WAIMEA BAY Across the road from the Audubon Center looms Waimea Bay, another fabled place that sports the largest surfable waves in the world. When surf's up in winter, the monster waves that roll in are so big they make the ground tremble when they break. Salt spray reaches as far as the highway. Thirty-foot waves are not uncommon. Fifty-foot giants have been recorded; though unsurfable, these are not tidal waves, just swells rising along the incredible North Shore. Each winter, the bay is the site of a big wave contest in honor of the late lifeguard Eddie Aikau who was lost at sea. The contest is only held if the waves exceed 25 feet and conditions are clean. In summer, Waimea is a pretty blue bay with a white-sand beach. The water is placid and the area perfect for picnicking and sunbathing. So when you visit Waimea, remember: Swim in summer, sunbathe in winter.

HALEIWA The Kamehameha Highway crosses Anahula River and a double rainbow–shaped bridge en route to this old plantation town with a new facelift. Fortunately, the designers who performed the makeover on this village had an eye for antiquity. They planned it so the modern shopping centers and other facilities blend comfortably into the rural landscape. The community that has grown up around the new town reflects a rare combination of past and future. The old Japanese, Filipinos and Hawaiians have been joined by blond-mopped surfers and laidback counterculturalists. As a result, this clapboard town with wooden sidewalks has established itself as the "in" spot on the North Shore. Its stylish nonchalance has also proved popular among canny travelers. Despite gentrification, Haleiwa holds on to its relaxed ambience. The surf scene still adds a definite style to Haleiwa.

NORTH SHORE SURF AND CULTURAL MUSEUM

✉️*North Shore Marketplace, 66-250 Kamehameha Highway, Haleiwa* 📞*808-637-8888* 🖱️*www.captainrick.com/surf_museum.htm* Surf's up at this museum, which displays related artifacts, boards and old photographs of the local community. A mini-theater shows videos of the sport. The museum also temporarily houses items from an 1824 shipwreck, providing a safe haven for the items while the wreck is being excavated. (There's jewelry for sale that was found by underwater metal detection.) The museum's other claim to fame is its possession of the last two boards used by famed surfer Mark Foo before he was killed in a surfing accident in 1994. Closed Tuesday.

LILIUOKALANI PROTESTANT CHURCH

✉️*66-090 Kamehameha Highway, Haleiwa* 📞*808-637-9364* The little church in Haleiwa is named for the queen who used to summer on the shores of the nearby Anahulu River, Queen Liliuokalani. This Protestant church dates back to the early 1800s, though the current building was constructed in the mid-1900s. If you have a chance to enter the church, take a look at the clock that was donated by the queen—it shows the phases of the moon as well as the hour, day, month and year.

WAIALUA A scenic detour takes you to this former sugar plantation town, via Haleiwa Road. There's not much to see here except the old **Waialua Sugar Mill**, which has been converted into office space. The mill closed its sugar operation in the mid-'90s and the cane fields around this area are being replanted with Waialua coffee. Plantation houses line the streets and it's an interesting area to look around.

THE ORIGINAL GLIDER RIDE ✆808-637-0207 ✍www.honolulusoaring. 177
com, info@gliderridehawaii.com For a faster route toward Kaena Point, pick
up Farrington Highway (Route 930). This country road parallels miles
of unpopulated beachfront, past wind-battered Mokuleia Beach and
arrives at Dillingham Airfield, where you can take a ride along the
Waianae Mountains. With over 30 years of experience, Mr. Bill knows
the ins and outs of the countryside. Calling about weather conditions
and making reservations are highly recommended.

9
NORTH SHORE LODGING

KAENA POINT NATURAL AREA RESERVE

Beyond Dillingham Air Field, the road continues for several miles
between a wild ocean and scrub brush–covered mountains before turning into a very rugged dirt track. Along this unpaved portion of roadway you can hike out about ten miles to **Kaena Point**
on Oahu's northwest corner. The hot, shade-free journey takes
you into this state-managed, 59-acre reserve, which stretches
around the corner to the Leeward Coast. It serves as a nesting
ground for laysan albatross, shearwaters and other seabirds,
which were once a food source for early Hawaiians, who used
the region for fishing and feather-collecting. Within the reserve, there is a *wahi pana*, or sacred Hawaiian site, known as a
laina a ka uhane, a leaping-off point where spirits of the dead
jumped into the afterlife. Its cultural significance lends a pal-
pable energy to the remote yet beautiful landscape, and eerie
ghost stories of Kaena Point continue to be told today. If you
make the trek to the point, be sure not to leave any valuables in
your car, as the end of the road is notorious for vehicle break-
ins. Kaena Point is also accessible from the south, past the
town of Makaha. (See Chapter Ten.)

LODGING

TURTLE BAY RESORT

$$$$ 443 UNITS ✉*57-091 Kamehameha Highway, Kahuku* ✆*808-293-8811,*
800-203-3650 ✆*808-293-9147* ✍*www.turtlebayresort.com*
For a resort experience in a rustic setting, consider this "rural" retreat,
which sprawls across 880 acres on a dramatic peninsula. With a broad
beach at the doorstep and mountains out back, the resort sits on an
overwhelming spot. (The one drawback may be the fairly constant
winds. But then again, you might enjoy the steady cool, sometimes
cold, breezes on this side of the island.) Add to that riding paths, two
golf courses, tennis courts, three swimming pools, a spa and a fitness
center. Every guest room features an ocean view.

BACKPACKER'S VACATION INN

$ 21 UNITS ✉*59-788 Kamehameha Highway, Haleiwa* ✆*808-638-7838*
✆*808-638-7515* ✍*www.backpackers-hawaii.com, info@backpackers-hawaii.com*
Surfers, scuba divers and budget-minded travelers will love Back-
packer's along Oahu's vaunted North Shore. The central building provides hostel-style rooms and features a TV lounge and kitchen. There's

also a back house with private rooms that share a kitchen and bath. Like a hostel, it's budget-priced. Across the street, and directly on the beach, there's a house with private apartments that include their own kitchen and bathroom and are moderately priced. In addition, there are nine restored plantation cabins with kitchens and baths set on a landscaped acre. The inn has guest laundry facilities and barbecue areas, which provide excellent opportunities for meeting other travelers.

KE IKI BEACH BUNGALOWS

$$–$$$ 11 UNITS ✉59-579 Ke Iki Road, Haleiwa ☎808-638-8229, 866-638-8229 📠808-638-8823 ✍www.keikibeach.com, info@keikibeach.com

Offering accommodations right on the beach, these bungalows are located between the Banzai Pipeline and Waimea Bay. You'll find moderate- and deluxe-priced duplexes and an ultra-deluxe-priced cottage, all on an acre-and-a-half of palm-shaded property. They are basic woodframe buildings with bamboo and rattan furnishings; all units have full kitchens. The complex includes barbecue facilities, hammocks and a wide beach. Accommodations are great for families.

KAWELA BAY BEACH HOUSE

$$$$ 1 UNIT ✉Kawela Bay; book through Pacific Islands Reservations ☎808-262-8133 📠808-262-5030 ✍pir@aloha.com

Although it's a bit far-flung, located some 30 minutes north of Haleiwa, this beach house is a great choice for those seeking a quiet, oceanfront retreat on the North Shore that doesn't cost an arm and a leg, as private cottages go. Set on a larger estate, the two-bedroom, one-bath house has a full kitchen and a fold-out couch in the living room. The decor is light and breezy, but it's cozy—while it can sleep four adults and two kids, it's best-suited to a small family or close friends. It sits right on a secluded white-sand beach that has good snorkeling and plenty of privacy. Minimum five-night stay.

CONDOS

THE ESTATES AT TURTLE BAY

103 UNITS ✉56-565 Kamehameha Highway, Kahuku ☎808-293-0600, 888-200-4202 📠808-293-0471 ✍www.turtlebay-rentals.com, etbinfo@hawaii.rr.com

Located on the grounds of the Turtle Bay Resort but independently operated, The Estates offers studio, as well as one-, two- and three-bedroom resort condominiums, each with stove, refrigerator, dishwasher, microwave, washer/dryer and cable television. There are five swimming pools and four tennis courts on the property, and guests can arrange golf and horseback riding through the resort. Rates begin at $115 for a studio and up to $350 for a three-bedroom unit.

TURTLE BAY CONDOS

50 UNITS   ✉ *56-565 Kamehameha Highway, Kahuku*   📞 *808-293-2800, 888-266-3690*
📠 *808-293-2169*   🖥 *www.turtlebaycondos.com*

This clean, minimalist-style accommodation has one-, two- and three-bedroom units with kitchen facilities, washer/dryer and private lanais that overlook either a nine-hole golf course or a garden area. In high season, studios are $110; one-bedrooms units with a loft sleeping up to four guests are $165; and two-bedroom units with a loft are $215.

DINING ⑨

KAHUKU GRILL

$$–$$$ PLATE LUNCHES   ✉ *56-565 Kamehameha Highway, Kahuku*   📞 *808-293-2110*

Appropriately enough, you'll find the Kahuku Grill not far from the old Kahuku Sugar Mill. The menu includes Hawaiian plate lunches as well as shrimp, seafood and steak dishes. Open for breakfast, lunch and dinner daily, it's plain and informal.

GIOVANNI'S ALOHA SHRIMP TRUCK

 hidden

$$ PLATE LUNCHES   ✉ *Beside The Mill, Kamehameha Highway, Kahuku*
📞 *808-293-1839*

Giovanni's serves gourmet plate lunches that the locals claim are the best on Oahu. There's a choice of scampi, lemon and butter shrimp or hot and spicy shrimp, and, like all plate lunches, they come with two scoops of rice. Picnic tables sit under an awning for this rain-or-shine outdoor eating spot.

TURTLE BAY RESORT

$$–$$$ PACIFIC RIM/AMERICAN   ✉ *57-091 Kamehameha Highway, Kahuku*
📞 *808-293-8811*   📠 *808-293-9147*   🖥 *www.turtlebayresort.com*

This resort features three dining options. **21 Degrees North** has sweeping ocean views and features contemporary island cuisine. Expect such delights as rosemary-crusted rack of lamb, Muscovy duck and seared *ahi* with wasabi mashed potatoes. At the **Palm Terrace**, overlooking the hotel's lovely grounds, you'll encounter moderately priced dining in an attractive environment. The restaurant, serving three buffet meals, offers everything from sautéed swordfish to calzone. At the **Hang Ten**, munch on a hamburger or fish tacos while lounging in the sun.

JAMESON'S BY THE SEA

$$–$$$ SEAFOOD   ✉ *62-540 Kamehameha Highway, Haleiwa*   📞 *808-637-6272*
📠 *808-637-3225*   🖥 *www.jamesonshawaii.com*

For relaxed sunset dining overlooking the ocean, try Jameson's. The inviting dining area features tropical touches like potted plants and rattan furnishing. For lunch there are sandwiches, chowders and fresh fish dishes; at dinner they specialize in seafood. Brunch on the weekend.

HALEIWA JOE'S SEAFOOD GRILL

$$–$$$ SEAFOOD   ✉ *66-011 Kamehameha Highway, Haleiwa*   📞 *808-637-8005*
📠 *808-637-8861*   🖥 *www.haleiwajoes.com*

The seafood here is not the best I've ever had, but the salads are large

How to Beat the Heat with a Sweet Treat

Since the early days of Hawaiian royalty, people have complained about Honolulu's shirt-sticking weather. Come summer, temperatures rise and the trade winds stop blowing. Visitors seeking a golden tan discover they're baking without browning. And residents begin to think that their city, renowned as a cultural melting pot, is actually a pressure cooker.

With the ocean all around, relief is never far away. But a lot of folks, when not heading for the beaches, have found another way to cool off: shave ice. Known as ice frappes among the Japanese originators and snow cones back on the mainland, these frozen treats are Hawaii's answer to the Good Humor man.

They're made with ice that's been shaved from a block into thin slivers, packed into a cone-shaped cup and covered with sweet syrup. Health-minded people eat the ice plain or with a low-calorie or sugar-free syrup, but some folks ask for a scoop of ice cream or sweet red beans (adzuki beans) underneath the shavings. Most people just order it with their favorite syrup flavors—grape, root beer, cola, cherry, orange, lemon-lime, vanilla, fruit punch, banana, strawberry and many more.

Whichever you choose, you'll find it only costs a couple bucks at the many stands sprinkled around town. Watch for stands up on the North Shore, too. As a matter of fact, any place where the sun blazes overhead, you're liable to find someone trying to beat the heat by slurping up a shave ice before it melts into mush.

MATSUMOTO'S ✉*66-087 Kamehameha Highway, Haleiwa* ☎*808-637-4827*
No doubt you'll see a long line outside this shop, Oahu's most famous shave ice store.

and refreshing, the coconut shrimp pretty good, and the atmosphere a little more upscale than most casual beachside places. Plus, the patio has a beautiful ocean view.

SCOOP OF PARADISE
$ ICE CREAM   ✉*Haleiwa Shopping Center, 66-145 Kamehameha Highway, Haleiwa*
☎*808-637-3456*

When it's time for dessert, head here for homemade ice cream, served plain or with mix-ins. They serve unique flavors like lilikoi cheesecake and Kona coffee, and also have shave ice.

PIZZA BOB'S
$ PIZZA   ✉*Haleiwa Shopping Center, 66-145 Kamehameha Highway, Haleiwa*
☎*808-637-5095*

Pizza Bob's has, you guessed it, pizza. It also has burgers and pastas and a wonderful outdoor covered patio for dining.

ROSIE'S CANTINA
$–$$ MEXICAN   ✉*Haleiwa Shopping Plaza, 66-165 Kamehameha Highway, Haleiwa*
☎*808-637-3538* 🖷*808-637-5086*

Mexican restaurants in Hawaii had fish tacos long before places on the mainland caught on. True to the islands, Rosie's offers them, rounding out a menu filled with the culinary features found in every south-of-the-border eatery. The breakfast menu features American standbys like pancakes and omelettes, while the dinner menu ranges from tacos and enchiladas to steaks and seafood.

KUA AINA SANDWICH SHOP

$ AMERICAN   ✉66-160 Kamehameha Highway, Haleiwa   ☎808-637-6067
📠808-637-4858

Join the surfers who pour into the joint, where they order hamburgers, french fries and mahimahi sandwiches at the counter, then kick back at one of the roadside tables. Great for light meals, this place is a scene and a half. Sources say that Barack Obama once happened upon legendary travel writers Pico Iyer and Paul Theroux sharing a meal here and impressed them with his intimate knowledge of their works.

FOOD FOR THOUGHT

$ VEGETARIAN   ✉Haleiwa Town Center, 66-165 Kamehameha Highway
☎808-780-7928   🖱www.foodforthoughthawaii.com

Parked behind the American Savings Bank, this eatery lives up to its "eco-friendly lunchwagon" label by using biodegradeable food containers and flatware and as much locally grown produce as possible. There are healthy options for vegetarians and omnivores alike: pita wraps with falafel or seared *ahi*, soy corn dogs, vegetarian chili cheese fries, and for those who have to order shrimp from a lunchwagon, a garlic shrimp plate. The parking lot is a rather unsightly place to eat, but there are tables for those who don't want take-out. Cash only.

CHOLOS HOMESTYLE MEXICAN RESTAURANT

$–$$ MEXICAN   ✉North Shore Marketplace, 66-250 Kamehameha Highway, Haleiwa
☎808-637-3059   📠808-637-1795   🖱www.choloshomestyle.com

Steaming fish tacos smothered in spicy salsa. Salty chips that leave oil on your napkin. Cold beer topped with lime. Mmmm. But I digress. Cholos is ideal after-beach fare. You can dine inside or out, and the gorgeous crafts on display are for sale.

COFFEE GALLERY

$ COFFEEHOUSE   ✉North Shore Marketplace, 66-250 Kamehameha Highway, Haleiwa   ☎808-637-5355   🖱www.roastmaster.com, coffeegalleryhawaii@yahoo.com

Years ago, Haleiwa was home to Da Cuppa Kope, a great café and gathering place. Today it's been supplanted by an even better coffeehouse, the Coffee Gallery, which roasts its coffee on-site. In addition to the best cappuccino on the island, this homespun restaurant, decorated with coffee sacks, serves homemade pastries, bagels, soups and a variety of sandwiches. They also have internet and free wi-fi access.

PARADISE FOUND CAFÉ

$ VEGETARIAN   ✉Inside Celestial Natural Foods, 66-443 Kamehameha Highway, Haleiwa   ☎808-637-4540

"Casual" is an understatement here, where barefoot beachgoers order up fresh fruit smoothies, soups, salads and vegetarian delights such as tempeh burritos and tofu lemongrass curry. They also have healthy takes on plate lunches, like the walnut tempeh plate. Vegan substitutions are easily accommodated at this friendly eatery.

OPEL THAI

$ THAI   ✉66-460 Kamehameha Highway, Haleiwa   ☎808-381-8091

Widely considered the best Thai food on the island, this clean lunchwagon consistently draws a crowd of visitors and local regulars. The humble owners, Opel and Aoy, seem to know everyone by name and go out of their way to customize orders. Among the most delicious items on the dry-erase-board menu are the rice-paper-wrapped vegetarian summer rolls made with fresh tofu, the thick, round garlicky noodles, and the pad thai made with a special housemade peanut sauce. Since Opel is a vegetarian, he capably makes any dish meat-free. Enjoy a leisurely lunch at the shaded wooden picnic tables as you watch the traffic go by. Cash only.

CAFÉ HALEIWA

$ AMERICAN   ✉66-460 Kamehameha Highway, Haleiwa   ☎808-637-5516

At this café, surfers swear by the omelettes, pancakes and "the Barrel"—a blend of eggs, potatoes, green salsa and cheese wrapped in a tortilla. Sandwiches and burgers round out the menu. Located in a century-old building featuring local artwork, surfboards and surfing memorabilia, this local favorite also serves an excellent quesadilla. No dinner.

NORTH SHORE COUNTRY OKAZU AND BENTO

$ LOCAL-STYLE   ✉Haleiwa Shopping Center, 66-197 Kamehameha Highway   ☎808-637-0055

Bright pink hot dogs, butter *mochi*, fried chicken and cone sushi...What do all these have in common? They're distinct local favorites, and they're all available at this tiny take-out joint in Haleiwa, one of the last *okazuya* standing on this side of the island. Assemble your own *bento* from a large variety of choices. Outstanding selections include the miso butterfish (available on Friday only), kabocha pumpkin and *shoyu* chicken. Get there early—well before noon—before all the good stuff is gone.

SHOPPING

THE ONLY SHOW IN TOWN
✉56-931 Kamehameha Highway, Kahuku   ☎808-293-1295   🖷808-293-8585   Calling itself The Only Show In Town is a slight (very slight) exaggeration, but claiming to be "Kahuku's largest antique and vintage collectible shop" is definitely warranted. Some store specialties include Japanese glass fishing floats, ivory, Coca-Cola memorabilia and unusual beads from around the world. Fittingly, this wonderful antique store is located in the old Tanaka Plantation Store, an early-20th-century woodframe building.

Trendy shoppers head for the little town of Haleiwa. Since Haleiwa is a center for surfers, it's a good place to buy sportswear and aquatic equipment as well as varied artworks and crafts.

STRONG CURRENT ✉ *66-208 Kamehameha Highway, Haleiwa* ☎ *808-637-3410* 📠 *808-637-3406* 🖰 *www.strongcurrenthawaii.com* Stocking everything imaginable that's related to surfing, here you'll find an abundance of books, videos, posters, boards and other appurtenances, all relating to a single theme.

IWA GALLERY ✉ *66-119 Kamehameha Highway, Haleiwa* ☎ *808-637-4865* 🖰 *www.thewaxrevolution.com/iwagallery* Here you'll find a unique collection of artwork by a number of local island artists, including hand-crafted candles.

OOGENESIS BOUTIQUE ✉ *66-249 Kamehameha Highway, Haleiwa* ☎ *808-637-4422* This shop has a creative selection of women's fashions.

NORTH SHORE MARKETPLACE ✉ *66-250 Kamehameha Highway, Haleiwa* You can watch glass artists fashion whales, sharks, reef fish and other aquatic creatures at **Oceans in Glass** (808-637-3366), pick up a new swimsuit at **North Shore Swimwear** (808-637-6859) or buy a surfboard and any of the associated gear at **Boardriders Club** (808-637-5026).

POLYNESIAN TREASURES

✉ *66-250 Kamehameha Highway, Haleiwa* ☎ *808-637-1288* 📠 *808-637-8535* This unassuming gift shop sells koa wood boxes, island art, homemade soaps and candles, and a wide variety of hand-crafted trinkets, including jewelry made with prized, locally gathered sunrise shells worth up to $3000.

NIGHTLIFE

LEI LEI'S BAR AND GRILL ✉ *Turtle Bay Resort, 57–049 Kuilima Drive, Kahuku* ☎ *808-293-2662* 🖰 *www.turtlebayresort.com* Among the relatively few nightlife options on the North Shore, Lei Lei's has established itself as the unofficial hangout for professional surfers and visiting Hollywood celebrities. The bustling, well-lit dining room overlooks the Turtle Bay Resort golf course (accessible from the left turn immediately past the security booth), and the staff is friendly and accommodating. During the winter surf season, the North Shore's bronzed and beautiful converge on Lei Lei's breezy outdoor lanai to see and be seen.

BREAKERS RESTAURANT AND BAR ✉ *66-250 Kamehameha Highway, Haleiwa* ☎ *808-637-9898* This surf-themed restaurant is also one of Haleiwa's most popular bars. Intense surf videos loop on a giant screen, and there is often live music on weekend nights. During football season, it's also a sports bar where diehard fans show up early in the morning to watch games on the overhead televisions and support their home teams over bloody marys.

BEACHES & PARKS

SUNSET BEACH
✉ *Kamehameha Highway*

🏖 🤽 🛶 ⛵ As far as surfing goes, this is the place! I think the best way to do Sunset is by starting from **Ehukai Beach Park** (off Kamehameha Highway about seven miles northeast of Haleiwa). From here you can go left to the "Banzai Pipeline," where crushing waves build along a shallow coral reef to create tube-like formations. To the right lies "Sunset," with equally spectacular surfing waves. Throughout the area the swimming is fair in summer; however, in winter it is extremely dangerous. From September to April, high waves and strong currents prevail. Be careful! Game fish caught around Sunset include *papio*, *menpachi* and *ulua*. Facilities at Ehukai Beach Park include picnic areas, restrooms and showers. Snorkeling here is poor.

PUPUKEA BEACH PARK
✉ *Kamehameha Highway at Pupukea Road*

🏖 🤽 Some of the island's best snorkeling is at this Marine Life Conservation District on Kamehameha Highway, six miles northeast of Haleiwa. This 80-acre park, fringed by rocky shoreline, divides into several sections. Foremost is "Shark's Cove," located on the north side of the fire station, which contains spectacular tidepools. Underwater caves draw divers (experienced only—there have been a number of drownings in these deep and maze-like caverns). Snorkelers will revel in the large, colorful schools of fish that float from reef to reef, nibbling at the coral. Commonly seen are parrotfish, goatfish, convict tangs, yellow tangs, butterflyfish, wrasses and triggerfish, and more often than not, turtles. The abundance of marine life is the happy result of the conservation district's no-fishing rules. Uneasy swimmers should be aware that the ocean depth drops to 50 feet just beyond the exposed reef area. Also, winter swells bring surges that can slam swimmers against the jagged reef; check with lifeguards before entering the water if conditions are not flat.

WAIMEA BAY BEACH PARK
✉ *Kamehameha Highway (Route 83) about five miles northeast of Haleiwa*

🏖 🤽 🛶 ⛵ If Sunset is *one* of the most famous surfing spots in the world, Waimea is *the* most famous. The biggest surfable waves in the world (30 feet in winter!) roll into this pretty blue bay. There's a wide white-sand beach and a pleasant park with a tree-studded lawn. It's a marvelous place for picnicking and sunbathing. During the winter crowds often line the beach watching top-notch surfers challenge the curl; in summer the sea is flat and safe for swimming; you can also bodysurf in the shorebreak and snorkel when the bay is calm during the summer (during winter months, use extreme caution near the water). *Papio*, *menpachi* and *ulua* are common catches. Facilities include a picnic area, restrooms, showers and a lifeguard.

LANIAKEA BEACH
✉*Kamehameha Highway (Route 83) one mile north of Haleiwa*

🏊 Just before you reach Haleiwa, you'll come to Laniakea. On days when there is surf, the gravel parking lot on the mountain side of the road is typically full. Three offshore surf spots offer left- and right-peeling waves: "Himalayas," "Laniakea" and "Holton's." A slippery, seaweed-covered reef that is exposed at low tide separates the ocean from the narrow strip of sand, which makes for treacherous snorkeling, but offers a great opportunity to view green turtles. On the east end of the beach, hordes of tourists descend to get a glimpse of the turtles that like to bask on the sand here. Walk west toward the wider beach in front of the private residences, and you're just as likely to spot a turtle. There are no showers, lifeguards, or other facilities at this beach.

HALEIWA BEACH PARK
✉*Kamehameha Highway (Route 83), Haleiwa*

🏊 🎣 ⛴ This is an excellent refuge from the North Shore's pounding surf. Set in Waialua Bay, the golden-sand beach is safe for swimming almost all year. You can snorkel, although it's only fair. Surfing is not possible here but "Haleiwa" breaks are located across Waialua Bay at Alii Beach Park. Facilities include a picnic area, restrooms, showers, a ball field, a basketball court and a playground. The primary catches at Haleiwa are *papio*, *menpachi* and *ulua*.

HALEIWA ALII BEACH PARK
✉*Kamehameha Highway (Route 83), Haleiwa* 📞*808-637-5051*
📠*808-637-5052*

🏊 🏄 🚴 Across from Haleiwa Beach Park, this is where you go to surf. Swells can top 20 feet here, which is why it's the site of several surfing and bodyboarding tournaments—you can watch the pros do things that seem to defy gravity. The main break here is called "Haleiwa," but when the surf is macking, tow-in surfers like to ride an outer reef break called "Avalanche." If you've come on one of the few days that surfing is not ideal, or if you're a beginner, bring your boogieboard and join the kids on the more manageable waves. If you're visiting in winter, you may be in luck: Lifeguards sometimes give free surfing lessons in the morning (it's a good idea to reserve a spot ahead of time; head for the lifeguard tower to sign up). Facilities include a picnic area, restrooms and year-round lifeguards.

KAIAKA BAY BEACH PARK
✉*66-449 Haleiwa Road*

🏊 🎣 ⛴ The setting at this peninsular park just outside Haleiwa is beautiful. There's a secluded area with a tree-shaded lawn and a short strip of sandy beach. A rocky shoreline borders most of the park, so it's more for picnics than water sports. You *can* swim and snorkel, but there's a rocky bottom. Fishing is good for *papio*, *menpachi* and *ulua*. The facilities here include a picnic area, showers and restrooms.

⛺ There are seven campsites available; a county permit is required.

MOKULEIA BEACH PARK AND MOKULEIA BEACH

✉On Farrington Highway (Route 930) about seven miles west of Haleiwa.
To the west of the park, this beach stretches for miles along a secluded coast.
You can hike down the beach or reach its hidden realms by driving farther
west along Farrington Highway (Route 930), then turning off onto any of the
numerous dirt side roads.

The 12-acre park contains a sandy beach and large unshaded lawn. An exposed coral reef detracts from the swimming, but on either side of the park lie beaches with sandy ocean bottoms. If you do swim, exercise caution, especially in the winter months; there's no lifeguard. There's good snorkeling in the summer, particularly when the ocean is calm and the sand unchurned. Lots of small fish—such as tangs, goatfish and triggerfish—populate the shallow reef that fronts the beach park, and the occasional eel can be spotted hiding in a hole. When winter swells arrive, surfing is possible in front of the park at "Park Rights" or at a hairy break across the channel to the west called "Daystar." Anglers try for *papio*, *menpachi* and *ulua*. Watch for skydivers, who often use the shoreline for their beach landings. Whatever your activity of choice, you'll have to contend with the noise of small planes from nearby Dillingham Airfield. The park is also an excellent starting point for exploring the unpopulated sections of Mokuleia Beach. Facilities include picnic areas, restrooms and showers. Note: Mokuleia is a high-theft area, so don't leave your belongings in the car if possible.

▲ No camping allowed until further notice.

MOKULEIA ARMY BEACH

✉Route 930 near the Dillingham Airfield

This is the widest stretch of sand along the Mokuleia shoreline, and probably the most untamed, which is probably one of the reasons that many scenes of the television show *Lost* were filmed here. Once maintained by the Army for the exclusive use of their personnel, it's now open to the public but has no facilities. The high surf in winter poses no challenge to natives, but surfing really isn't recommended; there have been fatalities here. The treacherous waters mean that you'll pretty much have the spot to yourself. Most folks are locals with a strong sense of loyalty to this spot.

CENTRAL OAHU & LEEWARD COAST

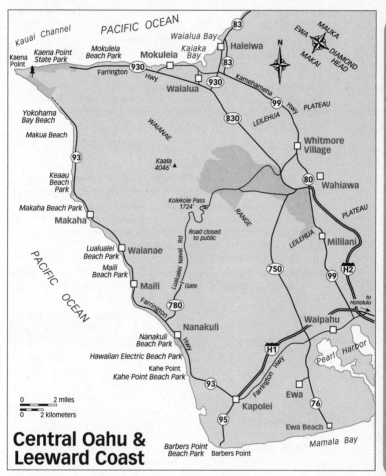

Central Oahu & Leeward Coast

Visitors often ignore Central Oahu and the Leeward Coast, which together make up the western half of Oahu. They'll buzz down Route 99, which intersects the island, on their way to or from the North Shore, and they'll avoid the Leeward Coast entirely, having been warned of potential problems with the locals. But they shouldn't. The very fact that people don't often visit these two places makes them worth going to for a glimpse of Oahu that hasn't been transformed by tourism.

CENTRAL OAHU

The 1000-foot-high Leilehua Plateau, a bountiful agricultural region once planted with sugar and pineapple, extends from the North Shore to the southern reaches of Oahu. Spreading across the middle of the island between the Waianae and Koolau ranges, this tableland nurtured the large plantations that once formed the backbone of Oahu's agricultural infrastructure. It is now being cultivated in diversified agriculture. It is also a vital military headquarters. Wheeler Air Force Base, Schofield Barracks and several other installations occupy large plots of land here.

From Haleiwa south to Wahiawa you can take Route 803, Kaukonahua Road, a pretty thoroughfare with excellent views of the Waianaes, or follow Route 99, the Kamehameha Highway, which passes through verdant pineapple fields.

SIGHTS

DOLE PINEAPPLE PLANTATION ⊠*64-1550 Kamehameha Highway, Wahiawa* ✆*808-621-8408, 800-697-9100* ✺*808-621-1926* ✎*www.dole-plantation. com, sales@dole-plantation.com* The plantation, often crowded with tourists, sells (who would have guessed?) pineapple products. They offer a train ride through the plantation and the World's Largest Maze, a 1.7-mile labyrinth made from more than 11,400 Hawaiian plants that covers two acres. They also offer self-guided tours of the **Pineapple Variety Garden**, a plot of land on the highway planted with a variety of pineapples, once a major agricultural staple of the island. Nowadays, most pineapples are grown elsewhere, so this really is a garden museum. Admission.

KUKANILOKO

⊠*Follow the dirt road across from Whitmore Avenue just north of Wahiawa.* The east fork of Route 99 becomes Route 80, which passes near a cluster of sacred stones marking the place where Hawaiian royalty gave birth, accompanied by chants, drums and offerings. Studded with eucalyptus trees, this spot has held an important place in Hawaiian history and religion for centuries.

KOLEKOLE PASS For a scenic and historic detour from Route 80, follow Route 80 until it links with Route 99. Take Route 99 west, pull up to the sentry station at Schofield Barracks and ask directions to the pass. On that "day of infamy," December 7, 1941, Japanese bombers buzzed through this notch in the Waianae Range. You'll be directed through Schofield up into the Waianaes. When you reach Kolekole Pass, there's another sentry gate. Ask the guard to let you continue a short distance farther to the observation point. From here the Waianaes fall away precipitously to a plain that rolls gently to the sea. There's an astonishing view of Oahu's west coast. If you are denied permission

WAHIAWA BOTANICAL GARDENS

PAGE 190

Silky white orchids, bright green palms and warm-hued ginger flowers spread across 27 acres—a feast for the senses

MAKUA CAVE

PAGE 196

Hundred-foot-high, millennia-old lava tube known as the mythical home to the shark god Kamahoalii

MAKAHA BEACH PARK

PAGE 201

Magnificent water-sport destination boasting a white-sand beach and waters ideal for snorkeling, surfing and swimming

L & L DRIVE-INN

PAGE 199

Hearty plate lunches and classic island breakfasts piled high with eggs, sausage, Spam and rice

ELENA'S HOME OF FINEST FILIPINO FOODS

PAGE 192

Traditional Filipino dishes emphasizing fresh vegetables and trademark flavors in a home-style eatery

to pass the sentry point, then take the footpath that begins just before the gate, leading up the hill. Near the top, you will have a partial view of both the Waianaes' western face and the central plateau region.

SCHOFIELD BARRACKS Originally established in 1909 to defend the northern approach to Pearl Harbor, today the barracks are a thriving, self-contained Army community, and one of the largest Army posts outside the continental U.S. Not to mention the fact that this was the location for *From Here to Eternity*, starring Burt Lancaster, Deborah Kerr and Frank Sinatra.

TROPIC LIGHTNING MUSEUM ✉*Schofield Barracks, Building 361, Waianae Avenue* ✆*808-655-0438* ✆*808-655-8301, linda.hee@schofield.army.mil* The interesting history of the barracks and the 25th Infantry is explained through exhibits and photos at this army building. Closed Sunday and Monday.

Central Oahu Sights

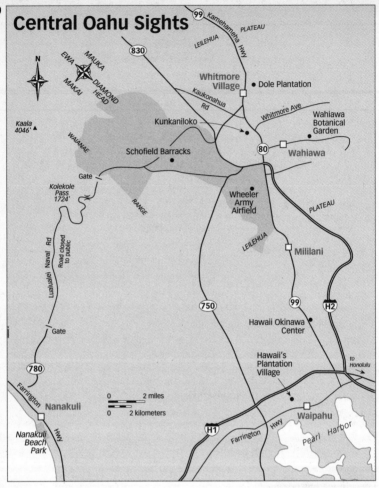

N

EWA — MAUKA — DIAMOND HEAD

MAKAI

99 Kamehameha Hwy

PLATEAU

LEILEHUA

830

Whitmore Village   • Dole Plantation

Kaukonahua Rd

Whitmore Ave

Wahiawa Botanical Garden

Kunkaniloko

80   Wahiawa

Kaala 4046' ▲

WAIANALE

Schofield Barracks

Gate

Kolekole Pass 1724'

RANGE

Wheeler Army Airfield

PLATEAU

Lualualei Naval Rd

Road closed to public

LEILEHUA

Mililani

750   99   H2

Gate

Hawaii Okinawa Center

Hawaii's Plantation Village

to Honolulu

780

Farrington   Nanakuli

0   2 miles
0   2 kilometers

H1

Waipahu

Nanakuli Beach Park

Farrington Hwy

Pearl Harbor

WAHIAWA BOTANICAL GARDENS

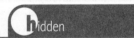

hidden

✉ *1396 California Avenue, Wahiawa* ☎ *808-621-7321* 📠 *808-621-7321*
🖱 *www.co.honolulu.hi.us/parks/hbg* Spreading across 27 acres, you'll
find a handsome retreat studded with tropical vegetation. Plants
include orchids, ferns, cacti and bromeliads, as well as helico-
nias, palms and gingers that thrive in a cool, moist climate. There
are also plants from Africa and Australia, Asian camphor trees
and gum trees from New Guinea. A walk through the gardens is a
feast for the senses, with fragrant flowers and spices filling the air
and colors as vivid as any you've seen before. The garden specializes in introduced and native rainforest plants. Self-guided tours
are available.

ROUTE 750   Route H-2 provides the fastest means back to Honolulu; the most interesting course is along Route 750, Kunia Road, which skirts the Waianaes, passing pineapple fields and stands of pine.

HAWAII'S PLANTATION VILLAGE

✉94-695 Waipahu Street, Waipahu ✆808-677-0110 📠808-676-6727 🖥www.hawaiiplantationvillage.org, hpv.waipahu@hawaiiantel.net Along the way back to Honolulu you can take in this partially recreated and partially restored village that spreads across three acres of Waipahu Cultural Park in Waipahu. Comprised of over two dozen buildings, it includes a Japanese Shinto shrine, a company store and a Chinese Society building. Hawaii's many ethnic groups are represented in the houses, which span several architectural periods of the 19th and 20th centuries. Together they provide visitors with a window into traditional life on a plantation. Guided tours are given every hour Monday through Saturday. Closed Sunday. Admission.

HAWAII OKINAWA CENTER

✉94-587 Ukee Street, Waipahu ✆808-676-5400 🖥www.huoa.org, info@huoa.org A small center in the town of Waipahu showcases the life and times of Okinawan immigrants to the islands. A gallery features historical items from the sugar era, including a grinder used to make tofu and a kitchen crock distiller for moonshine. You'll also find traditional crafts and a photo display. Closed weekends.

From Waipahu, Honolulu is about 15 miles east along Route H-1, or you can take Route 750 south to Ewa.

DINING

DA POKEMAN FISH MARKET

$ PLATE LUNCHES/LOCAL-STYLE   ✉36 North Kamehameha Highway, Wahiawa ✆808-622-4629

If you're hankering for fresh fish, including the raw fish delicacy known as *poke*, stop here. The food is simple, cheap, local-style and good, with an emphasis on bentos and plate lunches built around such entrées as teriyaki chicken and beef, pork cutlet and fried chicken. The daily fresh fish specials are always a winner.

SEOUL INN

$ KOREAN   ✉410 California Avenue, Wahiawa ✆808-621-9090

You can order a range of excellent Korean entrées here, including *kalbi* beef, fish *jun* and a number of hot and cold one-dish meals that combine fish, chicken, meat or tofu and abundant fresh vegetables. The meat *jun* is recommended, and the kimchi is hot and spicy; bring your own beer to cut the heat. The once dark dining room is now clean and bright, but you can always order take-out if you don't warm to the ambience.

SUNNYSIDE

$ AMERICAN   ✉ *1017 Kilani Avenue, Wahiawa*   ☎ *808-621-7188*

This eatery in Wahiawa is the choice for hearty homestyle meals and delicious baked goods made on the premises. The menu features waffles, pancakes and omelettes, as well as chicken cutlets, hamburgers, teriyaki mahimahi and liver and onions at $5 or less. The fruit and cream pies are legendary and whole pies must be reserved; the chocolate pudding pie should not be missed. Closed Sunday.

ELENA'S HOME OF FINEST FILIPINO FOODS

$ FILIPINO   ✉ *94-866 Moloalo Street, Waipahu*   ☎ *808-676-8005*

In Waipahu, Elena's is certainly worth a stop if you're craving a meal that's authentic, tasty and low-priced. You can start at 6 a.m. with their trademark omelette filled with pungent pork *adobo*, or try an early dinner of *pancit* noodles, *sari sari*, roast pig or other dishes that have the usual Filipino emphasis on fresh vegetables, pork and distinctive flavor. The homey, simple decor is as down to earth as the food. Breakfast, lunch and dinner are served.

ZIPPY'S WAIPIO

$ INTERNATIONAL   ✉ *94-1082 Ka Uka Boulevard, Waipahu*   ☎ *808-677-8842*
🖳 *www.zippys.com*

A ubiquitous part of Oahu life is the Zippy's fast-food chain, with 28 outlets around Oahu. You'll find them in nearly every major shopping center, from tony Kahala Mall to Ala Moana, and local neighborhoods from Kalihi to Kaneohe, too. Their appeal is familiarity, low prices, convenience and a wide assortment of satisfactory food that includes favorites such as roast pork, tripe stew, Portuguese bean soup, fresh corned beef and cabbage, Spam, oxtail stew, burgers and pork chops. Its signature chili is served with white rice (unless you order it on spaghetti). Zippy's Waipio is representative of the chain, with bright lights, booths and tables typical of a fast-food joint, all done up in red and white.

NANCY'S KITCHEN

$ LOCAL-STYLE   ✉ *Gentry Waipio Shopping Center, 94-1040 Waipio Uka Street, Waipahu*   ☎ *808-676-3438*

Check out this delightful spot for delicious local-style breakfasts and authentic Hawaiian fare like pork *laulau*, *lomilomi* salmon and *haupia*. A homey eatery, this is a good choice for a comfortable, low-priced meal away from the tourist track.

MILILANI FARMER'S MARKET ✉*Mililani High School, 95-1200 Meheula Parkway, Mililani* If you are in the area, check out this farmer's market, open from 8 a.m. to 11 a.m. on Sundays.

WAIKELE PREMIUM OUTLETS ✉*94-790 Lumiana Street, Waikele* ☎*808-676-5656* For bargains on designer clothes, bags, shoes and more, you can't beat this massive shopping complex just off Exit 7 on Route 1 heading west. The higher-end fashion outlets are found on the west side of Lumiana Street while big box stores like Borders and K-Mart anchor the other half of the shopping center. A free trolley brings visitors back and forth from Waikiki.

NIGHTLIFE

NANCY'S KITCHEN ✉*Gentry Waipio Shopping Center, 94-1040 Waipio Uka Street, Waipahu* ☎*808-676-3438* By day, this low-price local eatery is known for filling breakfasts and authentic Hawaiian fare. At night it does double duty as a casual sports bar with a family-style ambience.

LEEWARD COAST

Out along the west coast of Oahu, less than 30 miles from the sands of Waikiki, Hawaiian culture is making a last stand. Here on the tableland that separates the Waianae Range from the ocean, the old ways still prevail. Unlike the cool rainforests of the Windward Coast or the rain-spattered area around Honolulu, this is a region of stark beauty, resembling the American Southwest, with rocky crags and cactus-studded hills. Farther north, the spartan scenery gives way to wide vistas of massive mountains sloping gracefully to the sea.

Hawaiian and Samoan farmers tend small fields and raise chickens. Side roads off the main highway pass dusty houses and sunblasted churches before turning into dirt tracks that keep climbing past truck farms and old homesteads. For entertainment, there are birthday luaus, cockfights and slack-key guitar playing.

The Leeward Coast has become the keeper of the old ways, and residents jealously guard the customs and traditions that they see slipping away in the rest of the state. Although there have been reports of outsiders being hassled by local residents, the reality, in fact, is usually the reverse. Here, far from the madding crowds of tourists and tourist businesses, the true spirit of aloha is alive and well. But who knows for how long?

"Second City," a major development built near the town of Ewa, has added thousands of houses to the Central Oahu area, which has led to a dramatic increase in commuter traffic. And in the southwest corner of the island, the ultramodern JW Marriott Ihilani Resort & Spa in the Ko

Olina area is only the beginning of the inevitable encroachment along this side of the island.

SIGHTS

From Honolulu, you can visit the Leeward Coast region by traveling west on Route H-1 or Route 90. If you want to tour what once was a prime sugar-growing area, take Route 90 past Pearl Harbor, then turn left on Fort Weaver Road (Route 760).

EWA Fort Weaver Road leads to this plantation town. With its old sugar mill and trim houses, Ewa is an enchanting throwback to the days when sugar was king. This town is a slow, simple place, perfect for wandering and exploring.

HAWAIIAN RAILWAY ✉*91-1001 Renton Road, Ewa* ☎*808-681-5461* 📠*808-681-4860* ✑*www.hawaiianrailway.com, info@hawaiianrailway.com* The transportation of late-19th- to early-20th-century Oahu centered around the railroad. You can experience the past firsthand on a ride aboard this historical train, once owned by the defunct Oahu Railway and Land Company. The ride covers six miles (of the existing ten) and is fully narrated. There are historical locomotives on display, and you can picnic on the grounds. Open Sunday only. Admission.

HAWAIIAN WATERS ADVENTURE PARK ✉*400 Farrington Highway, Kapolei* ☎*808-674-9283* ✑*www.hawaiianwaters.com, questions@hawaiianwaters.com* Near Oahu's southwest corner, Routes H-1 and 90 converge to become the Farrington Highway (Route 93). From here, follow the signs to Hawaiian Waters, perfect for those who are afraid of getting a little sand in their shoes but love to ride waves or splash in the water. There are inner-tube slides, a 60-foot water slide, artificial waves and much more, spread over 25 acres. For less wet fun, mini-golf is also available. Closed Tuesday and Wednesday. A hefty admission.

The first beach along the Leeward Coast is **Barbers Point Beach Park**, a detour south on Route 95. However, continue along Route 93 and you'll come upon Oahu's latest development.

KO OLINA RESORT ✉*92-1480 Aliinui Drive, Kapolei* You might want to stop here and take a look at the scenery: Seven lagoons surrounded by silky sand dot this multifaceted complex, that includes a hotel, golf course and marina. It's a beautiful and little-visited spot. It does get windy, so hold on to your hat.

HAWAIIAN ELECTRIC BEACH PARK Farrington Highway continues along the coast to Kahe Point. The beach north of the point is the official Hawaiian Electric Beach Park, but it's more commonly called "Tracks" and is home to one of the west side's best surf spots by the same name. Keep going along Route 93 and you'll pass the towns of Nanikuli, Maili and Waianae.

WAIANAE If you turn up Mailiilii Street in the sleepy town of Waianae, you will pass placid Hawaiian homesteads and farmlands.

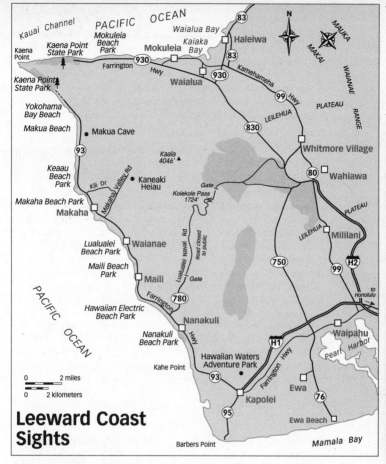

Leeward Coast Sights

This side road also provides sweeping views of the Waianae Range. On the northern side of town is Waianae Harbor, a small port hosting small fishing vessels as well as spiffy yachts.

MAKAHA BEACH ✉*Farrington Highway* Along Farrington Highway is Makaha Beach, one of Hawaii's most famous surfing spots, and the site of an annual international surfing championship. It's also a great place for shell hunting.

KANEAKI HEIAU _____

✉*Off Manunaolu Street* 📞*808-695-8174* 📠*808-695-8174* The **Makaha Valley**, extending from the ocean up into the Waianae Mountains, is home to this *heiau*, a 15th-century temple dedicated to the god Lono. Closed Monday and when raining or windy.

MAKUA CAVE

⊠*Farrington Highway* The highway continues along the coastline past several mostly deserted beaches and parks. Just before you reach Kaena Point State Park, you'll come upon Makua Cave, traditionally called Kaneana. According to legend, this massive, 150,000-year-old lava tube was home to the shark god Kamahoalii. This once-forbidden cave is 100 feet high and 450 feet deep, so there's plenty of room if you dare to explore.

KAENA POINT
NATURAL AREA RESERVE

Beyond Makua Cave, where the paved road turns to dirt, lies **Yokohama Bay**, with its curving sand beach and inviting turquoise waters. The rough road past Yokohama is only partially passable by auto, so if you want to explore the scenic point from this side of the island, you'll have to hike through this reserve located within Kaena Point State Park. It's between two and three miles to the northwest corner of Oahu, past lava-strewn tidepools teeming with marine life. Rays and sharks are often seen gliding around the tidal waters. On a clear day you can see Kauai; from November to May you might spy a humpback whale. Shearwaters, frigates, albatross and other waterbirds also nest in this coastal area. From the 1920s to the 1940s, there was a rail system in the islands, but it was too costly to maintain, especially around Kaena Point. Remnants of the tracks can be seen in the area. (Swimming and other water activities are not recommended; don't leave valuables in the car.) You can also access Kaena Point from the east, past Dillingham Airfield. (See North Shore chapter.)

HONOULIULI PRESERVE

⊠*The Nature Conservancy, 923 Nuuanu Avenue, Honolulu, HI 96817* ☎*808-537-4508* ☒*808-545-2019* ⏍*www.nature.org/hawaii, hawaii@tnc.org* Away from the crowds of Waikiki and the hubbub of downtown Honolulu and high in the mountains of Leeward Oahu, this preserve operated by The Nature Conservancy is helping to save some of the island's and the world's endangered flora and fauna. The organization is trying to ensure that the land on which these threatened species exist will be cared for so that the natural history of Oahu can be perpetuated, not only for the present generation but for those to come.

Home to more than 90 rare and endangered species, the 3582-acre forest preserve stretches along the southern Waianae Mountains and down their eastern slopes. This land once belonged to Hawaiian royalty, and *honouliuli* means "dark harbor," for the dark, dense land that stretches up the mountainside. Incorporated within its boundaries is what is left of a diverse native ecosystem once common on Oahu. The preserve harbors plant and animals species that are, or have the potential to be, endangered. Several birds, including the *pueo* (Hawaiian owl), the flycatching *elepaio*, the crimson-feathered *apapane* and the yellow-green *amakihi*, live in the Honouliuli forests. Two endangered tree snails endemic to Oahu and found nowhere else also call the preserve their home. Animals aren't the only living things that Honouliuli Preserve helps to spare. Three plants found here grow nowhere else on the planet. One of these is a mint species and two are flowering lobelia.

Because the preserve is in a remote part of the Waianae Mountains, The Nature Conservancy recommends visiting it only as part of a regularly scheduled—usually twice-monthly—guided hike or work project.

LODGING

JW MARRIOTT IHILANI RESORT & SPA

$$$$ 387 ROOMS ✉92-1001 Olani Street, Kapolei ☎808-679-0079, 800-626-4446 📠808-679-0295 ⊘www.ihilani.com

To get away from everything, you'll want to dig deep into your pockets for a short stay here. Backed by the Waianaes and facing a curved expanse of ocean, this hideaway is part of the 640-acre Ko Olina Resort. The pastel-painted guest rooms are spacious and the lavish bathrooms offer deep European soaking tubs to float in if the windy waters outside are too much for you. There's a golf course, six tennis courts, five restaurants and a spa. More importantly, you'll find a string of four lagoons, each with a crescent beach and a cluster of islets that protects the mouth of the lagoon.

BOB'S OCEAN HOUSE

$$$$ 1 UNIT ✉Book through Pacific Islands Reservations ☎808-262-8133 📠808-262-5030 ⊘pir@aloha.com

If you have a large group and want spacious accommodations, Bob's is right on the water and not far from the sandy shores of Makaha Beach. In fact, it has its own beach in summer (the same beach disappears in winter). It has four large bedrooms, four-and-a-half baths (including a huge, lavish master bath), a full kitchen and a big living room, as well as roomy, covered decks both upstairs and down; eight people can live together comfortably. A washer-dryer, DVD player and lovely views of the Waianae Mountains and water make this a relaxed, pleasant place to hang out.

MAKAHA GOLF RESORT

$$ 196 UNITS ✉84-626 Makaha Valley Road, Makaha ☎808-695-9544, 866-576-6447 ⊘www.makaharesort.net

A good choice in these parts—and a good deal—is this relaxed, island-style resort. Low-key, three-story buildings are nestled around gardens and an 18-hole golf course that has been dubbed one of the best on Oahu. Its air-conditioned rooms and suites, each with a private lanai, include mini-refrigerators, DVD players and coffeemakers. A putting green, pool, lounge and restaurant round out the amenities; children are welcomed.

CONDOS

MAKAHA VALLEY TOWERS

586 UNITS ✉️*End of Kili Drive, Makaha* 📞*808-695-9568*
🖱️*www.makahavalleytowers.org*

A highrise set along the slopes of Makaha Valley, units here range from studios to two-bedrooms, with nightly, weekly and monthly stays available. Rates vary and accommodations are handled by local realtors. One week studios $600, suite (monthly) $2600.

MAKAHA SHORES

88 UNITS ✉️*84-265 Farrington Highway, Makaha* 📞*808-696-7121* 📠*808-696-7121*
🖱️*www.makahashores.com, inquiries@makahashores.com*

This resort condo complex overlooks pretty Makaha Beach Park, one of Hawaii's top surfing beaches. There are studios and one- and two-bedroom units, each individually decorated by their owners. The minimum stay is one week. Rates start at $525 per week.

DINING

JW MARRIOTT IHILANI RESORT & SPA

$$–$$$$ INTERNATIONAL ✉️*92-1001 Olani Street, Kapolei* 📞*808-679-0079*
📠*808-679-0800* 🖱️*www.ihilani.com*

By way of resort restaurants, JW Marriott has both deluxe- and ultra-deluxe-priced dining rooms. Foremost is **Azul** (dinner only; brunch on Sunday), where the pork chops come with orange-butter sauce, the lobster is served in *pistou* and the ideas are Mediterranean. **Ushiotei** (dinner only; closed Tuesday and Wednesday) is the ultimate in Japanese cuisine. And **Naupaka Terrace**, a poolside terrace serving cross-cultural dishes for breakfast, lunch and dinner, is the Ihilani's answer to informality and easy elegance. Reservations are recommended.

CATHAY INN CHOP SUEY

$–$$ CHINESE ✉️*86-088 Farrington Highway, Waianae* 📞*808-696-9477*

A welcome restaurant on this sparsely populated strip of Waianae shoreline, this spot, with its friendly service, is a good choice for Chinese food like chow fun, egg *foo yong* and crispy *gau gee*.

HANNARA RESTAURANT

$ KOREAN/HAWAIIAN ✉️*86-078 Farrington Highway, Waianae*
📞*808-696-6137*

If you have yet to try hamburger steak, Hannara's is the place to do it. The hefty patty comes topped with sautéed onions and smothered in gravy, served, of course, with two scoops of rice. If you're not into so much rice, you can opt for Korean sides like kimchi or pickled radish. The Korean mixed plate and the

Hawaiian plate are also popular and filling choices. Breakfast regulars rave about the macadamia nut pancakes.

SURFAH SMOODEEZ CAFÉ

$ LOCAL-STYLE/HAWAIIAN ✉ *85-773 Farrington Highway, Waianae* ✆*808-478-9088*

The price is right at this local gem, where you'll find every manner of local favorites—*pasteles*, tripe stew, *laulau*, *shoyu* chicken, *kalua* pig—as well as heaping plate lunches. If you can't decide, Auntie Olivia's pork chops are *ono*, or you can go with a plain old cheeseburger. For those who are craving something fruity, there are 16 flavors of smoothies available. An ideal place to stop after a hot day at the beach.

L & L DRIVE-INN

$ PLATE LUNCHES ✉ *85-080 Waianae Valley Road, Waianae* ✆*808-696-7989* ✆*808-696-8803*

When I'm in Waianae, I have to stop at L & L, which serves breakfast, lunch and dinner. The breakfast combo includes eggs, Portuguese sausage, Spam and rice. Among the hearty plate lunches offered the rest of the day are breaded pork chop with hamburger steak and shrimp curry with chicken *katsu*.

NIGHTLIFE

JW MARRIOTT IHILANI RESORT & SPA ✉*92-1001 Olani Street, Kapolei* ✆*808-679-0079* The Ihilani is home to the **Hokulea**, a cozy lounge perfect for a quiet rendezvous. Hours vary with season.

PARADISE COVE LUAU ✉*Koolina Resort, 92-1089 Alii Nui Drive, Kapolei* ✆*808-842-5911, 800-775-2683* ✐*www.paradisecovehawaii.com* Of all the visitor luaus, this one is the best bang for your buck. Besides the standard shell lei greeting, complimentary mai tai, *imu* presentation, luau buffet and hula show, guests can also engage in spear throwing, dart sliding and lei making. You can even get a temporary Polynesian tattoo.

BEACHES & PARKS

BARBERS POINT BEACH PARK

✉*Kapolei; Take Campbell Industrial Park exit off Route 1 and follow Kalealoa Boulevard to the end. Turn right onto Olai Street and look for Barbers Point on the left.*

🏃 On the south end of the Leeward Coast in the area known as Kalaeloa, Barber's Point and nearby White Plains Beach offer forgiving waves that are ideal for beginning surfers. The waves are best in the morning before the wind makes the water choppy, and the lineup is rarely too crowded. It's rumored to be "sharky," but hey, the ocean is their home. There is a lifeguard on duty, as well as shower, restroom and picnic facilities.

KAHE POINT BEACH PARK

✉ *Farrington Highway (Route 93) about nine miles south of Waianae*

🏊 🐟 🛶 The ugly power plant you'll see here is the obvious reason for this park's nickname: "Electric Beach." It's actually thanks to that power plant that this beach is a unique snorkeling destination—two giant cooling pipes funnel warm water out to the ocean, and the warmer temperature around the openings attract lots of fish. To find the underwater pipes, look for the swirling bubbles on the surface. From the beach pavilion, it's a five- to ten-minute swim. Numerous fish species—among them triggerfish, butterflyfish, surgeonfish, tangs, jacks, snappers and more—swarm above the coral-covered pipes. Turtles and spinner dolphins are also common sightings. Be cautious about swimming in front of the pipes. The surge will send you instantly out to sea before you know what happened, and it's a long swim back.

HAWAIIAN ELECTRIC BEACH PARK (TRACKS BEACH)

✉ *Farrington Highway (Route 93) about seven miles south of Waianae*

🏊 🐟 ⛱ 🛶 Once privately owned, this park just north of Kahe Point Beach Park is now run by the county. Officially known as Hawaiian Electric Beach Park, locals just call it Tracks beach. Here there's a rolling lawn with palm and *kiawe* trees, plus a white-sand beach and coral reef. You can swim, snorkel, surf year-round and fish for *papio*, *ulua*, *moano* and *menpachi*. If you're a proficient surfer, you'll probably head for "Tracks," a top surfing break. The drawbacks are the lack of facilities (there are restrooms and a picnic area) and the park's proximity to the electric company.

NANAKULI BEACH PARK

✉ *89-269 Farrington Highway (Route 93) about five miles south of Waianae*
☎ *808-668-1137*

🏊 🐟 ⛱ 🛶 This park is so large that a housing tract divides it into two parts. The main section features a white-sand beach, *kiawe*-studded camping area and a recreation complex. It's simply a park with everything, unfortunately including weekend crowds. Needless to say, the swimming is good in the summer when the surf isn't too high; lifeguard on duty. There are winter breaks, "Parks" and "Middles," with right and left slides; watch out for heavy backwash. Fishing is sparse, but there's still *papio*, *ulua*, *moano* and *menpachi*. Facilities include restrooms, showers, a ball field, a basketball court and a volleyball court.

⛺ Tent and trailer camping are allowed, but a county permit is required.

MAILI BEACH PARK

✉ *87-021 Farrington Highway (Route 93) in Maili a few miles south of Waianae*

🏊 🐟 ⛱ 🛶 A long winding stretch of white sand is the high point of this otherwise unimpressive facility. The swimming is good in the summer; reef snorkeling is only fair. Be aware of the reef's steep dropoff. There are winter surf breaks with a right slide. The principal game fish caught here are *papio*, *ulua*, *menpachi* and *moano*. The park contains shade trees and a spotty lawn. There are picnic tables, restrooms and showers.

▲ Permitted weekends only with a county permit. Tent camping, with a county permit, is allowed in the summer at nearby Lualualei Beach Park.

MAKAHA BEACH PARK

✉ *84-369 Farrington Highway (Route 93) in Makaha, two miles north of Waianae*

 Some of the finest surfing in the world takes place right offshore here, at the break of the same name. This is the site of international competitions, drawing championship surfers from all across the Pacific. For more relaxed sports, there's a white-sand beach to sunbathe on and some good places to skindive. Swimming and snorkeling are both good when the sea is calm; otherwise, exercise extreme caution. Check with a lifeguard about water conditions. Anglers try for *papio*, *ulua*, *moano* and *menpachi*. The precipitous Waianae Mountains loom behind the park. There are picnic tables, restrooms and showers.

KEAAU BEACH PARK

✉ *83-431 Farrington Highway (Route 93) about five miles north of Waianae*

 Except for the absence of a sandy beach, this is the prettiest park on the west coast. It's a long, narrow, grassy plot spotted with trees and backdropped by the Waianaes. Sunsets are spectacular here, and on a clear day you can see all the way to Kauai. There's a sandy beach just west of the park. Unfortunately, a coral reef rises right to the water's edge, making entry into the water difficult. But once you're in there's great snorkeling, swimming and bodysurfing. Large pelagic fish, including amberjacks and rainbow runners, have been seen close to shore here, a treat for snorkelers. Divers can make the hardy swim out to an impressive ledge known as "Keaau Corner" when it's flat, and when it's not, surfers enjoy a long left break called "Free Hawaii." Note that, like other west-side beaches, the numbers of homeless that live at Keaau are growing. In response to concerns about safety, the city has closed several of the beach parks at night. Avoid dangerous situations by being sensitive and respectful to families living on the beach. There are picnic areas, restrooms and showers.

▲ Tent and trailer allowed. County permit required.

KAENA POINT STATE PARK (YOKOHAMA BAY)

✉ *At the end of the paved section of Farrington Highway (Route 93), about nine miles north of the town of Waianae*

This curving stretch of white sand is the last beach along Oahu's northwest coast. With the Waianae Range in the background and coral reefs offshore, it's a particularly lovely spot. Though officially a state park, the area is largely undeveloped and the remote beach is perfect for those seeking seclusion. On calm days, the bay's sparkling turquoise water is irresistibly inviting for swimming and snorkeling, and it's a great place to spot spinner dolphins. When the surf's up, the current moves swiftly, so it's best not to swim—exercise extreme caution. South and west swells create a pitching peak called "Yokohamas," or "Yokes" for short, that is suitable for shortboarding. Fish caught in the area include *papio*, *ulua*, *moano* and *menpachi*. Walk a few miles past tidepools teeming with life and you'll arrive at Kaena Point, the northwest tip of the island. Facilities include restrooms and lifeguards, but note that there is no potable water.

INDEX

LODGING

LODGING SERVICES

DINING

HIDDEN GUIDES

Adventure travel or a relaxing vacation?—"Hidden" guidebooks are the only travel books in the business to provide detailed information on both. Aimed at environmentally aware travelers, our motto is "Where Vacations Meet Adventures." These books combine details on unique hotels, restaurants and sightseeing with information on camping, sports and hiking for the outdoor enthusiast.

PARADISE FAMILY GUIDES

Ideal for families traveling with kids of any age—toddlers to teenagers—Paradise Family Guides offer a blend of travel information unlike any other guides to the Hawaiian islands. With vacation ideas and tropical adventures that are sure to satisfy both action-hungry youngsters and relaxation-seeking parents, these guides meet the specific needs of each and every family member.

HIDDEN GUIDEBOOKS

____ Hidden Arizona, $18.95
____ Hidden Baja, $14.95
____ Hidden Belize, $15.95
____ Hidden Big Island of Hawaii, $14.95
____ Hidden Boston & Cape Cod, $14.95
____ Hidden British Columbia, $18.95
____ Hidden Cancún & the Yucatán, $16.95
____ Hidden Carolinas, $17.95
____ Hidden Coast of California, $19.95
____ Hidden Colorado, $15.95
____ Hidden Florida, $19.95
____ Hidden Florida Keys & Everglades, $15.95
____ Hidden Georgia, $16.95
____ Hidden Hawaii, $19.95
____ Hidden Idaho, $14.95
____ Hidden Kauai, $14.95
____ Hidden Los Angeles, $14.95
____ Hidden Maui, $15.95
____ Hidden Montana, $15.95

____ Hidden New England, $19.95
____ Hidden New Mexico, $15.95
____ Hidden Oahu, $14.95
____ Hidden Oregon, $15.95
____ Hidden Pacific Northwest, $19.95
____ Hidden Philadelphia, $14.95
____ Hidden Puerto Vallarta, $14.95
____ Hidden Salt Lake City, $14.95
____ Hidden San Diego, $14.95
____ Hidden San Francisco & Northern California, $19.95
____ Hidden Seattle, $14.95
____ Hidden Southern California, $19.95
____ Hidden Southwest, $19.95
____ Hidden Tahiti, $19.95
____ Hidden Tennessee, $16.95
____ Hidden Walt Disney World, $13.95
____ Hidden Washington, $15.95
____ Hidden Wine Country, $14.95
____ Hidden Wyoming, $15.95

PARADISE FAMILY GUIDES

____ Paradise Family Guides: Kaua'i, $17.95
____ Paradise Family Guides: Maui, $17.95

____ Paradise Family Guides: Big Island of Hawai'i, $17.95

Mark the book(s) you're ordering and enter the total cost here ➾ [   ]

California residents add 9.75% sales tax here ➾ [   ]

Shipping, check box for your preferred method and enter cost here ➾ [   ]

❑ BOOK RATE   **FREE! FREE! FREE!**

❑ PRIORITY MAIL/UPS GROUND   cost of postage

❑ UPS OVERNIGHT OR 2-DAY AIR   cost of postage

[   ]

Billing, enter total amount due here and check method of payment ➾

❑ CHECK   ❑ MONEY ORDER

❑ VISA/MASTERCARD _____ EXP. DATE _____

NAME _____ PHONE _____

ADDRESS _____

CITY _____ STATE _____ ZIP _____

MONEY-BACK GUARANTEE ON DIRECT ORDERS PLACED THROUGH ULYSSES PRESS.

ABOUT THE
CONTRIBUTORS

Ray Riegert is the author of eight travel books, including *Hidden San Francisco & Northern California*. His most popular work, *Hidden Hawaii*, won the coveted Lowell Thomas Travel Journalism Award for Best Guidebook as well a similar award from the Hawaii Visitors Bureau. In addition to his role as publisher of Ulysses Press, he has written for the *Chicago Tribune*, *Saturday Evening Post*, *San Francisco Chronicle* and *Travel & Leisure*. A member of the Society of American Travel Writers, he lives in the San Francisco Bay area with his wife, co-publisher Leslie Henriques, and their son Keith and daughter Alice.

Catharine Lo, the update author for this edition, is a freelance journalist who moved to the North Shore of Oahu in 1998. She contributes stories regularly to *Hawai'i* and travel publications including *Hana Hou!*, *TravelAge West* and *Maui No Ka Oi* and was formerly editor at large for the *Honolulu Weekly*. Prior to moving to Hawaii, Catharine was a section editor for *Wired Magazine* in San Francisco. Her exploration of the islands has taught her the true meaning of paradise: a living land, a living ocean and a loving people who give more than they receive. She enjoys writing about the ocean and playing in it even more.